OYSTERS

OYSTERS

Recipes with the Fresh Taste of the Sea

CYNTHIA NIMS

Photography by Jim Henkens

SASQUATCH BOOKS | SEATTLE

This book is dedicated to all those—friends and family, chefs and farmers, writers and advocates—who keep me inspired in this wonderful world of food

CONTENTS

WHAT IS IT ABOUT OYSTERS?

THEY INSPIRE HIP OYSTER BARS, backyard grilling feasts, and elegant celebration meals. They evoke songs, poems, and fashion shows. They bring out our competitive streak to see who can shuck and slurp the most. They prompt pilgrimages to their home territory, which might include late-night forays to moonlit bays seeking the best of the season at its pinnacle of freshness. They satisfy our hunger, fuel our romance, and feed our souls. I've written quite a lot about Northwest foods over the years, and no other food seems to strike the kind of food-culture chord that oysters do.

Oyster culture is a natural part of our lives all along the Pacific Coast of the United States and Canada. Both culture in terms of the customs and values of us who live here and the practical business of raising oysters in this prolific growing environment. For some it's a particularly rich dose of both types of culture, as many oyster-growing operations are now run by third, fourth, even fifth generations of family members keeping their slice of local oyster heritage alive.

The sheer volume of production reflects the geography of this coast, with its countless bays, sounds, inlets, channels, and coves that provide ideal habitats for oysters. And the quality of those oysters is a direct product of the water they live in, nutrient rich and managed in ways to help preserve healthy seafood populations. The diversity of flavors that Pacific Coast oysters have echoes variants in the types of phytoplankton, zooplankton, and other microorganisms that thrive in the region's water, not to mention variations in water depth, temperature, tidal activity, and other environmental attributes.

This conglomeration of natural influences on the oyster's character has come to be known as *meroir*, the seaworthy version of terroir. We on the Pacific Coast are lucky to live in a place where the meroir produces superlative oysters that folks just can't seem to get enough of.

Oysters have a capacity to transport us, right there in our kitchen or on our oyster-bar stool, more than other foods. When we hold the creature in its pure form, it only takes a short leap of the imagination to put us on the shore where it was harvested. The fact that the shell may carry along some evidence of its marine cohorts makes it seem all the more vivid: barnacles, a tuft of seaweed, maybe a minuscule oyster or mussel. And that liquor that surrounds the oyster in its shell—it seems pure essence of the sea, a taste of place like none other.

I realize that not everyone is mad about oysters, nor necessarily feels transported when consuming them. But I will say that the mere mention of this book's topic launched more interesting conversations with both friends and strangers than I recall from any other project.

There was my weekend on Washington's Long Beach Peninsula, at the historic Shelburne Inn. I've known the owners, David Campiche and Laurie Anderson, for many years, originally in the context of doing wild mushroom research. On this recent early winter visit, I'd been to see Goose Point and Ekone oyster operations on Willapa Bay en route to teaching a wild mushroom class at the inn. As David put down a plate of his Hangtown fry (eggs cooked frittata style with oysters and bacon; he adds spinach and a dash of Parmesan) the next morning, he talked about growing up in that area. And how his Ilwaco High School football team was hard to beat because some of them worked at collecting oysters on the Willapa Bay mud flats, building up extraordinarily strong thigh muscles with each bushel they filled.

Another time I had just flown into San Francisco International Airport and was picking up my rental car. The fellow at the counter, being friendly while taking care of the paperwork, asked where I was headed. "Up to Tomales Bay," I said, "to have some oysters at Hog Island." "You know how I like to cook oysters?" he offered, without any prompting from me. "Just put them right on the grill and cook them until they pop open. Some Tabasco sauce. That's it." I nodded in total agreement. "Oh, and Hennessy Cognac, that's what I drink with those oysters." Hmm, now that was a pairing idea I hadn't considered before.

The road trips I took while researching this book amplified my realization that oysters are the source of hallmark Pacific Coast experiences. Oyster lovers can visit oyster farms, buy from the source, slurp oysters on the beach, enjoy a picnic within view of the oyster beds, and attend myriad oyster-centric events. There are many dynamic traditions built around oysters that exemplify the region's oyster engagement.

I cut my journalistic teeth on the subject of seafood as an editor at *Simply Seafood* magazine, published by a Seattle company founded by former fishermen who put out a couple of publications for the seafood industry as well. That magazine position was my first job back home after my culinary education in France. It was there that I wrote a 1997 article about the then renaissance of oyster bars. And it was thanks to that job that I found myself one chilly, dank late-fall morning on the doorstep of Julia Child's home in Cambridge, Massachusetts.

It's not as though she didn't know I was coming and wouldn't have let me in otherwise. But showing up with a cooler containing Olympia oysters and some first-of-the-season Dungeness crab in hand seemed to have swiftened my entry. Within moments I was in her warm kitchen and she shucked open an oyster, slurping it down with glee. That was just one of many occasions that have made clear to me how broad and devoted the fan base is for oysters from the Pacific Coast.

When it comes to exploring oysters, there are interesting parallels drawn to the world of wine. As we sip different wines from different places, sometimes side by side, it helps us better understand the range of options available as we form opinions about what suits our personal palate best. The same is true of sampling oysters, particularly when various types can be tasted at the same time for a clear comparison. This is the best way to appreciate how much diversity of flavor there is to be had with oysters. Soon you learn that not all oysters are the same, which invites only more delicious exploration.

Opportunities for just that kind of exploration abound along the Pacific Coast, fueled in large part by access to oysters through a number of channels. Beyond the usual retail store and restaurant options, some oyster farms sell direct to customers on-site, whether through a simple service window or in a small store with other oyster-friendly offerings. A few oyster growers have gone so far as to open restaurants at which they showcase their product from the oyster bed direct to the customer's plate.

But oyster-farm-to-table dining isn't a new phenomenon here. The origin of today's Oregon Oyster Farms and Dan & Louis Oyster Bar can trace to a mid-nineteenth-century shipwreck off Yaquina Bay, which precipitated an unscheduled introduction to the vast supply of oysters found in the bay. Meinert Wachsmuth was on board and didn't stay in the area at the time but retired there later. His son Louis Charles Wachsmuth is the one who took the oyster and ran with it in the early twentieth century, raising oysters on the coast and serving oysters in Portland. The family no longer owns the oyster-growing business, but its legacy lives on in both establishments. It also lives on in chef Cory Schreiber, great-great-grandson of Meinert, longtime chef/owner of Portland's beloved (and now closed) Wildwood restaurant and today chef/instructor at the Art Institute of Portland. He visited the family oyster beds many times growing up and hung out in the shucking room where the radio blasted as women shucked and gossiped all day long. If not through genetics alone, his fate of an oyster-rich life was surely sealed with the baby shower in his honor held at the family oyster bar.

So you see that it is a rich fabric that's woven with oyster culture all along the Pacific Coast. Family traditions, commercial industry, celebrations, recreation, history, conversation, and pure culinary enjoyment can all be fed by the humble oyster.

BASICS

KUSSHI OYSTERS
LIVE
LIVE
GEODUCK
(KING CLAM)
$23.99 lb.
LIVE
PENN
COVE
LIVE
MANILA
CLAMS
LIVE
MIYAGI
OYSTER
$13.99
LIVE
SHIGOKU
OYSTERS
$18.99 DOZEN
LIVE
PennCove
Select
OYSTERS $14.99 dz
LIVE
DEEP Bay
oysters
$13.99
doz

THE LIFE & TIMES OF THE MODERN OYSTER

HOW THEY GROW

What sets oysters apart from other creatures of the sea? As a mollusk, the oyster is related to a whole host of marine life, from abalone to octopus. Among those mollusks are shellfish—invertebrates with exoskeletons, or exterior skeletal structure—of which oysters fall in the class of bivalves. Like other bivalves, including clams, mussels, and scallops, an oyster is a filter feeder whose two (*bi*) hinged shells (*valves*) open to draw seawater across its gills, filtering out nutritious phytoplankton and other minute particles.

We easily see the differences in shape and size of the different bivalves. One characteristic you might not notice right off is that while most others have two identical shells, oysters have one cupped shell and one flat. They live differently too: clams burrow into the sand; mussels attach with byssal threads to rocks, piers, or other stationary objects; scallops propel themselves about and live more freely than the others.

Oysters stay put; in the wild they content themselves with the spot where they landed on the beach, neither burrowing nor flitting around.

Given the static life they lead, the oysters' form of reproduction is far from intimate. Most oysters spew out sperm and eggs into the water, and the larvae that are produced swim around for a few weeks until they are large enough to consider settling down. However, Olympia oysters and European flat oysters are brooders. Males dispense sperm and females nab it to fertilize eggs held within their shells. The female will brood the larvae for about ten days, then spit them out to make their way in the world.

Regardless of how they came to be, oyster larvae float freely for a week or two, then seek out an anchor from which to grow. Their preferred new home will be another oyster shell, which explains the tiny hitchhiker oysters you may find on the surface of full-grown oysters you're about to shuck. That's one indication that your oyster was reared in an area with particularly ripe conditions for oyster spawning. (This also explains why some recreational oyster rules require the oysters be shucked on-site and the shells be left on the beach.) Once an oyster has settled on this new home, it is now an oyster spat. If it survives its juvenile years into adulthood, a Pacific oyster can live twenty years or more.

The biology of an oyster isn't just about the oyster. Oysters have an interesting and important role to play in the ecosystem they inhabit. Some consider them to be a "keystone species," one that has a disproportionately large impact on the environment in which they live and grow. Others use the term "ecosystem engineers," referencing the function they have in supporting and boosting resources for other sea life around them.

The majority of oysters harvested on the Pacific Coast are farm raised, the product of aquaculture. That notion, rightfully so, can raise red flags in our minds. What about the degradation of mangroves caused by shrimp farming in Southeast Asia? And the feed additives and antibiotics used in salmon farming? With oysters, it's different. No feed or medicine is involved. And they contribute more to habitat enhancement than they do to habitat degradation.

Oysters can benefit waterways by simply doing what they do: filter water (as much as fifty gallons per day for large oysters). Their first priority is sourcing nutrients, but in doing so they're also cleaning the water. Clear water allows more sunlight to reach other organisms, which can help them thrive. Plus, the oysters themselves and the beds they inhabit create habitats for other creatures. And their processing of water helps move nutrients they don't require farther down the water column to appreciative species below.

All that, and they're delicious too. It's little wonder that countless agencies and organizations now rally to offer support to oyster populations. Habitat restoration, more intent management of water quality controls, further ecological research, enhancement and expansion of shellfish beds, public outreach about ecosystem issues—these are among the efforts to ensure oysters and other shellfish remain a dynamic part of the local seascape. The Washington Shellfish Initiative, as an example, was established to "protect and enhance" shellfish resources in the state. As I completed research on this book, work was underway in California and Oregon to develop shellfish initiatives for those states as well.

Growing oysters starts, for the most part, in land-based hatcheries where oysters spawn to create larvae. (Some oysters raised on Pacific Coast farms do begin life from "wild

set"—naturally occurring spawn—but it's not the norm.) When the larvae are large enough to settle, they attach to a hard surface on which they will develop their shells. If it's a whole oyster shell (called a "cultch"), a number of oysters will grow in a cluster from that shell. These oysters will generally be shucked for meat to be jarred. But some growers will break up the clusters when near maturity and toss the individual oysters back out to the bed to grow solo for a spell.

If the grower wants individually formed oysters ideal for the prime half-shell market, they will provide the larvae with oyster shells that are ground instead of whole. Each grain of the ground shell is large enough for just one single larva—which at that point measures about 0.3 millimeters—to attach itself, the perfect single-occupant home.

Hatchery facilities are expensive to develop and maintain, so there aren't many of them. Many oyster growers on the Pacific Coast rely on purchased larvae or "seed oysters" (spat oysters ready to be planted on an oyster bed) that they'll raise on their own property. Given the meroir effect, oysters take on distinctions of their home bed even when coming from a common seed source.

There are two basic approaches for growing oysters—bottom culture and off-bottom culture, with numerous variations and hybrids among them. Some oyster vendors and menus will reference the growing method as one element of the oyster's character. Based on the growing method chosen and other variables that are at play, cultured oysters will be harvested at about two to four years of age.

Bottom culture can be as simple as scattering juvenile oysters across a tideflat, letting nature do the work, and then coming back in a few years to harvest mature oysters. The oysters that survive predators, storms, exposure, and other challenges will be sturdy and resilient. You'll often see these oysters referred to as "beach grown." Bottom culture may also be done in broad, flat mesh bags attached to the ground; these oysters will still be bottom-raised but will have been secured and protected to some degree, making them a little less sturdy than beach grown. Some growers opt for the combination bag-to-beach method to gain the best of both approaches.

Among off-bottom options, longline is a common version. The cultch oysters with baby oysters attached are connected to ropes suspended a foot or two above the sea bottom in long rows. Or the oyster spat could go into mesh bags set on a rack raising them above the bottom. Other oysters grow suspended in lantern nets or trays from buoys or rafts, fully submerged 24/7. These methods provide oysters with more equal access to the plankton passing by, so they tend to grow more quickly than their bottom-culture counterparts. But they also tend to have less-sturdy shells when they don't get beach time.

With the advent of "tumbled" oysters, farmers can employ a technique that allows them to make up for limits traditional methods may have, while also customizing their product. Tumbling may be done by systems that amplify the tide's natural flow to more forcefully agitate the oysters within a bag or a bin. Floats attached to the outer edge of the bag will raise it upward with a high tide, then the bag will float downward when the tide recedes, so the oysters get tide tumbled twice each day. Other methods involve temporarily bringing the oysters on shore to tumble in a big cylindrical machine (think of your clothes dryer, without the hot air).

What tumbling accomplishes is breaking off just the fine outer edge of the oyster's shell. This elicits an instinct in the oyster to replenish that shell, which, over time, develops a more deeply cupped oyster with plumper meat. In modifying the architecture of the shell in that way, there is also invariably change in its design: these tumbled shells have less fluting and frilly layers, and instead have a smooth surface.

SEASONALITY

Oysters are produced year-round in most growing regions along the Pacific Coast. However, they are at their best, crispest, and most plump when conditions are cold, which is why we often associate the winter and early spring months with prime oyster time. That is when you are likely to see the most oysters in the greatest variety available in stores and on menus.

Warming water temperatures are generally what prompts spawning in oysters, the time when they commit energy to dispensing eggs and sperm, which is why oysters are often, at least traditionally, shunned during the summer months. There's nothing harmful about eating spawning oysters; they simply have thinner, softer meat that many find undesirable.

Contemporary oyster farming alleviates much of this concern with the option of raising oysters that are called "triploids," which have been bred to be essentially sterile so they don't respond to spawning impulses over the summer. And some varieties don't spawn on the same schedule as others, such as Kumamotos, making them great over the summer. Plus, colder waters, as those up in Alaska or in deeper parts of bays, prohibit spawning impulses completely.

EASTERN
PACIFIC
EUROPEAN FLAT
OLYMPIA
KUMAMOTO

PACIFIC COAST OYSTERS

Pacific (*Crassostrea gigas*)

Though not native to the West Coast of North America, the Pacific oyster has become by far the most significant species grown in the region, and it is grown around the world as well. As native Olympia oysters began disappearing in the early twentieth century, the Pacific oyster was brought from Japan to see if it might take well to these waters. It did, and it also grew larger and more quickly than Olympias, soon becoming the dominant local oyster. The exact size and shape of a Pacific oyster will vary depending on where and how it was grown, but it often has a distinctive fluted—sometimes almost ruffly—shell.

You will seldom see an oyster sold as simply a "Pacific oyster," particularly if there are any other oysters around. Given this prolific species' geographic spread, there would be a lot with the same name. Pacific oysters most often get to be known by the place name of where they were harvested, such as Dabob Bay or Pickering Passage oysters. Though nongeographic names work too, as with Chelsea Gem oysters from Washington's Eld Inlet or Summer Ice oysters from British Columbia's Jervis Inlet.

Kumamoto (*Crassostrea sikamea*)

The Kumamoto oyster is another transplant to the West Coast from Japan. The Kumamoto is small, rarely longer than two inches, with a deep cup and firm, mild meat that is easy to enjoy. Little wonder Kumamotos (or "Kumos" to aficionados) are so popular and make for a great starter oyster for those first slurps. These oysters hold up well over summer because they don't follow the same spawning schedule as most Pacific oysters. They also didn't naturalize to this region's waters as well as Pacifics did, requiring more protection and care, so only a handful of producers farm Kumamotos.

Regardless of where they are grown, these oysters will generally be sold simply as "Kumamoto oysters," though some oyster bar menus or retail displays may list at least the state, if not the bay, from which the Kumamoto was harvested.

Olympia (*Ostrea lurida*)

The Olympia oyster is small in size (under two inches long) and big in flavor (often coppery metallic like its *Ostrea* kin, the European flat oyster). The Olympia is the only oyster native to the West Coast of North America and was named Washington State's official oyster in 2014. Native populations were nearly wiped out completely by the mid-1900s, thanks to overharvest and a toxic environment propelled in part by flourishing pulp and paper mills. But extensive and continuing efforts to revive Olympia populations all along the Pacific Coast have shown success, so the oyster is showing up more again.

Fragile little things, Olympias take some TLC in their rearing and also grow slowly, despite their diminutive size, so all in all, growing Olympias is not the most compelling of business prospects. But the payoff can be big, as these little guys are cherished as one of the premier specialty oysters available. Fans are generally opportunistic, indulging whenever the oysters appear.

Eastern (*Crassostrea virginica*)

As the name suggests, the Eastern oyster is native to the East Coast of North America where it is a prolific species that, like the Pacific, is most often sold by distinctive place names.

When it became clear the native Olympia oyster stocks were waning in the late nineteenth century, the Eastern was the first attempted replacement oyster. Shiploads of seed oysters were sent from the East Coast, and they did pretty well for some time and were well received. But transcontinental seed sourcing proved inefficient and costly, and before long the Pacific came along, with growers turning attention to that easily acclimated variety. For many years little or no Eastern oysters were grown on the West Coast.

The revival of Pacific-grown Eastern oysters came in the past couple of decades, with both Hog Island Oyster Co. on Tomales Bay in California and Taylor Shellfish Farms on Totten Inlet in Washington growing *C. virginica* oysters. In fact, the great-grandfather of Bill Taylor (vice president of Taylor Shellfish) was growing them on Totten Inlet over a century ago. The modern Totten Inlet Virginica has come to be one of the favorites among oyster bar devotees.

European flat (*Ostrea edulis*)

The European flat oyster is the pinnacle variety typically associated with the northwest of France, where the region's famous Belon oysters are considered a special delicacy. The species has been gravely challenged in recent years by a parasite. While this species produces delicious results grown on the Pacific Coast, it is slow growing and delicate and its seed is hard to come by, so some local growers who once grew European flats have cut back on production. Lopez Island Shellfish on Lopez Island in Washington recently released, however, the Shoal Bay flat, using seed produced there on the farm. And down in California, Hog Island Oyster Co. has been working to propagate seed from their own brood stock. Their flat oyster goes by the name French Hog

and is in limited production, though you may see it occasionally on their oyster bar menus. Like Belons, European flat oysters grown here have a pronounced and bold flavor, rich with coppery minerals, which is a cherished characteristic for enthusiasts.

PACIFIC COAST GROWING REGIONS

I'll start with my home state of Washington, which is the biggest producer of oysters on the Pacific Coast, not to mention one of the largest in the country. A glance at a map paired with a basic understanding of what oysters look for in a home (protected bodies of nutrient-rich saltwater with doses of fresh water for balance), and you'll see that the Puget Sound, Hood Canal, Willapa Bay, and other smaller waterways are lavish oyster territory.

California, a state with countless other agricultural resources, has a different geography with fewer oyster-friendly bays. Humboldt Bay is the top oyster-producing area in the state, which, along with Tomales Bay, represents the bulk of oyster production in California. There are also some oyster producers farther south, including in and around Morro Bay. San Francisco Bay was, in its time, a resource, but the supply of native oysters there quickly dwindled during the gold rush era, both from overharvest and because of ecological disruption from mining operations. Efforts are underway to reestablish the bay's marine health, including reviving habitats for oysters.

Oregon's ocean coast is rather linear, though it does feature a handful of bays that are conducive to growing oysters. The most prolific among them are Tillamook Bay and Coos Bay, followed closely by Yaquina Bay. Netarts Bay also produces oysters, though it has limited production simply based on its resource capacity. Netarts Bay is, however, home to one of the largest oyster hatcheries on the Pacific Coast, Whiskey Creek Shellfish Hatchery.

British Columbia is a large province with quite a lot of coastline, but its oyster-growing production is concentrated primarily in and around the Strait of Georgia, particularly in the Comox Valley area. Over half of the province's oyster production comes from Baynes Sound. The second most productive area is to the north near Lund, from Okeover Inlet, Quadra Island, and Cortes Island growing areas nearby. There are even some hearty souls who work on the western, more rugged side of Vancouver Island.

And yes, there are oysters in Alaska, the great land of seafood. But while so many other species thrive that far north, it's not a natural habitat for oysters, since the waters are too cold to induce them to spawn naturally. Growers there begin with oyster seed (which may need to come from the Lower 48) and they must be a little patient, because the cold water temperatures slow growth. But the lush waters then go on to produce delicious oysters with bright and vivid flavor. And given the cold waters and lack of spawning, they're also an ideal year-round selection.

PACIFIC COAST OYSTER BAR CULTURE

"Don't throw out the brine, that's the best part!" This I overheard in an oyster bar as an oyster devotee instructed a friend who apparently was a slurping novice. It was said with kindness, certainly, but with an emphatic punctuation that left no doubt. Oyster lovers are a passionate bunch, and they invariably want to share that passion with others.

The Acidification Factor

One of the newest and most challenging realities facing oyster (and other shellfish) growers is ocean acidification. As a scientific study, change in the pH levels of ocean water isn't new. But it wasn't until the first decade of this century that increased attention was given to the connection between the pH change and the die-off of larval oysters.

Carbon emissions, as it happens, don't only float skyward toward the atmosphere but are also absorbed into the planet's waters. For a number of years that was considered to be a good thing, since it decreased the amount of CO2 in the atmosphere. But increased CO2 in the water raises the level of the water's acidity, which is a problem for shellfish and other calcium-dependent creatures. The chemical reactions associated with these changes impede the oyster's ability to form a viable shell, a process that begins within hours of hatching. Without that initial shell, the oyster's chances of survival dissolve.

For hatcheries (which may raise their own oysters as well as sell larvae or more mature seed to other growers), adapting to current conditions includes careful study and modification of their operations. In cooperation with scientists, they are making strides to assure continued production of healthy oysters by establishing conditions under which larvae are able to produce strong shells. Once an oyster's initial shell is well established, the oyster will mature and grow an increasingly larger shell in the natural environment with little issue.

Much has yet to be learned about ocean acidification and how we can mitigate its effects on the health of marine life. What's been seen so far has been eye-opening and has motivated a great deal of scientific investigation and experimentation that will be underway for some time.

So if you're not currently an oyster fiend, find someone who is and just go along for the ride!

Oyster consumption venues come in all forms. The simplest is the personal shuck-and-slurp, with your feet planted anywhere near a good source of oysters. No cooking to do, no manners to mind, no reservations to make. You, an oyster, and an oyster knife. The other end of the spectrum comes in white-tablecloth finery, oysters perched on an elegant porcelain plate, maybe a splash of champagne mignonette or a dab of caviar. In between? There are endless options for how and where you might eat oysters. One benefit of living in such prolific oyster-growing territory is that they show up in a wide range of dining experiences.

The ultimate oyster-centric destination is an oyster bar. Conviviality is a large part of the oyster bar experience. It's akin to the best of sushi-eating experiences, when you're sitting at the sushi bar and chatting with the sushi chef about what's newest/freshest/most interesting among that evening's selections. It's a completely different experience from sitting at a table twenty feet away and ordering off the menu.

The same is true in an oyster bar. You can chat with the shucker about what oysters from the roster are the plumpest and most delicious that day, ask about distinctions between the varieties, and pick up some shucking tips. And maybe, if you're in the right place at the right time, you might get a shucker's treat, like the Sumo Kumamoto (an older, slightly larger version of the beloved oyster bar choice) I was given at a Taylor Oyster Bar one afternoon when they'd just been delivered. A half dozen on the half shell can be delightful in any restaurant setting, but it's at the oyster bar where the eater is oyster-engaged at a higher level.

Now it's time to think about eating some of these briny delights. And I must lead off with a visit to Swan Oyster Depot in San Francisco. Frills? None here. Nor the most comfortable seats, nor much room for your food on the slender counter shared by you and a dozen-plus others. The wait's generally very long out on the sidewalk. It's cash only. So many things could count against this place. But once you sit down, the geniality, the simplicity of the menu (nothing cooked to order, most is raw or precooked and chilled), and the quality of the seafood draw you in. You go here in the right frame of mind and ready to slip into Swan time for a unique oyster (and crab, shrimp, cured salmon, etc.) experience. They've been doing something right for over a hundred years.

For the Pacific Coast oyster bar with the most long-standing and interesting history, though, my vote goes to Dan & Louis Oyster Bar in Portland. It may not have been in operation quite as long as Swan has, but its roots go back earlier. Oregon Oyster Farms on Yaquina Bay dates to 1910 (a few years earlier under a different name) and owner Louis Charles Wachsmuth based his business operations in downtown Portland. By the late 1910s he'd opened a small side business of selling shucked oysters—low overhead, minimal staff needed. Over the next couple of decades the offerings grew to include oyster stew, seafood cocktails, and seafood salads. It grew too into a dedicated space nearby, operating as the full-service Dan & Louis Oyster Bar by the late 1930s.

Dan & Louis Oyster Bar is still in operation today, and it maintains a strong dose of authentic nostalgia. The oysters are still great—fresh and served simply as they should be. Other parts of the menu may be less inspiring, but the place remains true to its heritage, for which—in my mind—they deserve great credit. If they or Swan Oyster Depot decided to revamp their spaces for some modern panache, the character and local culture they represent would be, in my opinion, lost. I very much hope both are around for decades to come.

Anyone can open a new oyster bar. But no one can open one that's got a century or so under its belt. I'm a big proponent of appreciating and supporting both the old and the new.

One thing that baffles me about Seattle is that it has no Swan Oyster Depot, no Dan & Louis Oyster Bar. It's a city with plenty of seashore, a long commercial seafood history, and many generations of devoted seafood lovers—and yet our oyster bar heritage is limited. It took three-quarters into the twentieth century to see oysters register much on Seattle's culinary radar. A *Seattle Times* article from December 1978 written by John Hinterberger discusses the then proliferation of oyster-slurping venues, including F.X. McRory's, Shuckers Oyster Bar, and the soon-to-be-opened Emmett Watson's Oyster Bar, all of which are still in operation today. But in that context he points out the interesting fact that "a mere three years ago . . . Seattle had no oyster bar."

But new oyster bars? Seattle has those in spades. The first-generation wave includes the aforementioned trio, with Elliott's Oyster House and The Brooklyn joining in the 1980s. The latest spate is quite a dynamic bunch with The Walrus and the Carpenter, three locations of Taylor Oyster Bars, Bitter/Raw, Ballard Annex Oyster House, Little Gull at Westward, and the bar at Blueacre, among others. All along the Pacific coast, you'll find many dozens of places like these—from L & E Oyster Bar in Los Angeles to Rodney's Oyster House in Vancouver—where longtime devotees and newbies alike can get their fill of just-shucked treasures. And you'll find Pacific Coast oysters showing up around the country too, from the venerable Grand Central Oyster Bar in New York City to smaller neighborhood spots. Oyster fans have plenty of opportunity to slurp eastern and western varieties together to appreciate their distinct characteristics.

Even the newest kids on the block can manage to feel rather like old souls. There's not much to improve about the classic art of choosing outstanding oysters, shucking them with care, perching them on ice, and giving them to appreciative customers. At least not if you're doing it right.

Oyster accoutrements range from lemon wedges and cocktail sauce to freshly grated horseradish and mignonette. Maybe on occasion it's a zesty frozen topping. Or signature variations on the mignonette theme. At Blueacre in Seattle, I've had a soy-ginger sauce and a house cocktail sauce made with fresh horseradish. At Hog Island oyster bars in California, they serve their signature Hog Wash sauce made with rice vinegar, shallot, jalapeño, cilantro, and lime juice.

And you're certainly not limited to raw slurping. One of the most enjoyable things about this growing array of oyster outlets is seeing what else is on tap—how they round out their raw bar menu. Because after that first dozen or two oysters, you may be ready for something else. Like other raw seafood, ceviche, smoked fish, fried or baked oysters, seafood cocktails, chowder, maybe some pickled vegetables, and interesting salads. You can compose a pretty phenomenal meal from among the offerings. An oyster bar is the perfect destination to enjoy some great food, check out new oysters you haven't tried before, gain some ideas for things you might want to cook at home, and generally feed your oyster inspirations.

Shuckers Dozen Today
Shigoku
Kumamoto
Olympia
Totten Inlet
Virginica

IN THE KITCHEN

BUYING & STORING OYSTERS

The key consideration when shopping for oysters is to buy them from a merchant that goes through a decent amount of oysters. Frequent turnover means a higher likelihood of getting a fresher product—not to mention that it means they're familiar with handling and selling oysters. If the pile of in-shell oysters looks a little forlorn and haphazard to one side of a seafood case, rather than piled on ice and arranged with care, it might be a clue they're not prime oyster sellers.

Direct yourself to specialty seafood markets, markets that have tanks or dedicated shellfish displays (Asian markets in particular often have great seafood selections), and supermarkets that clearly go out of their way to bring in top-quality product and take good care of it until it's in your hands. Some farmers' markets may have oyster farmers among their vendors, a wonderful direct-from-the-producer option. And if you don't have these options where you live, know that oysters are surprisingly resilient travelers, and you can order them to be shipped a day or two from harvest to your doorstep (see Oyster Shopping Guide, page 134).

When shopping for jarred oysters, check the "sell by" date on the jar, which is generally a couple of weeks from the date it was packed. Regardless of that date, once you open the container you should use the oysters within a day or so. Also check that the packaging is securely sealed and there's no leaking or punctures (as may be the case with a plastic tub). The oysters should be plump and evenly colored, and fully submerged in liquor, which should be clear.

For in-shell oysters, these are alive and need to stay alive until you prepare them. Some stores may have them in salt-water tanks. But out of water, oysters hold up quite well in the right conditions: cold (35 to 38 degrees F), with air to breathe, and a moist environment.

Live oysters in the shell don't come with a sell-by date stamped on them, but each bag of oysters is required by law in both the United States and Canada to have a shellfish tag attached. It includes information such as identification of the producer, description of the product, date of harvest, and place of harvest. Whatever business entity receives the oysters must keep the tag available for viewing upon request as long as that batch of product lasts, then keep the tag on file for ninety days from receipt. Don't be afraid to ask to see that tag!

To ensure in-shell oysters are alive, the shells should be tightly closed; like clams and mussels, they may gape a bit on occasion but they don't gape quite as much. The shells should definitely close when tapped, and if not, toss them out. A bit of chipping on the outer edge of the oyster shell is of little concern, but if any chips or cracks expose the oyster interior, discard that one as well.

If there's a hollow sound that results from tapping an oyster with another oyster or some other small hard item, it's likely the oyster has lost much of its liquor. Pass on these if you have a chance before purchase. Follow your senses and your gut instinct. If you open an oyster and it looks small in the shell, deflated, and not plump and moist, it's not in prime form. It may not be bad to eat, but it won't be a great eating experience. And if you open an oyster that smells off or funky, don't hesitate to toss it out.

When you get your shelled oysters home, refrigerate them right away. (If it's a warm day and/or you'll not be returning directly home from the store, ask for a bag or two of crushed ice at the seafood counter to keep the oysters cold in transit.) The paper or plastic wrapping should be opened up, allowing the oysters to breathe. The oysters will be best enjoyed soon after purchase, but live oysters in their shells, stored properly, will hold well for three or four days (or longer, but don't push it).

You've got a few options for storing oysters in your refrigerator, depending on space available and how many oysters you have. The easiest, I find, is to put the oysters in a colander, set the colander inside a bowl just large enough to hold it, and cover the oysters with a damp (but not dripping wet) kitchen towel. Try to arrange the oysters in a vaguely horizontal (cupped-side down) fashion to preserve the maximum amount of liquor. Or, if you've got the refrigerator space for it, you could lay the oysters out flat in a rimmed baking sheet or large oblong baking dish, covered with a damp towel. Lastly, if you have a lot of oysters and/or you can spare the space, empty out one of the bin drawers from the refrigerator, put some crumpled newspaper in the bottom (to help soak up liquid that invariably will collect), arrange the oysters in it (usually still in their bags, but be sure the bags are open to allow them to breathe), and top with that damp towel.

Some folks swear by storing their oysters with ice, which is fine—but not really necessary in the refrigerator. It's important, if doing so, that the oysters are arranged in a way to ensure they will not be sitting in the water that runs off the melting ice. Oysters do not survive long in fresh water.

Any time you are cooking or serving the oysters in their shells, rinse them well first. If they're particularly dirty, scrub them with a stiff brush under cool running water. But if just moderately dirty, you can put them in a colander under cold running water and rather aggressively shake and toss the oysters so they knock against each other to help dislodge dirt and other debris. Don't submerge the oysters in water.

To store jarred oysters, be sure they stay fully chilled in the refrigerator until needed, sitting upright to avoid leaking.

SIZING THEM UP

One of the more interesting, and frankly frustrating, things I realized in working on this book is that there aren't a lot of industry standards with regard to sizes assigned to oysters for consumer sales.

When it comes to jarred oysters, container sizes vary among producers, but eight-, ten-, and sixteen-ounce jars are quite common. Though some brands may have other offerings, the sizes of oysters in those jars will generally range from yearling, on the smaller end, to extra-small, small, and medium. I haven't seen jarred oysters larger than medium and, given how big some of those mediums are, I think it's just as well.

It would be delightful if we knew, for example, that every ten-ounce jar of small oysters was going to contain eight oysters, but that's not the case. Some jars may have seven, others nine. And those oysters may not be of exactly the same size. In many recipes, one oyster more or less, or inconsistent sizing, isn't necessarily a deal breaker, but distribution among your dinner guests may just not be as even as hoped.

Oysters sold in the shell may not have any size listed, though a glance will give you an idea of their relative size. Generally they run from yearling/petite to extra-small, small, medium, and large. The latter are sometimes called barbecue or grill oysters, since they're beyond most oyster eater's capacity to eat any other way. I think of them as knife-and-fork oysters. We'll seldom see the jumbo oysters, larger still, which are prized in Asia and tend to go directly to that devoted market.

Which to choose, in the shell or in the jar? Jarred oysters are certainly convenient to use in any recipe for which you won't be cooking or serving the oysters in the shell. However, you can save shells after one meal, clean them very well, and later add jarred oysters to them for baking or grilling in the shell. For slurping on the half shell, live in-shell oysters are the only way to go.

For many recipes, either form will work, so the ingredient lists may offer options for both freshly shucked (you buy the oysters in the shell and shuck them yourself) or jarred (my general term for any container of preshucked oysters). Again, jarred will be quicker. But when you want to be more certain of the number and size of oyster you'll have to work with, in the shell gives you more control. It does mean shucking (see Shucking Oysters, page 31), but the benefit will be twofold: greater assurance of the oysters being the same size and you can buy exactly the number of oysters you need.

I haven't found much similarity between the sizes assigned to oysters in the shell and those in a jar. Generally the jarred version is larger: a "medium" from the jar is bigger than the meat just shucked from a "medium" oyster. This is why I may call for small to medium in-shell oysters or extra-small to small jarred oysters in the recipes.

OPINEL
INOX

SHUCKING OYSTERS

The art of opening oysters has many approaches. Half-shell pros often shuck simply holding the oyster and knife in their hands, not working on a counter. To me, it feels really awkward to shuck without a solid surface on which to securely hold the oyster. But likewise, one pro friend tried to show others the counter technique, and it just didn't feel right to him. So to each his own; either method works and will become comfortable once you get the hang of it. Just take some precautions as you go.

Protecting your hands is of number-one importance. Gloves are made just for this purpose, composed of rubbery material or steel mesh. For in-hand shuckers, a glove is a must! It's not only to protect from potential knife-to-hand contact, but also because many oyster shells have quite sharp edges that can cut just by holding them firmly in your hand. Items already in your kitchen can be used too, such as a heavy kitchen towel or oven mitt.

Next up is the oyster knife. I prefer using one that has a blade more slender and long than broad and stubby; I find it easier to maneuver in and around the oyster. Be sure the handle has some texture to it to help ensure a good grip even when your hand is wet. Never use a paring knife or other sharp kitchen knife for shucking oysters, as the thin blades may not be strong enough and you risk greater injury should the blade slip in the wrong direction. That being said, an oyster knife should have a fine enough edge to cut, rather than mangle, the adductor muscle from the shell.

Once you've got your hand protection, a good knife, and some outstanding oysters in your possession, it's time to shuck.

Having initially slipped the oyster knife into the hinged joint at the back of the oyster, carefully slide the blade across the top shell to separate it from the top side of the adductor muscle.

With the top shell now removed, slide the blade under the oyster to sever the bottom side of the adductor muscle.

I opt for the counter method and use a thick, terry-cloth kitchen towel to hold the oyster securely. Fold the towel lengthwise in thirds or quarters to produce a few layers of thickness. Set the oyster on the towel near one end, with its cupped-side down and pointed hinge end facing your dominant hand. Fold the rest of the towel up and over the oyster, holding the oyster down toward the rounded end with your non-dominant hand and leaving the hinge still exposed.

Firmly grasp the oyster knife and use the tip of the knife to wedge carefully between the oyster halves at the hinge. Sometimes this is easy, and sometimes it takes more determination. But keep at it and you will find the hinge gives and the knife tip will slip between the shells. The trick here—and I still fail at this now and then—is to have just the tip of the knife slip in, rather than barging in with the whole blade. The latter is not a catastrophe, but it often means the oyster meat will be a bit marred as a result. It's still perfectly edible, though.

Variations on the Shucking Theme

There are myriad ways to shuck an oyster. Julia Child, for one, was a proponent of the bottle opener, also known as a church key. This is the simple old-school metal tool with one flatter end for flipping off bottle caps and a pointy end for puncturing cans. The idea is to insert that pointy end into the hinge spot and apply pressure to pop open the shell. I have found this works well on oysters that have just-right hinge access but is less effective on oddly shaped or harder-to-open shells. And you'll still need a small knife for cutting the adductor muscle.

Far from old-school is the liquid nitrogen approach, or cryo-shucking. Nathan Myhrvold and his culinary team (creators of the massive six-volume Modernist Cuisine released in 2011, a project I was lucky enough to be part of) developed a technique by which a very quick and very cold freeze forces the adductor muscle to seize with virtually no impact to the rest of the oyster meat. About fifteen seconds in liquid nitrogen (roughly negative 325 degrees F) is all it takes. The oyster is left to return to a "normal" chilled temperature in the refrigerator, in which time the adductor muscle releases from the shell and the oyster is essentially self-shucked.

Then there are what I can only consider to be overengineered contraptions, oyster shucking tools that are inflexible (not all oysters are the same—sizes, hinges, shell types vary) and too unitasker for my interest. And they tend to be expensive. For your money, get a good oyster knife, learn to shuck, and spend the rest on delicious oysters instead.

Once the blade tip has slipped in, turn the knife handle to pry apart the shells a bit more. Then run the blade of the knife flat against the top shell of the oyster, separating the adductor muscle. The muscle is in the top-right quarter portion of the oyster relative to the hinge, to give you an idea of where to direct your efforts. Lift off and discard the top shell and gently slide the knife blade under the oyster as well to slice through the lower adductor muscle and fully separate the oyster. If you're serving it on the half shell and nicked the oyster earlier, you can flip the oyster over in its shell so the other side is facing (I won't tell).

HEALTH & SAFETY

Oysters are high in zinc, which tends to immediately bring to mind the oysters' longstanding reputation as an elixir of love. But most nutritionists tend to focus more on the fact that zinc helps promote a healthy immune system, maintain our sense of smell and taste, and build proteins, among other benefits. In fact, oysters contain more zinc than any other food.

Other nutritional plusses include being a very good source of protein, iron, vitamin B12, and omega-3 fatty acids, while relatively low in overall fat, calories, and sodium (yes, sodium, despite thinking of them as salty-briny). And though oysters contain what may seem like a high level of cholesterol (about forty-two milligrams per three-ounce serving), there are newer understandings of how the cholesterol we consume (what's known as dietary cholesterol) impacts—or may not, as recent findings have shown—the cholesterol in our bodies (blood cholesterol). This helps temper the oyster's oft-cited reputation as being bad for cholesterol-sensitive diets. Their nutrient profile has been found in at least one study to support the "good" HDL cholesterol levels in our bodies and can help lower the "bad" LDL cholesterol.

One of the dietary concerns related to oysters in this part of the world is *Vibrio parahaemolyticus*, a naturally occurring bacterium that—in large concentration—can cause gastrointestinal illness. It proliferates in warmer waters, which in these parts tend to occur in shallower bays and estuaries, primarily in the hottest months of summer. Waters on the West Coast of the United States don't produce *Vibrio vulnificus*, a more virulent form found in the East. Thorough cooking (reaching an internal temperature of 145 degrees F for a duration of fifteen seconds, measured using an instant-read thermometer) eliminates the harmful effects of *V. parahaemolyticus*.

Under the auspices of the National Shellfish Sanitation Program, a number of federal and state agencies in the United States participate in close monitoring of oyster habitats as well as supporting other mechanisms—such as the shellfish tag every commercial bag of oysters must include—to do all they can to ensure a safe oyster eating experience. When a problem is detected, oyster harvest in the area is closed until water temperatures drop to safe levels.

Be sure to only buy oysters from a reputable merchant that's selling them from licensed growers. Recreational harvest of shellfish is managed by state and provincial departments of fish and wildlife (or game, as the case may be). Be sure to check these agencies for information about harvest allowances, license requirements, seasonal openings, etc. before harvesting any oysters yourself.

Consuming raw or undercooked shellfish can carry risks for women who are pregnant, the very young, the very old, and those with compromised immune systems.

WHAT TO DRINK WITH OYSTERS

I'll start by saying that I'm not a big proponent of following "rules" regarding what beverage goes with what food. We all have vastly different palates and preferences; we taste foods and flavor combinations in distinctly personal ways. So I believe that "whatever you want" is a perfectly valid answer to the perennial "what should I drink with [fill in the blank]?" question.

That being said, there are some guidelines that come from objective consideration of the ingredients at hand and what's been learned from past experience. For the sake of this exercise, I'll consider the ingredient to be a raw oyster on the half shell. As with any food, the "what to drink" question is answered as much by how it's prepared and what other ingredients are added as by the main ingredient you start with. A creamy oyster stew (page 110), grilled oysters with tomato and bacon (page 86), and pan-fried oysters on a salad (page 99) take us down different paths based on their preparations. That exploration gets at universal principles of beverage pairing that are beyond the scope of this book. I realize many oyster slurpers do like to add a squeeze of lemon or tiny drizzle of mignonette, which in small doses shouldn't impact these pairing ideas that follow. Those oyster accents are accomplishing the same thing that well-paired beverages will do: they add a touch of savory acidity and bracing character to complement the rich, briny flavor of the oyster.

So let's consider what a beautiful, just-shucked half-shell oyster brings to the table. In broad terms, its flavor elements might include varying degrees of minerality, richness, brininess, vegetal flavors (cucumber, seaweed, lettuce, herbs), hints of green melon, and some earthy notes.

Complementary flavors to look for in potential beverage partners would include tart, crisp, mineral, citrus, herbal, spicy, vegetal, and smoky characteristics. As with any good partnership, ideally the two components will elevate each other when combined, with neither—no matter how delicious it may be—dominating the other. Though, granted, where "dynamic and bold partnership" ends and "one-sided domination" begins is a matter of opinion.

Half-shell oysters are about as simple as it gets, and they often lead us toward serving equally simple sips alongside: a glass of bubbly or white wine, icy vodka, chilled beer. There's little risk of competitive flavors, especially when leaning toward selections that are dry and brisk, not fruity, sweet, or overpowering.

Even though two of my oyster-loving friends, cocktail experts Robert Hess and Audrey Saunders, have an incredibly well-stocked bar and the talent to whip up a cocktail to suit any occasion, Robert says, "We will typically drink Champagne with oysters. The acid and texture of the bubbles provide a perfect counterpoint, and the crisp yet subtle flavor of the Champagne doesn't compete with the brininess of the oysters. It's all about finding the right balance."

There is a lot to be said for Champagne and dry sparkling wines as perhaps the ultimate pairing for oysters—including most of the recipes in this book.

Another friend, oyster evangelist Jon Rowley, has made a fine art out of finding the best still wines to pair with oysters. Over twenty years ago he established the Pacific Coast Oyster Wine Competition, inspired by a passage from Ernest Hemingway's *A Moveable Feast*, part of which reads: "I ate the oysters with their strong taste of the sea and their faint metallic taste that the cold white wine washed away, leaving only the taste of the sea . . ." Jon reads the full passage at the start

of each judging session as something of an anthem to put the judges in the right frame of mind.

Like my cohort judges, I chew an oyster with each sample, sip a bit of the wine, and see how well they play together on my palate, looking for a wine that "finishes clean and that exalts the oyster by not getting in the way of the next oyster," as Jon directs. From past judging notes, my favorite wines included descriptions like "bright and mineral," "touch of acid," "clean finish so oyster shines," and "refreshing and crisp." The wines that clashed most for me had strong floral and fruit characters. No points for any wine that bulldozed across the tongue and wiped out the oyster flavor.

This competition has featured wines from Washington, Oregon, and California—in celebration of the "what grows together, goes together" ethos. Among the wines that make the top-ten list, sauvignon blancs have been common, which echo one of the classic French oyster-wine choices, Sancerre—also made with sauvignon blanc grapes. Pinot gris/grigio (same grape, different name) wines are frequent winners as well, with an occasional dry chenin blanc.

It's hard to go wrong with a crisp, dry, slightly acidic white wine. Or a glass of Champagne. But you want more variety than that, right? How about beer? As much as I love beer, it's not often the drink I pair with oysters. Maybe it is because my favorite beers are strong with hops, and I find their distinct floral-resin-bitter flavor overwhelms raw oysters. Lighter, brighter options like lagers and pilsners are great candidates. And, as unlikely as it may seem, sipping a stout alongside oysters has a huge following, particularly Guinness, which I imagine to be an especially enchanting pairing when slurping an Irish oyster on its home turf. (I'm putting that experience on my bucket list.) Some adventurous brewers going back decades have even produced stout made *with* oysters, as has the brewery at Spinnakers Gastro Brewpub in Victoria, British Columbia, using Hollie Wood oysters from Baynes Sound a bit up-island.

When it comes to spirits, I'm tempted to skip right over vodka and head straight to gin, because it has so much more flavor to contribute. Sampling vodka with half-shell oysters during my research, as part of a larger study of how different spirits fared in the oyster-pairing department, I thought it was fine. Clean and brisk, not unpleasant, no particular complaints. It just didn't contribute much.

Gin's prominent ingredient is juniper, and with its bracing, slightly evergreen character it is a good start for complementing oysters. From there, gins can contain any number of botanical ingredients that generally lean toward oyster compatibility. Not only do those botanicals mesh well with the oysters' natural flavor, the touch of brine from the oysters elevates the botanical character, like you'd expect from a pinch of salt in a recipe. I would only caution that gins with strong floral components might clash with, rather than complement, a raw oyster.

Another spirit that leaped quickly to mind was aquavit. Not dissimilar to gin, aquavit is a spirit flavored with spices and herbs. Also like gin, it can be made with a broad range of flavor combinations; I would lean toward those that include herbal and savory-spice elements (fennel, dill, coriander) rather than warm spices (allspice, star anise).

The spirit-pairing study I mentioned was casual in format but serious in intent. I invited Jake Kosseff, partner/wine director at Miller's Guild in Seattle, to join me and we settled in for an afternoon of experimenting. A couple dozen oysters at a time, with three or four spirits at a time, straight up, pure and simple. In addition to the vodka and gin noted, the other white spirit we tried was a blanco tequila, which we liked at least as much as the gin. Its slight earthiness tempered the brine a touch, and other flavors in the oysters became more pronounced. Both the oysters and the tequila tasted better together.

The big surprise as we moved through different spirits was how well brown spirits partnered with the raw oysters. I would have categorically dismissed the whole lot of them, from bourbon to single malt Scotch, believing them inherently overwhelming to that little nugget of briny delight. Not so fast.

The three Scotches we tried—one Lowland (Auchentoshan), one Speyside (Glenlivet), and one Islay (Laphroaig)—all fared astonishingly well. (Okay, I will admit the Laphroaig put me over the edge—under any circumstance it's just too powerful for me.) The Scotches' sharpness contrasts the richness of the oysters but with restraint. The lightly smoky-wood character from barrel aging lingers on the palate and melds nicely with lingering oyster flavors. And the peat factor brings a hint of saltiness to the Scotch that amplifies compatibility with the oyster's brine.

Cocktails are a whole other kettle of fish, and there are just too many options to distill here. But if you start with some of these spirits and consider the general array of flavors that complement oysters—citrus, spicy, herbal, tart, crisp—you get an idea of where to start with cocktail combinations.

RECIPES

RAW

Zippy Oyster Shots

MAKES 12 OYSTER SHOTS

2 tablespoons freshly squeezed lemon juice

1½ teaspoons wasabi powder, plus more to taste

1¼ cups tomato juice

¼ cup minced celery stalks

2 tablespoons minced celery leaves

Kosher salt

12 freshly shucked extra-small to small oysters (see Shucking Oysters, page 31), with their liquor

Oyster shots—or shooters, if you prefer—represent a broad category of serving options that need just a shucked oyster, a shot glass or something like it, and a splash of vividly flavored sauce. Given the name and the glass it's traditionally served in, no wonder many oyster shots include a dose of some alcohol as well. This booze-free version is appropriate for all age groups, though grown-ups can certainly spike theirs with a bit of vodka.

This is an occasion when evenly sized, freshly shucked small oysters are best. Drizzle a bit of their captured liquor into the tomato-juice mixture if you like.

Chill 12 shot glasses or other small glasses in the refrigerator for about 1 hour before serving.

In a medium bowl, stir together the lemon juice and wasabi powder until evenly blended. Add the tomato juice, celery stalks, celery leaves, and a pinch of salt. Stir to evenly blend and let the juice mixture sit for about 15 minutes. Taste for seasoning, adding more salt if needed. If you want a stronger kick, blend another ½ teaspoon of the wasabi powder with 1 teaspoon of water and add it to the juice mixture. Let it sit again for 5 to 10 minutes.

Spoon a bit of the mixture into the bottom of each shot glass, which will help prevent the oyster from sticking to the glass. Add an oyster to each and top with the rest of the juice mixture. Serve right away.

How to Serve Half-Shell Oysters

The most ardent oyster fans I know recoil at the idea of splashing anything at all on the just-shucked gem sitting in its pearly shell. The only garnish they condone is the natural liquor in the shell with the oyster, which I can appreciate. I used to rarely, if ever, dip into the sauces offered on oyster platters. As is, you taste the very purest expression of oysterness that's available to us.

But as an open-minded oyster eater, I've come to work more variety into my slurping experiences and have realized that very light touches of complementary flavors can subtly brighten and accentuate the oyster's own flavor. A judicious dose is key. If you douse your oyster in mignonette or cocktail sauce and the flavor overwhelms the oyster, it's kind of missing the point.

The famous Portland-born gastronome James Beard had this to say about half-shell oysters in his *American Cookery* cookbook published in 1972: "At their best, oysters are eaten on the half shell with nothing to enhance them except lemon, a bit of grated fresh horseradish, or a mignonette pepper sauce. If you do not like the natural flavor of oysters, and find that you must cover them with quantities of red cocktail sauce, then perhaps you shouldn't be eating them."

Well, there you have it. I will take a different stance, though. For those new to raw slurping, for whom the first swallow of oyster just feels too big a leap, I say, sure, douse away during the getting-acquainted phase. Over time you can slowly decrease the douse to a tiny drizzle, increasing the prominence of the oyster itself.

What follows is a game plan for serving oysters on the half shell, with recipes for mignonettes, granités, and relishes as accompaniments (see pages 53 to 65). Note that for all the recipes, the yield is an approximation. The amount of topping used per oyster will vary with the slurper (from a drizzle to a douse) and with the size of the oysters. I recommend not pregarnishing the oysters, instead setting the topping in a bowl alongside or in the center of the oyster tray, with a small spoon guests can use to accentuate their own just before slurping. An exception is the frozen granités, which you should distribute on the oysters and serve right away.

Choose a rimmed tray on which you can set the just-shucked oysters. Something sturdy, watertight to contain ice melt, and with deep enough sides to hold at least an inch of ice. It can be a fancy tray if you have one, or a serving platter, but frankly once the ice and oysters are piled on, guests won't see much of the tray itself. And with delicious oysters to distract them, they won't much care what's holding them. I've used basic rimmed baking sheets at times. If you like the idea of those stainless-steel trays set on a raised stand like you see in oyster bars, check out a restaurant supply store in your area.

Ice is important for half-shell oysters that will be sitting for any time before guests enjoy them. For the oysters to nestle well into the ice—both to sit securely (not tipping out their luscious liquor) and to assure maximum shell contact with ice—it's best to use crushed ice rather than larger cubes. Ask at the seafood counter if they're willing to share some of their crushed ice with you.

Prepare the tray or platter with ice before you begin shucking, so the oysters can go directly onto the ice. The oysters can be shucked thirty to sixty minutes in advance and tucked into the refrigerator until ready to serve. This is a nice option so you can avoid shucking while your guests wait, particularly if you're not a whiz at it yet and would benefit from the lack of distraction to concentrate.

When it comes to the slurping itself, many prefer the timeless approach of lifting the oyster to bring the edge of its shell to their lips, then tipping the oyster and its liquor into their mouth. It's certainly the most sensory option: you feel the craggy shell in your hand and smell the distinct whiff of the fresh sea that's held in the shell before tasting the cold, plump oyster. Others prefer a daintier method of using a cocktail fork to lift the oyster from its shell, with the option of then sipping the liquor from the shell separately. Depending on how well you know your oyster-eating crowd, you may want to have some seafood forks on hand in case they prefer this latter option.

Types of Toppings

Mignonettes

This class of oyster sauce is known for brisk, bracing flavor, which serves as an ideal contrast to the rich and briny flavor of a raw oyster. Though mignonettes are most commonly made with vinegar, I offer one version with another oyster-friendly acidic ingredient: lemon juice (see page 55). They are very quick to make, and offer room for variation, whether using different vinegars (red, white, herb, sherry; I'd avoid sweeter balsamic) or different seasonings (pink peppercorns, fresh herbs, a bit of minced chile pepper).

Granités

Granités, sometimes called granitas, are a brisk and vibrant icy complement to half-shell oysters. Note that freezing temperatures dull the flavor of the ingredients, so the base mixture should be on the perky, flavorful side to begin with.

For freezing the mixtures, a shallow pan is ideal, so the mixture will freeze more quickly. I tend to use a pie pan, but it could be any number of vessels that are a couple inches deep and eight to ten inches across. Different materials can require different freezing times, so be mindful that exact times needed between stirs may vary. Generally, a metal pan quickens the freezing time relative to a glass pan or plastic container.

This is an easy technique but requires a bit of attention. You need to stir the mixture at regular intervals so it freezes with a flaky texture rather than freezing solid into a block. At first the icy flakes will be rather big, but as you stir over time and it freezes more, the texture will become more like coarse snow and lighten both in texture and color. If the granité does freeze solid, don't fret. Let it sit at room temperature long enough to soften again and continue with the freezing/stirring. Or you can break it into a smaller pieces and pulse in the food processor to finely chop; this will be best used right away.

Relishes

These oyster toppings are more substantial than the others in this chapter, with flavors that are vivid but not quite as pronounced as traditional mignonettes. Based on finely chopped vegetables, they also provide a bit of complementary crunch to play off the oyster. The uncooked relishes are vaguely reminiscent of salsa, and when you consider how diverse salsa variations are today—using ingredients from roasted tomatoes to pomegranate seeds—you get an idea of how diverse relish options can be for topping your oysters.

Champagne Vinegar–Roasted Shallot Mignonette

MAKES ABOUT ½ CUP, *enough for about 4 dozen half-shell oysters*

1 medium shallot

⅓ cup champagne or white wine vinegar

Freshly ground black pepper

The very classic mignonette commonly served with oysters is little more than red wine vinegar with minced shallot, the bright and brisk flavor a complement to the briny-rich oyster. You can make that by stirring together one-third cup red wine vinegar, two tablespoons minced shallot, and a grinding or two of black pepper. This twist on that classic first roasts the shallot whole to soften its sharp flavor, and uses white wine vinegar rather than red. Still brisk in flavor, it's a bit smoother than the original.

Preheat the oven to 400 degrees F.

Trim the root end from the shallot and peel away the papery outer skin. Wrap the shallot in a piece of aluminum foil and roast until it is tender when squeezed, about 30 minutes. Set aside to cool.

Finely chop 2 tablespoons of the cooled shallot. Save the rest for another use (vinaigrette dressing, rice, pasta).

In a small ramekin or other small serving dish, stir together the shallot, vinegar, and pepper to taste. The mignonette can be served right away, or allowed to sit for 1 to 2 hours. Refrigerate if making more than 2 hours in advance. (See the tips for serving raw oysters, page 49.)

Lemon-Rosemary Mignonette

MAKES ABOUT ½ CUP, *enough for about 4 dozen half-shell oysters*

1 tablespoon loosely packed fresh rosemary leaves

¼ cup boiling water

⅓ cup freshly squeezed lemon juice

Rosemary and oysters may not seem the most natural of combinations. Rosemary is an herb with some punch, no doubt, but balanced with the bright lemon it makes a really delicious accent to oysters.

Put the rosemary in a small heatproof bowl, and pour the boiling water over. Set aside to steep for about 30 minutes. Drain, reserving both the rosemary and the water.

In a small ramekin or other small serving dish, combine the lemon juice with 2 tablespoons of the rosemary water. Finely mince enough of the rosemary leaves to measure ¼ teaspoon and stir them into the lemon juice mixture. The flavors will be best if allowed to sit for 1 hour before serving. Refrigerate if making more than 2 hours in advance. (See the tips for serving raw oysters, page 49.)

Rice Vinegar–Ginger Mignonette

MAKES ABOUT ½ CUP, ***enough for about 4 dozen half-shell oysters***

1 (2- to 3-inch) piece peeled fresh ginger (about 2 ounces), plus a bit more if needed

⅓ cup unseasoned rice vinegar

2 teaspoons finely minced pickled ginger

Both fresh and pickled ginger add distinct flavor to this mignonette. Look for the thinly sliced ginger (often pink, sometimes a natural buff color) commonly served with sushi. It may be sold with other Asian ingredients in a refrigerated case, or you may find small condiment-size containers near prepared sushi.

Finely grate the fresh ginger, using a Microplane grater if you have one. Put the grated ginger in a small fine sieve set over a small bowl and press on the ginger with the back of a spoon to extract the juice. You need about 2 teaspoons for this recipe; if you have a bit less and have no more ginger to juice, you can add a bit more of the pickled ginger instead.

In a small ramekin or other small serving dish, combine the ginger juice, rice vinegar, and pickled ginger. Refrigerate if making more than 2 hours in advance. (See the tips for serving raw oysters, page 49.)

Pear–Black Pepper Granité

MAKES ABOUT 3 CUPS, ***enough for about 4 dozen half-shell oysters***

1 ripe pear, cored, seeded, and peeled (about 10 to 12 ounces)

½ cup water

3 tablespoons white wine vinegar

½ teaspoon freshly ground black pepper

Aside from citrus fruits, I am rarely inspired to combine oysters with fruit. This is a delicious exception, with the pear's mellow form of sweetness complemented by the punch of black pepper.

Coarsely chop the pear and puree it in a food processor with the water, vinegar, and pepper until very smooth. The mixture should have a pourable consistency; add a bit more water if needed.

Freeze and stir the mixture (see note below).

To serve, take the granité from the freezer and scrape it again with a fork to loosen it. Top each oyster with some of the granité and serve right away (see the tips for serving raw oysters, page 49).

Basic Freezing Technique

Pour the granité mixture into a shallow pan, such as a 9-inch-diameter cake or pie pan. Clear a spot in your freezer where the pan can sit evenly, and freeze the mixture until it begins to set around the edges, 15 to 25 minutes. Take the pan from the freezer and use a fork to break up the solid bits and stir them back into the remaining liquid, crushing any larger pieces under the fork. Freeze for another 15 to 25 minutes or so, then stir the mixture with the fork as before. Continue this process until all of the liquid has frozen and the granité has a light, coarse-snow texture. This might take 1 to 1½ hours total. If you're not using the granité soon, scrape it into a freezer-proof, airtight container and freeze. The texture is best if served within 1 to 2 hours, but the flavor will hold for 4 to 5 days.

Grapefruit-Basil Granité

MAKES ABOUT 3 CUPS, *enough for 4 dozen half-shell oysters*

1½ cups freshly squeezed pink grapefruit juice (from about 2 large or 3 medium grapefruit)

2 tablespoons red wine vinegar

1 tablespoon finely minced fresh basil

2 teaspoons sugar

The bracing acidity of grapefruit is one of my favorite counterpoints for oysters, here with a touch of extra aroma and flavor from fresh basil.

In a small bowl, stir together the grapefruit juice, vinegar, basil, and sugar until the sugar is dissolved.

Freeze and stir the mixture (see Basic Freezing Technique, page 57).

To serve, take the granité from the freezer and scrape it again with a fork to loosen it. Top each oyster with some of the granité and serve right away (see the tips for serving raw oysters, page 49).

Cucumber-Shiso Granité

MAKES ABOUT
2½* CUPS, *enough for 3½ dozen half-shell oysters

1 small English cucumber or medium regular cucumber (about 12 ounces)

3 tablespoons freshly squeezed lime juice

2 tablespoons minced fresh shiso

Kosher salt

Shiso is a spiky-edged, deep-green herb used in Japanese cuisine. A relative of mint, it has quite a different flavor, grassy-earthy with almost a touch of lemon. It can be hard to find in stores, but it makes a great garden herb if you have some space for it. You can use mint instead for equally refreshing results.

Trim and peel the cucumber (remove the seeds if not using English cucumber) and cut it into 1-inch pieces. Puree the cucumber in a food processor until a very smooth, juicy pulp is created. Add the lime juice, shiso, and a pinch of salt, and blend for another 30 seconds or so.

Freeze and stir the mixture (see Basic Freezing Technique, page 57).

To serve, take the granité from the freezer and scrape it again with a fork to loosen it. Top each oyster with some of the granité and serve right away (see the tips for serving raw oysters, page 49).

“Cocktail” Relish

MAKES ABOUT 1¼ CUPS, *enough for about 4½ dozen half-shell oysters*

1 cup finely chopped tomato

2 green onions, white and light-green parts minced

1 tablespoon ketchup

1 tablespoon freshly squeezed lemon juice

1 teaspoon prepared horseradish

½ teaspoon

Tabasco sauce

Kosher salt

This recipe echoes elements from classic cocktail sauce, but it’s a chunkier version for a more toothsome twist. Feel free to use a different pepper sauce than Tabasco; brands vary in intensity of heat, so adjust the amount used to suit your taste.

In a small bowl, stir together the tomato, green onions, ketchup, lemon juice, horseradish, Tabasco, and a good pinch of salt. Let the relish sit for about 30 minutes, stirring occasionally, to allow the flavors to blend.

Transfer the relish to a small ramekin or other small serving dish and refrigerate until ready to serve, up to 1 hour (see the tips for serving raw oysters, page 49).

Kimchi-Cucumber Relish

MAKES 1 CUP, ***enough for about 4 dozen half-shell oysters***

¾ cup peeled and seeded finely chopped cucumber

¼ cup finely chopped kimchi

1 teaspoon unseasoned rice vinegar, plus more to taste

¼ teaspoon soy sauce, plus more to taste (optional)

Kimchi—traditional Korean fermented vegetables, often cabbage—brings bold, spicy flavor to whatever context in which it's served. Its character is tempered a bit with a bright, crisp complement from cucumber. If you're a big fan of kimchi, feel free to amend the proportions, using a half cup each of the cucumber and kimchi. As is, this offers a milder kimchi flavor that most oyster slurpers should enjoy.

In a small bowl, stir together the cucumber, kimchi, rice vinegar, and soy sauce. Taste for seasoning, adding a bit more vinegar or soy sauce to taste. Let the relish sit for about 30 minutes, stirring occasionally, to allow the flavors to blend.

Transfer the relish to a small ramekin or other small serving dish and refrigerate until ready to serve, up to 1 hour (see the tips for serving raw oysters, page 49).

Fennel-Aquavit Relish

MAKES ABOUT 1¼ CUPS, ***enough for about 4½ dozen half-shell oysters***

1 small fennel bulb, with green fronds if possible

¼ cup aquavit

Kosher salt

This over-twenty-one relish has some spirited character from aquavit, the traditional Scandinavian spirit infused with any from among a range of herbs and spices. Many bottles will at least hint at the ingredients that flavor their product; if you have a choice, lean toward those with fennel-dill-anise elements, though most aquavit should work fine here.

Trim the fennel bulb (see note below), reserving the green fronds. Coarsely chop the bulb and pulse it in a food processor until finely chopped. You can finely chop the bulb by hand, if you prefer, but the agitation by the food processor blades helps draw some of the flavorful juices from the fennel.

Chop enough of the fennel fronds to measure 1 to 2 tablespoons. In a small bowl, stir together the fennel bulb, fennel fronds, and aquavit with a pinch of salt. Let the relish sit for about 30 minutes, stirring occasionally, to allow the flavors to blend. Transfer the relish to a small ramekin or other small serving dish and refrigerate until ready to serve, up to 1 hour (see the tips for serving raw oysters, page 49).

Preparing Fennel Bulb

Trim the stalks from the fennel. Reserve the tender green fronds if using in the recipe and discard the stalks (or save them for a batch of fish or vegetable stock). Cut away the tough base from the bulb and set the bulb upright on the cutting board. Halve it vertically. If the outer layer is thick and tough or bruised and blemished, discard it. Cut out the tough core from each half, then chop or slice the fennel as needed.

Gazpacho Relish with Tequila Chaser

MAKES 1 SCANT CUP RELISH, ***enough for about 3½ dozen half-shell oysters and 6 to 8 chasers***

1 cup finely chopped tomato

½ cup peeled, seeded, and chopped cucumber

2 tablespoons chopped fresh cilantro

2 tablespoons chopped green onion, white and light-green parts

2 tablespoons freshly squeezed lime juice

2 tablespoons olive oil

2 teaspoons chopped jalapeño

½ teaspoon finely chopped garlic

Pinch ground cumin

Kosher salt

About ½ cup blanco or silver tequila

One of the world's great chilled soups is gazpacho, which comes in many forms but most often brings to mind the red tomato-based soup with crisp cucumber and aromatic character from garlic and herbs. Those flavors beautifully complement raw oysters, as it happens. The liquid portion, to which a splash of tequila is added, is a delicious bonus.

In a food processor, combine the tomato, cucumber, cilantro, green onion, lime juice, oil, jalapeño, garlic, cumin, and a pinch of salt and pulse for 20 to 30 seconds until finely chopped and well blended, scraping down the sides of the bowl once or twice. There should still be a little texture; you don't want to make a smooth puree.

Spoon the mixture into a fine sieve set over a bowl and let sit for 15 to 20 minutes to drain off the flavorful liquid; stir now and then to help it drain evenly. You should have a generous ¼ cup or almost ½ cup of liquid. Add about the same amount of tequila as you have juice to the liquid and refrigerate until ready to serve. Spoon the relish into a small ramekin or other small serving dish and refrigerate until ready to serve, up to 1 hour. When serving, restir the chaser and serve a couple tablespoons each in shot glasses (see the tips for serving raw oysters, page 49).

BAKED & GRILLED

Baked Oysters with Tender Leeks & Thyme

MAKES 2 MAIN COURSE SERVINGS ***or 4 to 6 appetizer servings***

Rock salt, for baking

2 tablespoons unsalted butter

4 medium or 3 large leeks, trimmed and cleaned (see note on following page), white and light-green portions thinly sliced

1 teaspoon minced fresh thyme, divided

½ teaspoon finely grated lemon zest, divided

Kosher salt and freshly ground black pepper

¼ cup fine dried bread crumbs

2 tablespoons finely grated Parmesan cheese

¼ cup dry white wine

12 medium to large oysters in their shells, shells well rinsed

This is a versatile recipe that can be served as a main course, appetizer, or cocktail bite from a platter. If you have spare rock salt on hand, you can form small mounds on the serving plates to help hold the oyster shells even.

Set the oven rack in the center of the oven. Preheat the oven to 450 degrees F. Line a rimmed baking sheet with rock salt or cut a piece of aluminum foil twice as long as the baking sheet and crumple it on the surface of the pan.

Melt the butter in a medium skillet over medium heat. Add the leeks and cook, stirring often, until they begin to soften, 2 to 3 minutes. Stir in ¾ teaspoon of the thyme, ¼ teaspoon of the lemon zest, and a good pinch each of salt and pepper. Reduce the heat to medium, cover the skillet with its lid or a piece of aluminum foil, and cook, stirring occasionally, until the leeks are quite tender, 10 to 12 minutes longer. The leeks should not brown; reduce the heat if needed.

While the leeks are cooking, in a small bowl, stir together the bread crumbs and Parmesan with the remaining ¼ teaspoon thyme and ¼ teaspoon lemon zest. Set aside.

Uncover the leeks, stir in the wine, and cook until the liquid has mostly evaporated, 1 to 2 minutes. Take the skillet from the heat and set aside to cool.

CONTINUED

Shuck the oysters (see Shucking Oysters, page 31), discarding the top shell. Cut the adductor muscle from the bottom shell, leaving the oyster in place. A little oyster liquor is good, but pour off excess if there is quite a lot of liquor in some of the shells. Nestle the oysters into the rock salt or aluminum foil on the baking sheet so they sit evenly and securely. Top the oysters with the leek mixture, spreading it out a bit to cover the oysters. Sprinkle the bread crumb mixture evenly over the leeks.

Bake until the oysters are plump and the bread crumbs are nicely browned, 8 to 10 minutes. Use tongs or an oven mitt to transfer the oysters to individual plates or a platter, perching them as evenly as you're able. Serve right away.

Cleaning Leeks

The thin layers of a leek can sometimes harbor grit, so it's best to clean them before using. First trim away the root end and the darker-green top portion, which is quite tough (though it can be used in a batch of stock). Then split the leek lengthwise and run cool water through the layers of the leek to draw off any grit. Pat it dry with a kitchen towel and use as directed.

Oysters Baked with Devil Sauce

MAKES 4 MAIN COURSE SERVINGS ***or 8 to 12 appetizer servings***

Rock salt, for baking

For the sauce

1 tablespoon olive oil

¼ cup minced shallot or onion

½ cup dry vermouth

2 tablespoons tomato paste

1 tablespoon Dijon mustard

2 teaspoons Worcestershire sauce

About 1 teaspoon Tabasco or other hot sauce, plus more or less to taste

Kosher salt

24 medium oysters in their shells, shells well rinsed

This is my take on the barbecue sauce theme, which is a popular accent for grilled and baked oysters. So many barbecue sauces have a sweet element that I find clashes with oysters, so I go full-on savory with a bold, devilish flavor.

Set an oven rack about 5 inches below the top element. Preheat the oven to 450 degrees F. Line a rimmed baking sheet with rock salt or cut a piece of aluminum foil twice as long as the baking sheet and crumple it on the surface of the pan.

To make the sauce, heat the oil in a medium skillet over medium heat. Add the shallot and cook, stirring occasionally, until tender, 3 to 4 minutes. Add the vermouth and cook until the liquid has reduced by about half, 2 to 3 minutes. Take the pan from the heat and add the tomato paste, mustard, Worcestershire, Tabasco to taste, and a pinch of salt. Stir well to combine and let the sauce cool to room temperature.

Shuck the oysters (see Shucking Oysters, page 31), discarding the top shell. Cut the adductor muscle from the bottom shell, leaving the oyster in place. A little oyster liquor is good, but pour off excess if there is quite a lot of liquor in some of the shells. Nestle the oysters into the rock salt or aluminum foil on the baking sheet so they sit evenly and securely. Top the oysters with the sauce, about ½ teaspoon each, and bake until the oysters are plump and juices around the edge are bubbling, 8 to 10 minutes. Use tongs or an oven mitt to transfer the oysters to individual plates or a platter, perching them as evenly as you're able. Serve right away.

Green Curry Oyster & Spinach Puffs

MAKES 32 PUFFS

8 to 10 ounces jarred small to medium oysters, drained

2 tablespoons unsalted butter

½ cup minced onion

2 tablespoons prepared green curry paste

4 packed cups washed fresh spinach (about 4 ½ ounces or 1 small bunch), coarsely chopped, or half of 1 (10-ounce) package frozen chopped spinach, thawed, excess liquid squeezed out

Kosher salt and freshly ground black pepper

About 1 pound puff pastry, thawed

Look for prepared puff pastry in the freezer section of your grocery store. If you can find all-butter puff pastry (which might mean hitting a specialty shop or gourmet grocery), the flavor really is best. Because different producers make puff pastry sheets in different sizes, you might need to amend the size and shape of yours a bit. Be sure to plan ahead, as the frozen pastry needs to thaw completely before you use it.

Set 2 oven racks at the centermost positions. Preheat the oven to 425 degrees F. Line 2 baking sheets with parchment paper or silicone baking mats.

Coarsely chop the oysters and lay them on paper towels to draw off excess moisture, which will help keep the pastry from becoming soggy.

Heat the butter in a medium skillet over medium heat. When the butter has melted, add the onion and cook, stirring occasionally, until aromatic but not browned, 1 to 2 minutes. Stir in the curry paste to evenly blend with the onion. Add about half of the spinach and cook, stirring, until mostly wilted, then add the remaining spinach. Continue cooking until the spinach is evenly tender and bright green, and any excess moisture has cooked off, 3 to 4 minutes longer. (If using thawed frozen spinach, add it to the pan all at once and cook for a few minutes until well blended with the onion.) Season to taste with salt and pepper.

Transfer the spinach mixture to a medium bowl and let cool. When cooled, stir in the oysters.

Unfold half of the puff pastry onto a lightly floured work surface. Roll it out a bit so that the dough is roughly 12 by 12 inches and about ⅛ inch thick. (Other dimensions are okay, depending on the shape of the sheet you begin with, but the final lengths of the sides should be divisible by 3 inches.) Cut the dough into 3-inch squares, preferably using the rolling blade of a pastry or pizza cutter.

Spoon about 1 teaspoon of the oyster mixture just off-center onto a pastry square and flatten it a bit. Very lightly brush the pastry edges with water and fold one corner over to meet its opposite side, forming a triangle. Press the edges well with your fingers to seal, set the triangle on one of the prepared baking sheets, and continue forming triangles with the remaining ingredients.

Use kitchen shears or the tip of a small knife to snip a small vent in the top of each pastry triangle. Bake until the pastry is well puffed and moderately browned, 15 to 18 minutes, switching the baking sheets halfway for even baking. Let the pastries cool for about 5 minutes before transferring the puffs to a platter or plates for serving.

Cutting Dough

It might be natural to reach for a knife when a recipe calls for cutting raw dough into portions, but the tool I reach for instead is a rolling pastry cutter. The stationary blade of a knife can tug at the dough rather than cleanly slicing through it. A rolling blade, as on a pastry or pizza cutter, glides easily over the dough more efficiently and cleanly than a knife.

Oyster & Kale Gratin with Brown-Butter Crumbs

MAKES 4 MAIN COURSE SERVINGS
or 8 appetizer servings

6 tablespoons unsalted butter, divided, plus more for buttering

2 bunches kale (about 12 ounces each), tough stems removed

1 large shallot, thinly sliced (about ¾ cup)

½ cup freshly grated Parmesan cheese (about 2 ounces)

Freshly ground black pepper

1½ cups half-and-half, plus more if needed

20 to 24 jarred small to medium oysters, with their liquor

½ cup fine dried bread crumbs

Scalloped oysters is one of those classic recipes that is easy to make and richly satisfying. How could it be otherwise with oysters, bread crumbs, cream, and butter all baked together? This is an update on that idea, adding some flavorful kale and a delightful crunch from a topping of buttery bread crumbs. Either regular curly kale or lacinato kale can be used; the latter may take an extra minute or two to wilt.

This makes a great wintry main course, perhaps with roasted or braised root vegetables alongside. It can be served as an appetizer as well.

Preheat the oven to 400 degrees F. Butter a 12-inch gratin dish or similar shallow baking dish.

Stack 4 or 5 of the kale leaves at a time and cut across them into strips 1 to 2 inches wide.

Melt 2 tablespoons of the butter in a large skillet over medium heat. Add the shallot and cook, stirring occasionally, until tender, 3 to 4 minutes. Add a couple handfuls of the kale and cook, stirring, until it is about half wilted, then add another handful of kale. Continue adding the kale in batches as room becomes available in the skillet. The kale does not need to become fully tender, just evenly wilted; this should take about 8 to 10 minutes total.

CONTINUED

Arrange the kale and shallot mixture in an even layer in the gratin dish. Sprinkle the Parmesan over the kale and season with pepper to taste. In a small bowl, stir together the half-and-half with 3 to 4 tablespoons of the oyster liquor. Pour all but ½ cup of the mixture over the kale. Bake until the kale is tender, the cheese is just beginning to brown, and the liquids bubble around the edges,
15 to 20 minutes.

While the kale is baking, melt the remaining 4 tablespoons butter in a medium skillet over medium heat. After the butter has melted, continue cooking until the milk solids have turned a medium brown and the butter smells slightly nutty, 2 to 3 minutes longer. Take the skillet from the heat, add the bread crumbs, and stir until evenly blended.

Take the gratin dish from the oven. Arrange the oysters evenly over the kale and drizzle them with the reserved half-and-half mixture. Scatter the bread crumbs evenly over the oysters and return the gratin dish to the oven to bake until the oysters are plump and the bread crumbs are nicely browned, 8 to 10 minutes. Let the gratin sit for a few minutes before serving.

Alder Smoked Oysters

MAKES 36 SMOKED OYSTERS

For the brine

3 cups warm water

¼ cup kosher salt

3 tablespoons packed light brown sugar

1 tablespoon minced or pressed garlic

1 tablespoon finely grated peeled fresh ginger

½ teaspoon freshly ground black pepper

....

36 freshly shucked medium to large oysters (see Shucking Oysters, page 31) or jarred small to medium oysters, drained

2 cups alder or apple wood chips

These oysters are a wonderful snack as-is for cocktail hour on small crackers, or use them in the Crostini with Smoked Oysters (page 80). You could toss them with pasta, add some to a potato salad, or add a bit of smoky character to one of the soups (as an accent, not instead of the fresh oysters). There are plenty of possibilities.

Oysters being so much smaller than, say, a brisket or other large pieces of meat typically smoked, be sure to check if your grill grate has a fine enough grid to securely hold the shucked oysters. If not, use a grilling rack. Those intended for grilling vegetables are ideal, allowing smoke contact from both sides. Or you could use a large metal cooling rack that has a fine, crosshatch grid, though you might want to commit it to future grilling/smoking projects rather than expecting to use it again to cool a batch of sugar cookies.

If you have a smoker, of course this is an ideal time to use it, following the manufacturer's instructions. Your total smoke time may vary, based on the level of heat and distance the oysters are from the heat source.

To make the brine, in a large bowl, stir together the water, salt, sugar, garlic, ginger, and pepper until the salt and sugar have dissolved. Let the brine cool to room temperature.

Add the oysters to the cooled brine. They should be fully covered; add a bit more cold water if needed. Cover and refrigerate the oysters for 1 to 3 hours.

When ready to smoke the oysters, prepare an outdoor grill for indirect heat. If you have temperature control, 225 to 250 degrees F is about right. Soak the wood chips in cool water for at least 30 minutes. Lightly oil the grilling rack.

Drain the oysters from the brine, rinse them lightly under cold water, and dry them on paper towels. Arrange the oysters on the grilling rack; they can be close but should be touching each other as little as possible.

Half fill a small aluminum pan with water and put it between the coal piles in your charcoal grill or to one side of a gas grill. Drain the wood chips and scatter about half of them over the coals or put them in your grill's smoker box.

Set the rack with the oysters on the grill, away from the heat source. Quickly cover the grill to retain the maximum heat and smoke. Smoke the oysters until they are firm and nicely bronzed, 1½ to 2 hours (internal temperature should read 145 degrees F for 15 seconds, measured using an instant-read thermometer). Replenish with a few wood chips as needed, and add a few more charcoal pieces every 30 minutes or so.

Take the grilling rack from the grate and let the oysters cool. If not serving right away, store the oysters in an airtight container and refrigerate for up to 3 days.

Crostini with Smoked Oysters

MAKES 18 CROSTINI

3 tablespoons olive oil, divided, plus more if needed

½ cup finely chopped onion

1 (14-ounce) can chickpeas, drained and rinsed

⅓ cup freshly squeezed lemon juice, plus more if needed

2 teaspoons finely grated lemon zest

Kosher salt and freshly ground black pepper

18 smoked oysters (about 4 to 5 ounces), at room temperature

18 slices baguette, lightly toasted

As a kid I'd happily snack on smoked oysters plopped on whatever type of cracker was at hand. From that simple starting point, I dress things up a bit with a couple of my favorite ingredients: lemons and chickpeas. This is a perfect cocktail hour nibble or game-night snack. Look for small-batch smoked oysters from regional companies (see Oyster Shopping Guide, page 134, for some options). Better yet: smoke your own (see Alder Smoked Oysters, page 78).

Heat 2 tablespoons of the oil in a medium saucepan over medium heat. Add the onion and cook, stirring occasionally, until tender and aromatic, 3 to 4 minutes. Add the chickpeas, lemon juice, and lemon zest with a good pinch each of salt and pepper. Cook, stirring occasionally, until the chickpeas have softened a bit, 5 to 7 minutes.

Take the pan from the heat, add the remaining 1 tablespoon oil, and use a potato masher or sturdy whisk to mash the chickpeas to a texture that's cohesive and spreadable but still a bit chunky. Taste for seasoning, adding salt, pepper, or a bit more lemon juice if needed. The chickpea mixture can be made up to 1 day in advance and refrigerated, covered. Allow the chickpea mixture to come to room temperature before serving. You may need to add a tablespoon or two of water to return it to a spreadable consistency.

To serve, spread a generous tablespoon of the smashed chickpeas onto the toasted bread. Top each slice with a smoked oyster and arrange the crostini on a platter.

How to Serve Grilled Oysters

When grilling oysters, be sure you're starting with cleaned, shut-tight oysters. Avoid choosing very small oysters for grilling; they may be harder to manage on the grill and tend to be prime for slurping anyway.

You have two options: grilling the oysters preshucked on the half shell or whole in their shells. The benefits of preshucked include more even cooking, you can easily tell when they're done, a sauce or topping can be added before grilling so it melds more with oysters as they cook, and all the work's done in advance. Once grilled, just eat! The con arguments for preshucking include the extra step of shucking, plus the fact that, if the shells aren't perched evenly, toppings or sauces risk dripping out of shells during cooking and when transferred from the grill.

For cooking the oysters whole in their shells, just set them on the grill; no further preparation is required. The trick here is that some oysters will tell you when they're ready by popping their shells, others won't, leaving you to guess when to pull them off and risking that some get a little overcooked. Also, the sauces or toppings are more of an add-on accent rather than mingled with the oysters while cooking. And you likely still need to do a bit of shucking to open some, though less than preshucking requires. Note that on occasion you may get an oyster that explodes a bit from the heat, so using the grill lid with in-shell oysters is recommended.

Both methods are good; it's your choice. Either way, start with a grill that's preheated for direct medium-high heat. Total grill time will vary with different styles of grill, temperature, size of oysters, and whether the grill is covered or not.

Preshuck Grill Method

Shuck the oysters (see Shucking Oysters, page 31) and sever the lower adductor muscle. Drain off some of the liquor from each shell so the oyster is moist but not swimming; this helps avoid diluting the sauces during cooking, but if you're cooking the oysters au naturel you can leave all the liquor. Top the oysters with one of the sauces that follow (pages 85 to 87). (You can do so up to an hour ahead, keeping the oysters chilled on rimmed trays until they're ready to grill.) Use long-handled tongs to set the oysters on the preheated grill, perching the shells as evenly as you're able. Grill until the oysters are plump, their edges have curled, and juices around the edge are bubbling, about five to seven minutes. Use the tongs to transfer the oysters to a platter or individual plates for serving, alerting guests to wait a few minutes before diving in.

Grill Whole Method

Set the whole cleaned oysters directly on the preheated grill, cupped-side down, perching the shells as evenly as you're able. Grill, covered, until the shells have popped a bit or you see active bubbling around the edges of the shells, five to ten minutes, perhaps a few minutes longer for larger oysters and/or thicker shells. Use long-handled tongs to transfer the opened oysters to a tray, and when cool enough to handle, use a shucking knife to remove the top shell and to sever the lower adductor muscle in each oyster, if needed. Top with one of the sauces that follow.

Baking Oysters

Baking oysters in their shells is a great all-weather variant on outdoor grilling. Set the cleaned oysters cupped-side down on a rimmed baking sheet or large roasting pan or baking dish. Bake in a 425-degree-F oven until the oysters pop open a bit, or until you see liquids actively bubbling around the edges of the shells, indicating they should be good to go. This might take eight to twelve minutes depending on the size and shell thickness of the oysters; in the dry heat of the oven you want to avoid overcooking or the oyster meat will dry up quite a lot. Any oysters that don't open may need a bit of shucking help, or you can also preshuck and bake if you prefer.

Arugula-Almond Pesto

MAKES ABOUT ¾ CUP, *enough for about 3 dozen grilled oysters*

1 clove garlic

2 cups moderately packed arugula (about 2 ounces)

½ cup slivered almonds

¼ cup olive oil, plus more if needed

Kosher salt and freshly ground black pepper

The meaty character of this relish makes the oysters taste extra substantial, almost burger-like. This relish would be a particularly good choice for a main-course grilled option, with a crisp coleslaw alongside. A teaspoon or so of finely chopped chipotle chiles en adobo can add another level of robust and spicy flavor if you like.

Put the garlic clove in a food processor and pulse a few times to finely chop, scraping down the sides once or twice. Add the arugula, almonds, and oil with a good pinch each of salt and pepper. Puree until smooth, scraping down the sides as needed. The pesto should be on the thick side, but spread out a bit when scooped up in a spoon. Add a dash more oil or a bit of water if needed. If making the pesto in advance, you can cover and refrigerate it for up to 24 hours, but allow it to come to room temperature before serving (see the oyster grilling tips on page 81).

Smokey Tomato-Bacon Relish

MAKES 1 SCANT CUP, *enough for about 2½ dozen grilled oysters*

4 strips thick-cut smoked bacon, cut lengthwise in half and across into ¼-inch pieces

¼ cup finely chopped shallot or onion

1 cup finely chopped tomato

Kosher salt and freshly ground black pepper

It's fun to play around with the basic premise of pesto using different greens and nuts, sometimes with garlic and/or Parmesan cheese, sometimes without, depending on how it will be used. In this recipe the peppery character of arugula is a delicious contrast to the rich oysters, and the vivid green makes a striking presentation to boot.

Cook the bacon in a medium skillet over medium heat, stirring often, until most of the fat has rendered and the bacon is lightly browned, 5 to 7 minutes. If there looks to be more than about 1 tablespoon of fat, pour the excess off (it can be saved for another use), then add the shallot and cook until tender and aromatic, about 2 minutes. Stir in the tomato and cook until it has softened, the excess liquid has evaporated, and the mixture has thickened slightly, 3 to 4 minutes. Season to taste with salt and pepper and set aside until ready to serve. If making the relish in advance, you can cover and refrigerate it for up to 6 hours, but allow it to come to room temperature before serving (see the oyster grilling tips on page 81).

Garlic-Sage Butter

MAKES ABOUT ½ CUP, *enough for about 2 dozen grilled oysters*

½ cup unsalted butter, at room temperature

1 tablespoon finely minced fresh sage

1 teaspoon minced or pressed garlic

Kosher salt

NOTE: The butter is used as is if you are shucking the oysters before grilling. If you are cooking the oysters whole in their shells, the seasoned butter should be melted and drizzled over the cooked oysters just before serving.

Garlic butter on grilled oysters is one of life's simple pleasures. I ramp up the flavor a bit here using fresh sage. Flat-leaf parsley or chives would be delicious here too, or consider a combination of all three.

In a small bowl, combine the butter, sage, and garlic with a good pinch of salt. Stir together with a fork, mashing and stirring well to be sure the mixture is evenly blended. If not grilling the oysters for 1 hour or more, refrigerate the butter, which can be made up to 2 days in advance. Allow the butter to soften at room temperature before using (see the oyster grilling tips on page 81).

FRIED & SAUTÉED

Pan-Fried Oysters with Fennel Tartar Sauce

MAKES 2 MAIN COURSE SERVINGS *or 4 to 6 appetizer servings*

For the fennel tartar sauce

¾ cup mayonnaise

½ cup finely chopped fennel bulb (see note, page 64)

3 tablespoons finely chopped cornichon or dill pickle

2 tablespoons chopped fennel fronds or minced chives

1 tablespoon white wine vinegar or freshly squeezed lemon juice, plus more if needed

Kosher salt and freshly ground black pepper

····

¾ cup unbleached all-purpose flour, plus more for flouring

½ teaspoon kosher salt

→

This is one of the most popular ways to cook oysters: oysters, some seasoned flour, and a bit of fat (butter, oil, bacon fat, you choose) are all you need. For a gluten-free variation, you can use other types of flour such as chickpea or rice. You may need a bit extra in order to fully coat the oysters, as not all flours coat the same.

In a pinch, any delicious tartar sauce will be a fine complement, but the savory crunch of this fennel version is worth the few extra minutes to whip it together. Not all fennel bulbs come with tender green fronds still attached, but try to find a bulb that does. The greens make a nice herbal accent in the tartar sauce. If you've got fronds to spare, scatter them—whole or just coarsely chopped—over the oysters just before serving.

To make the tartar sauce, combine the mayonnaise, fennel bulb, cornichon, fennel fronds, and vinegar and stir well to blend. Season to taste with salt and pepper and refrigerate until ready to serve, preferably for at least 1 hour in advance to allow the flavors to blend.

Preheat the oven to 200 degrees F. Line a rimmed baking sheet with brown paper or paper towels and set an oblong wire rack on top, if you have one. Lightly flour another baking sheet or a tray for holding the coated oysters.

CONTINUED

¼ teaspoon freshly ground black pepper

24 freshly shucked medium oysters (see Shucking Oysters, page 31) or jarred small oysters, drained

Mild olive oil or vegetable oil, for frying

On a large plate or in a shallow bowl, stir together the flour, salt, and pepper. Add a few of the oysters at a time, tossing well to evenly coat with the flour mixture, then lift them out and shake off the excess flour. Set the coated oysters aside on the floured baking sheet and continue coating the remaining oysters. Reserve the excess flour.

Heat about ¼ inch of oil in a large heavy skillet, such as cast iron, over medium heat. Keep in mind that the heavier the pan, the longer it will take to preheat.

While the pan is heating, quickly retoss the oysters 3 or 4 at a time in the flour to ensure an even coating. When the oil is hot, carefully add about 6 of the oysters (don't crowd the pan; cook fewer if needed) and cook until nicely browned, about 3 minutes. Turn the oysters and brown on the other side, 2 to 3 minutes longer. Transfer the oysters to the prepared baking sheet and keep them warm in the oven while frying the remaining oysters. Add a bit more oil to the pan and allow the oil to reheat if needed between batches.

Taste the tartar sauce again just before serving, adjusting the seasoning if needed. Arrange the oysters on individual plates with a generous spoonful of the sauce alongside and serve right away.

Oyster Sliders with Togarashi Slaw

MAKES 12 SLIDERS

For the togarashi slaw

¾ cup mayonnaise

⅓ cup finely chopped green onion

Kosher salt

½ medium cucumber (about 6 ounces), peeled and seeded

1 bunch radishes (about 8 ounces), trimmed

1 medium carrot, trimmed, peeled, and cut into about 2½-inch lengths

1 cup moderately packed finely shredded Napa or savoy cabbage

2 tablespoons unseasoned rice vinegar

¾ teaspoon toasted sesame oil

½ teaspoon *shichimi togarashi*

→

A riff on the New Orleans po'boy, Asian character comes through with the Japanese spice blend shichimi togarashi, which often includes red pepper flakes, dried orange peel, dried seaweed, and sesame seeds. Keep the oysters in their briny liquor until just before coating in the crumbs, for just the right amount of moisture for the panko to cling to.

To make the slaw, in a medium bowl, stir together the mayonnaise, green onion, and a pinch of salt. Set aside.

Use a food processor with the grater plate or the large holes of a box grater to grate the cucumber. Squeeze the excess liquid from the cucumber and put it in a large bowl. Grate the radishes and carrot and add them, along with the cabbage, to the cucumber. Add about ⅓ cup of the mayonnaise mixture (reserving the rest as a spread for the buns), the rice vinegar, sesame oil, and *shichimi togarashi*, and toss well to mix. The vegetables should be just lightly coated.

Set aside while preparing the oysters, stirring the slaw occasionally. (If making the slaw more than 1 hour in advance, cover the bowl and refrigerate, along with the remaining mayonnaise mixture, allowing it to come to room temperature before serving; note that the vegetables will lose some of their crunch and the slaw will become wetter the longer it sits.)

CONTINUED

••••

2 cups panko bread crumbs, divided

Mild olive oil or vegetable oil, for frying

12 freshly shucked small to medium oysters (see Shucking Oysters, page 31) or jarred extra-small to small oysters, with their liquor

12 slider buns

NOTE: You can also serve the oysters and slaw on larger single-serving hoagies or other sandwich rolls. Or skip the bread and serve the fried oysters on the slaw in cleaned oyster shells or Asian soup spoons for cocktail party fare.

Preheat the oven to 200 degrees F. Line a rimmed baking sheet with brown paper or paper towels and set an oblong wire rack on top, if you have one. Scatter about ½ cup of the panko in another rimmed baking sheet or tray for holding the coated oysters.

Heat about ¼ inch of oil in a large heavy skillet, such as cast iron, over medium heat. Keep in mind that the heavier the pan, the longer it will take to preheat.

Spread the remaining 1½ cups panko on a plate. Add a couple of oysters to the panko, scatter some of the panko over the oysters, and press gently to help the crumbs adhere. Set the oysters aside on the crumb-covered tray and continue coating the remaining oysters. Let the oysters sit for about 5 minutes, then lightly coat them once more to be sure they're evenly covered.

Add half of the oysters to the skillet (don't crowd the pan; cook fewer if needed) and fry until nicely browned, about 3 minutes. Carefully turn the oysters and fry on the other side, 2 to 3 minutes longer. Transfer the oysters to the prepared baking sheet and keep them warm in the oven while frying the remaining oysters.

Halve the buns if they're not already split. Spread the remaining mayonnaise mixture on the bottom half of the buns. Taste the slaw for seasoning, adding more salt or *shichimi togarashi* to taste. Spoon the slaw onto the buns and top with the oysters. Cap off the sandwiches with the top buns and serve right away, with any remaining slaw alongside.

Oyster Okonomiyaki (Savory Japanese Pancake)

MAKES 4 TO 6 APPETIZER SERVINGS

For the sauce

2 tablespoons mayonnaise

1 teaspoon Worcestershire sauce

1 teaspoon mirin

1 teaspoon soy sauce

••••

¾ cup unbleached all-purpose flour

½ cup water

12 freshly shucked extra-small to small oysters (see Shucking Oysters, page 31) or jarred yearling to extra-small oysters, plus ¼ cup liquor (if less liquor is available, add water to make ¼ cup)

½ teaspoon kosher salt

2 large eggs

1½ cups moderately packed finely shredded green cabbage

Okonomiyaki is one of those dishes that is as much an idea as a recipe; there are a great many variations on ingredients used and how the recipe is composed. My favorite is Osaka style, ingredients blended first in a batter and cooked together. The pancake should be not too thick, so that it cooks evenly. This makes an ideal snack or first course.

This recipe makes two medium pancakes that are easier to cook than one large one, particularly when it comes to flipping. You can make this as one larger pancake instead, cooking each side one to two minutes longer, though flipping gets trickier.

To make the sauce, stir together the mayonnaise, Worcestershire, mirin, and soy sauce. Set aside.

Preheat a large skillet, preferably nonstick, over medium heat. Preheat the oven to 200 degrees F.

While the skillet is heating, make the batter. Put the flour in a large bowl and whisk in the water, oyster liquor, and salt until smooth and well blended. If the oysters you're using are on the bigger side, you may want to cut each in half. Whisk the eggs into the batter, then add the oysters, cabbage, mushrooms.

Set aside about 2 tablespoons of the dark-green portion of the green onions for garnish, and add the remaining amount to the batter. Stir gently to thoroughly blend.

1½ cups thinly sliced shiitake mushrooms (about 3 ounces)

4 large or 6 small green onions, trimmed and thinly sliced at an angle

3 teaspoons mild olive or vegetable oil, divided

Bonito flakes or *furikake*, for serving (optional) (see note)

When the skillet is heated, add 1½ teaspoons of the oil and gently swirl the pan to evenly coat the bottom. Restir the pancake mixture, then add half of it to the skillet, doing your best to distribute the oysters evenly. Spread the mixture out and press gently to form an even layer. Cook until the pancake is nicely browned on the bottom and looks dry on the surface, 6 to 7 minutes. Use your largest spatula to carefully flip the pancake and cook until the other side browns and the vegetables are fully tender, 6 to 7 minutes longer. (If the pancake breaks up a bit when flipping, don't fret, simply reform and reshape it as best you can; it'll still taste fantastic.) Transfer the pancake to a baking sheet and keep it warm in the oven while cooking the second pancake in the same way, adding the remaining 1½ teaspoons oil to the skillet and stirring the pancake mixture again before adding it to the skillet.

Gently slide both *okonomiyaki* onto a chopping board. Restir the sauce to mix and drizzle it over the pancakes. Scatter the reserved green onions over, then the bonito flakes. Cut each *okonomiyaki* into 6 wedges and serve.

NOTE: Bonito flakes are whisper-thin slices of dried tuna and are a common garnish for *okonomiyaki*; when they hit the warm pancake the heat makes the flakes flutter a bit, quite dramatic! If you're unable to find bonito flakes, some types of *furikake* (a Japanese rice seasoning blend) include bonito flakes and that seasoning combination is quite good on the pancake as well. You can also skip this extra dash of garnish altogether.

Endive & Radicchio Salad with Fried Oysters & Hazelnuts

MAKES 2 TO 3 MAIN COURSE SERVINGS
or 6 appetizer servings

4 large heads Belgian endive (about ¾ pound)

1 small head radicchio (about 8 ounces)

1 cup hazelnuts (about 4 ounces), lightly toasted and skinned, divided

¾ cup fine dried bread crumbs

Kosher salt and freshly ground black pepper

3 tablespoons red wine vinegar

1 teaspoon Dijon mustard

¼ cup mild olive oil, plus more for frying

2 tablespoons hazelnut oil (optional)

18 freshly shucked small to medium oysters (see Shucking Oysters, page 31) or jarred extra-small to small oysters, with their liquor

There are a lot of delicious complementary things going on in this salad: tender and crunchy, earthy and briny, fresh and bitter. You can prepare the greens and dressing and coat the oysters up to an hour in advance, refrigerating the greens and oysters. The greens should be dressed and the oysters cooked just before serving. If you don't have hazelnut oil on hand, you can simply use more of the olive oil for the dressing. As a variation you could swap out the radicchio and use four ounces of arugula instead. Whether using jarred or just-shucked oysters, keep them in their briny liquor until just before coating in the bread crumbs, as it will offer just the right amount of moisture for the crumbs to cling to.

Preheat the oven to 200 degrees F. Line a rimmed baking sheet with brown paper or paper towels and set an oblong wire rack on top, if you have one.

Trim the stem ends from the endive and discard any blemished outer leaves. Cut each endive in half lengthwise and cut away the triangular core from the base. Cut across each half into roughly ¾-inch pieces. Put the endive in a large bowl.

Halve the radicchio and cut away the tough core. Discard any blemished outer leaves. Cut across each half into slices about ¼ inch thick and add them to the bowl with the endive. Cover with a damp kitchen towel or paper towels and set aside.

CONTINUED

ENDIVE & RADICCHIO SALAD WITH FRIED OYSTERS & HAZELNUTS, CONTINUED

Put ½ cup of the hazelnuts in a food processor and pulse until finely ground (take care not to overgrind or you might end up with hazelnut butter). Add the bread crumbs and a good pinch each of salt and pepper, and pulse a few times to blend. Transfer the mixture to a plate. Coarsely chop the remaining ½ cup hazelnuts.

In a small bowl, whisk together the vinegar and mustard with a good pinch each of salt and pepper. While whisking, drizzle in the olive and hazelnut oils.

Heat about ¼ inch of olive oil in a large heavy skillet, such as cast iron, over medium heat. Keep in mind that the heavier the pan, the longer it will take to preheat.

While the oil is heating, toss 2 or 3 oysters at a time in the nut-crumb mixture, coating each oyster well and patting to remove excess. When the oil is heated, carefully add about 6 of the oysters (don't crowd the pan; cook fewer if needed) and cook until nicely browned, about 3 minutes. Turn the oysters and brown on the second side, 2 to 3 minutes longer. Transfer the oysters to the prepared baking sheet and keep them warm in the oven while frying the remaining oysters. Add a bit more oil to the pan and allow it to reheat if needed between batches.

Rewhisk the dressing to mix, then pour it over the endive and radicchio and toss well to evenly coat. Arrange the salad on individual plates and top with the oysters. Sprinkle with the remaining ½ cup hazelnuts and serve right away.

Cracker-Coated Oysters with Dilled Cream

MAKES 2 MAIN COURSE SERVINGS *or 4 to 6 appetizer servings*

¾ cup unbleached all-purpose flour, plus more for flouring

Kosher salt and freshly ground black pepper

½ cup whole or 2 percent milk

1½ cups finely crushed crackers (about 4 ounces or one sleeve), such as saltines or Ritz (see note on following page)

24 freshly shucked medium oysters (see Shucking Oysters, page 31) or jarred small oysters, with their liquor

Mild olive or vegetable oil, for frying

½ cup heavy cream

1 tablespoon minced fresh dill

These oysters get a triple-dip, so the cracker coating has extra-crispy results. This retro style of pan-fried oysters could be served with good ol' tartar sauce (like my fennel version on page 91) or cocktail sauce (the relish on page 61 would be a great option). But this simple cream sauce, essentially a savory whipped cream seasoned with fresh dill, offers something a bit different.

Preheat the oven to 200 degrees F. Line a rimmed baking sheet with brown paper or paper towels and set an oblong wire rack on top, if you have one. Lightly flour another baking sheet or a tray for holding the coated oysters.

On a large plate, put the flour with a generous pinch each of salt and pepper and stir to combine. Put the milk in a shallow bowl. Put the cracker crumbs on another large plate.

Toss a few of the oysters in the flour until evenly coated (see The Wet & the Dry, page 102). Pat to remove excess flour, then add the oysters to the milk and gently turn to evenly moisten. Lift the oysters, allowing excess milk to drip off, then coat them well in the cracker crumbs. Set the coated oysters on the floured baking sheet and continue coating the remaining oysters. Let the oysters sit for about 10 minutes so the coating sets. (The oysters can be coated up to 1 hour in advance and refrigerated until ready to cook.)

CONTINUED

NOTE: For the cracker coating, roughly crush the crackers with your hands, then pulse in a food processor or put in a heavy plastic bag and crush with a rolling pin to form fine crumbs. Don't over-process; the crumbs should still have some texture, not be too fine.

Heat about ¼ inch of oil in a large heavy skillet, such as cast iron, over medium heat. Keep in mind that the heavier the pan, the longer it will take to preheat.

While the oysters are sitting and the oil is heating, whip the cream in a medium bowl until medium peaks form. Whisk in about 2 tablespoons of oyster liquor, if you have some, then add the dill and a pinch of salt and continue whipping until the cream is well thickened. Set aside. (If the kitchen is quite warm, you can put the cream in the refrigerator, but it should ideally be room temperature when served.)

When the oil is heated, carefully add about 6 of the oysters (don't crowd the pan; cook fewer if needed) and cook until nicely browned, about 3 minutes. Turn the oysters and brown on the second side, 2 to 3 minutes longer. Transfer the oysters to the prepared baking sheet and keep them warm in the oven while frying the remaining oysters. Add a bit more oil to the pan and allow it to reheat if needed between batches.

Arrange the fried oysters on individual plates, add a generous dollop of the dilled cream alongside, and serve right away.

The Wet & the Dry

When a recipe calls for you to coat food in a succession of dry and wet ingredients, the trick is to devote one hand to dry elements (patting flour, moving to milk, patting crumbs, moving to tray) and the other hand to wet elements (oysters into flour, coating in milk and/or egg, and moving to crackers). The wet fingers stay wet, the dry ingredients stay dry, and you avoid a gooey combo of gloppy fingers and ingredients.

Hangtown Hash with Fried Eggs

MAKES 4 SERVINGS

12 to 18 freshly shucked small to medium oysters (see Shucking Oysters, page 31) or jarred extra-small to small oysters, drained

4 strips thick-cut bacon, cut across into ½-inch pieces

1 medium onion, finely chopped

3 medium Yukon Gold or other waxy potatoes, scrubbed and cut into ¼-inch dice

Kosher salt and freshly ground black pepper

¼ cup chopped fresh flat-leaf parsley

2 tablespoons chopped fresh chives

2 tablespoons unsalted butter

4 large eggs

This is a variant on Hangtown fry, which is essentially an omelet or frittata made with fried oysters and bacon. Here oysters, bacon, potato, and onion are combined in a flavorful hash on which to perch a fried egg—or poached or scrambled, whatever suits your fancy. Just add fruit, coffee, and maybe a piece of toast for brunch. For a breakfast-for-dinner option, this recipe will serve two as a main course.

Preheat the oven to 200 degrees F.

If some of the oysters you're using are on the large side, cut them in half or quarters. Small oysters will be fine left whole.

Cook the bacon in a large ovenproof skillet, preferably nonstick, over medium heat until lightly browned and most of the fat has rendered, 3 to 5 minutes. Scoop out the bacon to a plate and set aside. Pour off all but about 2 tablespoons of the bacon fat; the rest can be saved for another use.

Reheat the skillet over medium heat and add the onion. Cook, stirring, until the onion begins to soften, 3 to 5 minutes. Add the potatoes and a good pinch each of salt and pepper and toss to combine. Cover the skillet, reduce the heat to medium-low, and cook, stirring occasionally, until the potatoes are nearly tender, about 10 minutes. Remove the lid and continue cooking until the potatoes are tender and lightly browned, 5 to 7 minutes longer.

CONTINUED

Add the oysters and increase the heat to medium. Cook, stirring gently but frequently, until the oysters are plump and their edges curl, 3 to 4 minutes. Take the skillet from the heat and stir in the bacon, parsley, and chives. Taste the hash for seasoning, adding more salt or pepper to taste, and set the skillet in the oven to keep the hash warm until ready to serve. (If you don't have a griddle or another large skillet for cooking the eggs, transfer the hash to a baking dish to keep it warm in the oven and wash the skillet before continuing.)

Preheat a griddle or another large skillet over medium heat and melt the butter. Crack the eggs onto the griddle and fry 3 to 4 minutes undisturbed for sunny-side up, or 2 to 3 minutes per side for over easy, or to your taste.

To serve, spoon the warm hash onto 4 individual plates, top the hash with a fried egg, and serve right away.

Behind the Name

Hang a few desperados and suddenly a town's got a reputation. That's what came of the central California city we know today as Placerville in the Sierra Nevada foothills, which earned the Hangtown nickname in the mid–nineteenth century. A couple of accounts of the Hangtown fry recipe's origins differ slightly but represent a common inspiration. One nodded to a convicted criminal wanting to burden the local coffers with his last meal request, the other credits a newly rich prospector wishing to flaunt his wealth. Either way it came down to the triad of eggs, bacon, and oysters, three of the most expensive ingredients for that time and place. They may be relatively less expensive today but the combination still tastes indulgent. With a little dose of history tossed in.

Ale-Battered Oysters & Chips

MAKES 4 SERVINGS

Vegetable oil, for deep-frying

2 russet potatoes (about 1½ pounds), well scrubbed and dried

Kosher salt

For the Batter

1½ cups unbleached all-purpose flour

1½ cups (12-ounce bottle) pale ale, plus more (or a splash of water) if needed

½ teaspoon kosher salt

••••

24 freshly shucked medium to large oysters (see Shucking Oysters, page 31) or jarred small to medium oysters, drained

Fennel Tartar Sauce (page 91) or store-bought, for serving

Lemon wedges, for serving

This is a delightfully simple batter that takes moments to whip together—just flour, ale, and salt. There's pretty good flexibility relative to the beer you use, though I'd stay away from distinctly flavored beers like hoppy IPAs or dark stouts. The potato-frying method may sound odd, but it's inspired by one I picked up from the bright folks at Cook's Illustrated and have used many times. There's no fussing about oil temperature or double-frying as is often recommended.

Preheat the oven to 200 degrees F. Line a rimmed baking sheet with brown paper or paper towels and set an oblong wire rack on top, if you have one.

Put a few inches of oil in a Dutch oven or other large, deep, heavy saucepan; it should come no more than halfway up the sides of the pan. Cut the potatoes lengthwise into ⅜-inch-thick slices, then cut those slices lengthwise into roughly ⅜-inch-wide strips. Add the potatoes to the oil and set the pan over medium-high heat. The oil will slowly come to a boil in about 7 to 10 minutes; gently stir occasionally with a wire skimmer or long-handled metal tongs during this time to ensure the potatoes aren't sticking to each other. When the oil is boiling, continue cooking the potatoes, stirring just very gently on occasion to avoid sticking, until the potatoes are evenly and well browned, 15 to 20 minutes longer. Carefully lift out and transfer the fries to one side of the prepared baking sheet, sprinkle lightly with salt, and set in the oven to keep them warm while frying the oysters.

Adjust the heat under the pan if needed to arrive at about 350 degrees F (use a deep-fry or candy thermometer to check the temperature).

While the oil is adjusting, make the batter. In a medium bowl, combine the flour, ale, and salt, and whisk gently to mix. The batter should have the consistency of heavy cream; if it's too thick, add a bit more beer or water.

Dip 6 of the oysters into the batter, allowing excess to drip off, and slide them carefully into the oil. Fry until nicely brown, about 3 minutes. Transfer the oysters to the baking sheet with the fries and return the baking sheet to the oven. Continue coating and frying the remaining oysters, allowing the oil to reheat between batches as needed.

Arrange the fried oysters and potatoes on individual plates, add a generous dollop of tartar sauce alongside with lemon wedges, for squeezing, and serve right away.

STEAMED & POACHED

Oyster Stew

MAKES 4 TO 6 SERVINGS

6 tablespoons unsalted butter, divided

3 cups half-and-half

16 to 20 ounces jarred yearling or extra-small oysters, with their liquor

Kosher salt and freshly ground black pepper

Oyster Crackers (page 116) or store-bought, for serving

This stew is the essence of oysters and one of the most timeless ways of preparing them. Simple as it is, there are many variations, usually related to the liquid element: anything from just milk to full-on cream. In fact, old menus I've seen offered options for the diner, such as a milk stew for sixty cents or the richer cream version for seventy-five. I opt for hybrid here with half-and-half, though feel free to play around with the degree of creaminess to suit your taste.

Melt 4 tablespoons of the butter in a heavy-bottomed medium saucepan over medium heat. Warm the half-and-half in a small saucepan over medium-low heat. Cut the remaining 2 tablespoons butter into 4 to 6 even pieces and set aside.

Add the oysters and their liquor to the melted butter. Cook, shaking the pan gently now and then, until the oysters have plumped a bit and their edges begin to curl, 2 to 3 minutes. Add the warm half-and-half with a small pinch each of salt and pepper. Cook over medium heat, stirring gently now and then, until hot, 2 to 3 minutes.

To serve, ladle the stew into individual warmed shallow bowls. Top each stew with a piece of the reserved butter and another grinding of black pepper. Serve right away, with oyster crackers alongside for sprinkling over the stew.

Oysters en Escabeche

MAKES 6 TO 8 SERVINGS

For the marinade

1 cup olive oil, plus more if needed

1 tablespoon sweet paprika (regular or smoked)

¼ cup red wine vinegar

1 bay leaf, preferably fresh, torn into 3 or 4 pieces

1 teaspoon kosher salt

••••

24 small oysters in their shells, shells well rinsed, or jarred yearling to extra-small oysters, with their liquor

Crackers or sliced baguette, for serving

NOTE: For marinating the oysters, choose a small, squat dish in which the oysters will be fully covered by the marinade, ideally one with a tight-fitting lid so you can just shake gently now and then to ensure even marinating.

Every escabeche I'd encountered before seemed to have a lot going on: slivered vegetables, chiles, various seasonings in addition to the vinegar-heavy base. But while in Galicia in northwest Spain, I tasted the local mussels en escabeche and the dish was blessedly simple and outrageously delicious: olive oil, a touch of vinegar, paprika. It inspired this approach with oysters, which makes a wonderful appetizer or cocktail snack.

This is a recipe for which the spice's freshness is paramount, particularly a spice like paprika that is relatively mellow to begin with. This may be the perfect time to invest in some fresh paprika; I buy bulk spices in smaller portions that I'm likely to go through pretty quickly. In place of regular sweet paprika (which means "not spicy" in this case, as for "sweet" bell peppers), you can also use Spanish smoked paprika.

In a small saucepan over low heat, stir together the oil and paprika and warm for about 15 minutes to draw the paprika flavor into the oil. Take the pan from the heat and let it cool for 5 to 10 minutes, then stir in the vinegar, bay leaf, and salt. Set the marinade aside.

If using in-shell oysters, steam them open (see note on page 123), 5 to 10 minutes. While still warm, but not too hot to handle, remove the oysters from the shells (some shells may not have fully opened, so you will need a shucking knife to help here) and add them to the marinade. Stir to be sure the marinade is evenly coating the oysters and set aside just until cooled to room temperature.

CONTINUED

If using jarred oysters, put the oysters and their liquor in a small saucepan and warm, stirring gently now and then, until the oysters plump up and their edges curl, 4 to 5 minutes. Set the pan aside for a few minutes to cool a bit, then lift the oysters from the pan with a slotted spoon and add them to the marinade. Stir to be sure the marinade is evenly coating the oysters and set aside just until cooled to room temperature.

Transfer the cooled oysters and marinade to a medium nonreactive container; the oysters should be fully submerged in the marinade; add a bit more oil if needed. Cover and refrigerate for at least 2 hours, or longer if the oysters are on the bigger side. The oysters can marinate for up to 3 days before serving. Stir now and then to reblend the seasonings and ensure even marinating.

To serve, allow the oysters to come to room temperature. Discard the bay leaf. Transfer the oysters to a serving dish, drizzle some of the marinade over, and serve with crackers or baguette alongside.

Fresh Bay

Bay is rarely among the fresh herbs tucked into our window boxes or backyard gardens. But when I needed some fresh bay to test a recipe about twenty years ago, I bought a little four-inch pot of the herb, used what I needed for the recipe, and transplanted it to my patio garden. I still have that same bay—now a small tree—and can't tell you the last time I used a dried bay leaf. Dried bay has its place in stocks and stews, but fresh bay has a whole different character, with more vivid flavor that is almost reminiscent of nutmeg. Use it as you would dry bay, though it is versatile enough to even use in desserts.

Oyster & Celery Root Bisque

MAKES 6 SERVINGS

3 tablespoons unsalted butter

2 cups finely chopped onion

2 cups finely chopped celery, preferably the tender interior stalks

¾ cup dry white wine

1 large or 2 small celery roots (about 1½ pounds), trimmed and diced

3 cups water, plus more if needed

Kosher salt

16 to 20 ounces jarred small to medium oysters, with their liquor

Freshly ground black pepper

About ½ cup loosely packed tender celery leaves

Dry sherry, for serving (optional)

This recipe uses both the common form of celery we know well and the less common celery root, a rather gnarly looking ball that grows underground and has a subtle, earthy celery flavor. The root needs to be peeled with a knife rather than a vegetable peeler, as the skin is quite craggy in parts and thicker than you might think. First cut off the top and bottom of the root to expose the white flesh, then cut downward around the sides to remove the rest of the skin. Try to avoid cutting away too much of the white flesh.

A bisque is often enriched with cream, but you won't even miss the cream in this soup—it still tastes quite luxurious. For a little extra flavor, you could chop some smoked oysters and scatter a bit in the center of each serving along with the tender celery leaves. The soup is delicious too using half the amount of oysters, though the oyster flavor is quite subtle then.

Melt the butter in a large saucepan over medium heat. Add the onion and celery stalks and cook, stirring often, until the vegetables begin to soften and turn translucent, 5 to 7 minutes. (They should not brown; reduce the heat if needed.) Add the wine and simmer over medium-high heat until the liquid has reduced by about half and the vapor no longer smells strongly of wine, 2 to 3 minutes.

Add the celery root and water with a large pinch of salt and bring just to a boil over medium-high heat. There should be enough liquid so that the celery root floats a bit; add about ½ cup more water if needed. Reduce the heat to medium-low, cover the pan, and simmer until the celery root is very tender, 30 to 35 minutes. Add the oysters and their liquor and simmer until the oysters are plump and the edges have curled, 3 to 5 minutes.

Using an immersion blender, or by transferring the mixture in batches to a food processor or blender, puree the vegetables and oysters until very smooth. Reheat the bisque gently over medium-low heat. Season to taste with salt and pepper.

Pile the celery leaves on a cutting board and cut across them into shreds.

To serve, ladle the bisque into individual shallow warmed bowls and add a small mound of the celery leaves to the center, along with a drizzle of sherry. Serve right away.

Oyster Crackers

MAKES ABOUT 4 CUPS CRACKERS, ***enough for a couple dozen servings of soup, or snacking for 8 to 12 people***

2 cups unbleached all-purpose flour, plus more for kneading

1 teaspoon kosher salt

½ cup warm water (105 to 110 degrees F), plus more if needed

2 teaspoons (1 envelope) active dry yeast

⅓ cup unsalted butter, melted and slightly cooled

Oyster crackers are easy enough to come by in the snack aisle of your grocery store. But with not too much effort, you can make a batch from scratch and add extra homemade panache to the Oyster Stew (page 110) or pretty much any soup. Heck, they make a great snack as is for cocktail hour.

In a medium bowl, stir together the flour and salt, then make a well in the center. Pour the warm water into the well and sprinkle the yeast over, stirring it gently into the water. Let the mixture sit until the yeast is frothy, about 5 minutes. Gently stir to start blending the wet and dry ingredients, drizzle the butter over, and continue stirring until a cohesive dough forms. If the dough is a bit dry, add another 1 to 2 tablespoons warm water. Knead the dough on the counter for a few minutes, with a little flour if the dough's sticky, until smooth and satiny. Put the dough back in the bowl, cover with a kitchen towel, and set aside in a warm place until doubled in bulk, about 1 hour.

Preheat the oven to 375 degrees F. Line 2 baking sheets with parchment paper or silicone baking mats.

Turn the dough out onto the counter, punch it down, and cut the dough in half. On a lightly floured work surface, roll out one half of the dough to a square about 7 by 7 inches with a thickness of about ¼ inch. With the rolling blade of a pizza cutter or plain (not fluted) pastry wheel, cut the dough into ½-inch strips in each direction, making ½-inch squares. Use a spatula to transfer sections of the squares to the baking sheet, then separate them so they don't touch while baking. Bake until the crackers are well puffed and lightly but evenly browned, 15 to 18 minutes. Some crackers around the edges of the baking sheet may be done sooner than those in the center; transfer them to a wire rack (or a plate, some racks may not have fine enough mesh to hold the crackers) to cool and continue baking the rest for a few minutes longer. Repeat with the remaining dough portion.

When all the crackers have cooled, transfer some to a basket or bowl for serving, for guests to sprinkle over their own chowder or nibble. Store any remaining crackers in an airtight container for up to 1 week.

Oyster Chowder

MAKES 4 TO 6 SERVINGS

3 strips thick-cut bacon, cut across into ¼-inch pieces

1 medium leek, trimmed and cleaned (see note on page 70), white and light-green parts thinly sliced

8 ounces Yukon Gold potatoes, scrubbed and cut into ¼-inch dice

3 cups half-and-half

16 to 20 ounces jarred yearling or extra-small oysters, with their liquor

Kosher salt and freshly ground black pepper

Minced fresh chives or flat-leaf parsley, for serving

Chive blossoms, for serving (optional)

While the Oyster Stew (page 112) is simplicity itself, this recipe isn't too many paces beyond that. Leeks and bacon bring earthy flavor and aroma to the mix, but the oysters still lead the charge in this simple, unthickened soup (not at all like a thick clam chowder). Feel free to scatter some oyster crackers over before serving if you like, maybe even your own homemade version (see page 118). You can skip the bacon, in which case you might want to use a bit more sliced leek and/or diced potato.

Fry the bacon in a medium, heavy-bottomed saucepan over medium heat until aromatic and much of the fat has rendered, 3 to 5 minutes. (The bacon shouldn't brown much, reduce the heat if needed.) If there is more than a couple tablespoons of fat, pour off the excess (it can be saved for another use).

Add the leek to the pan and cook, stirring occasionally, until tender but not browned (as before, reduce the heat if needed to avoid browning), 3 to 5 minutes. Add the potatoes and half-and-half, bring just to a low boil, then reduce the heat to low, cover the pan, and simmer gently until the potatoes are tender, 10 to 12 minutes.

Add the oysters and their liquor and simmer, uncovered, over medium heat, stirring gently now and then, until the oysters are plump and their edges are curled, 3 to 4 minutes. Season the chowder to taste with salt and pepper.

To serve, ladle the chowder into individual warmed shallow bowls, sprinkle with the chives and chive blossoms, and serve right away.

Steamed Oysters with Sake-Ginger Butter Sauce

MAKES 4 TO 6 APPETIZER SERVINGS

¾ cup dry sake

1 tablespoon finely grated peeled fresh ginger, plus more for serving

5 tablespoons unsalted butter, cut into 6 to 8 pieces and chilled

Kosher salt

12 small to medium oysters in their shells, shells well rinsed

This is a French butter sauce with an Asian flavor, made by whisking chilled butter into reduced sake that's been spiked with fresh ginger. Spooned over simply steamed oysters, the results defy how easy it is to make.

In a small saucepan, combine the sake and ginger and stir with a whisk to mix. Set the pan over medium-high heat and boil until reduced to about 2 tablespoons, 5 to 7 minutes. Reduce the heat to low and whisk in the butter, a couple pieces at a time, allowing each addition to melt creamily into the sauce before adding the next. When all the butter has been added, whisk in a good pinch of salt, then set aside. Avoid overheating the sauce or the butter may become oily; low heat is important.

Steam the oysters (see note on following page), about 12 minutes.

Gently rewarm the sauce over low heat for 1 to 2 minutes, whisking constantly.

Remove the top shell from each oyster and loosen the lower adductor muscle if needed. Arrange the oysters in their bottom (cupped) shells on individual plates. Spoon the warm butter sauce over, top with a tiny dab of fresh grated ginger, and serve right away.

How to Steam Oysters

Put the oysters in a large pot, arranging them as evenly as you're able (they shouldn't be more than 2 oysters deep). Pour about 1 cup of water over, cover the pot, and set over medium-high heat. Within a few minutes of the water boiling, the oysters may begin to open. Use tongs to transfer them to a large bowl and cover them with a towel or aluminum foil to help keep them warm. Continue steaming the remaining oysters until all have opened, or according to the time indicated in the recipe, whichever comes first. If there are any remaining unopened oysters, let them cool until you can handle them easily and use a shucking knife to open them.

Cider-Poached Oysters on Toast

MAKES 6 SERVINGS

18 freshly shucked small to medium oysters (see Shucking Oysters, page 31) or jarred extra-small to small oysters, drained

2 cups hard apple cider, plus more if needed

3 tablespoons unsalted butter, plus more for buttering

¾ cup finely chopped crisp tart apple, skin on (such as Braeburn, Granny Smith, or Fuji)

3 tablespoons unbleached all-purpose flour

¼ cup heavy cream

Kosher salt

6 slices (not too thick) country-style bread

About 3 tablespoons minced fresh chives, for serving

The production of hard ciders has grown quite a lot in recent years; you'll likely see a number of options available at the store. Avoid sweeter styles for this recipe, opting instead for a dry cider that will complement the oyster flavor best. Apples naturally contain malic acid, which has a characteristic slightly sour flavor that complements the oysters wonderfully. You might want to get enough of the cider to sip some alongside as well.

In a medium saucepan over medium-high heat, combine the oysters and the hard cider. Bring just to a low boil, then reduce the heat to medium-low and simmer, gently stirring occasionally, until the oysters are plump and their edges curl, 3 to 4 minutes. Drain, reserving the oysters and the liquid separately and discarding any grit left behind in the bottom of the saucepan. Set the oysters aside. Measure 2 cups of the liquid, discarding any extra or adding more cider if needed.

Rinse the saucepan, then melt the butter in it over medium heat. Add the apple and cook, stirring often, until partly tender, about 2 minutes. Sprinkle the flour over, stir to evenly blend with the butter, then continue to cook,

CONTINUED

stirring, for 2 minutes (it might get rather thick, which is okay). Stir in the reserved poaching liquid and cook, stirring often, until thick enough to coat the back of the spoon, 3 to 4 minutes. Stir in the cream and season to taste with salt. Return the poached oysters to the sauce and warm gently over low heat for a few minutes.

While the oysters are warming, toast the bread. Lightly butter the bread, then halve each piece diagonally. Set the toast pieces, slightly overlapping, in the center of individual plates. Spoon the oysters and sauce on the toast, scatter chives over, and serve right away.

OYSTER EXCURSIONS

TRAVELING AT THE INSISTENCE of our stomachs is nothing new. Food lovers often plot their weekend road trips and vacation getaways around specific foods they want to savor. Oyster lovers have a rich array of options, from visiting oyster beds and breathing in the sea air where the beloved bivalves thrive, to attending rowdy and rambunctious celebrations in honor of the oyster. These are just a sample of what you may want to put on your calendar or add to an upcoming vacation itinerary.

YEAR-ROUND (OR ALMOST)

Hog Island Oyster Farm

There are a number of options here at the Tomales Bay location of Hog Island Oyster Co. in Marshall, California. At the "Hog Shack" walk-up window, you can purchase oysters, other seafood, and picnic provisions to go. Or hit their outdoor cafe, The Boat Oyster Bar, for shucked oysters, grilled oysters, charcuterie, cheese, salads, and other items for an al fresco meal. For a more in-depth experience, consider signing up for one of their farm tours. There's a taste of Hog Island at their San Francisco and Napa restaurants as well.
HogIslandOysters.com

The Oyster Saloon at Hama Hama Oysters

In addition to the retail store open year-round at their farm on Hood Canal in Lilliwaup, Washington, Hama Hama also has the outdoor Oyster Saloon (hours vary seasonally) where they serve oysters raw and roasted, plus chowder, steamed clams, and other seafoods (and some non-seafood too!). All seating is outdoors, but you can reserve an A-frame shelter. *HamaHamaOysters.com*

Taylor Shellfish Farms

The Shelton, Washington, home base of Taylor Shellfish Farms in south Puget Sound has a retail store, as does the Samish Bay location to the north. On Samish Bay you'll also find a picturesque shoreside picnic area with tables, and you can order some shucked oysters, grilled oysters, and other options from their seasonal menu of items. For an urban Taylor Shellfish experience, hit one of their three oyster bars in Seattle. *TaylorShellfishFarms.com*

Westcott Bay Shellfish

This farm on beautiful San Juan Island in Washington offers on-site pick-up of their oysters and other shellfish (advance ordering online is an option). You can lunch on the farm as well. Memorial Day to Labor Day, their Tide Tables outdoor dining area features grilled oysters, half-shell oysters, other seafoods, and light fare using only island-sourced ingredients. The rest of the year, the Net Shed offers indoor dining and an expanded menu. Lunch schedule varies seasonally, reservations highly recommended. Farm tours are also offered. *WestcottBayShellfish.com*

ANNUAL & SEASONAL EVENTS

Slurp

This annual spring event put on by the Pacific Coast Shellfish Growers Association connects oyster lovers with local growers who are on hand to shuck their just-harvested oysters. There is also a celebrity slurp-off, local beverages, other seafood from local chefs, music, and other offerings. Proceeds go to support restoration projects and other efforts to support a healthy ecosystem.
PCSGA.org/slurp

Hama Hama Oyster Rama

The date floats a bit, but they aim for some time in April or early May while it's still cool enough for oysters to be in prime form and (likely) warm enough for folks to want to gather for an outdoor party, with a low tide to offer access to the oyster beds. For the one-day gathering on Washington's Hood Canal, there are food booths, an oyster relay and other oyster-y games, live music, and a beer garden—but really, spending time on that beach and communing with the oysters is the heart and soul of the event.
HamaHamaOysters.com

Arcata Bay Oyster Festival

In honor of the important oyster industry heritage on California's Humboldt Bay (within which Arcata Bay sits), this festival, held in June each year, is a day packed with creative oyster fun. Among highlights are the Shuck and Swallow Contest, where teams of two vie to shuck and slurp the most oysters, and an oyster-calling contest (call it Humboldt quirky). About half of the many food booths offer oyster items as well.
ArcataBayOysterFestival.com

Shelton OysterFest

The first weekend of October is blocked out for many Northwest oyster lovers, because there is nowhere else to be but in Shelton, Washington, for a two-day indulgence of oysters. There are cook-offs, food booths (the grilled oysters are always my favorite), and live entertainment. But here too are serious shucking competition heats that will take the weekend's top shucker to the national shucking competition at the St. Mary's County Oyster Festival in Maryland.
OysterFest.org

Oyster New Year

Early November, Elliott's Oyster House hosts one of the biggest oyster parties Seattle sees each year. A few dozen oyster growers are on hand shucking their oysters at the seemingly-never-ending oyster bar—true bliss for the biggest among oyster fans. Many oyster-friendly beers and wines are poured, and there is an array of other foods, live music, and a "most beautiful oyster" contest, among other fun. It's all for a good cause too: proceeds go to the Puget Sound Restoration Fund.
ElliottsOysterHouse.com/oyster-new-year/

Tofino Oyster Festival

On the rustic and wonderful west coast of Vancouver Island, Tofino, British Columbia, puts on quite a party to celebrate local oysters late November each year. A new iteration of what had been the popular Clayoquot Oyster Festival for over 20 years, the three-day event includes a gala with oyster dishes from local chefs, and—an event I can't wait to attend myself—The Mermaid's Ball, a sea-themed costume party with a bounty of oysters to slurp. The "Shucker's Showdown" is a chance to catch the action as pros compete.
TofinoOysterFest.com

OYSTER RESOURCES

A FEW FAVORITE BOOKS

A GEOGRAPHY OF OYSTERS **by Rowan Jacobsen (2007)**
Subtitled "The Connoisseur's Guide to Oyster Eating in North America," this book covers an impressive range of territory relating to oysters. The coolest is Jacobsen's detailed discussion of specific oysters grown from Canada's Maritime provinces down around the Gulf Coast and up the Pacific coast to Alaska. Jacobsen is one well-traveled oyster lover.

HEAVEN ON THE HALF SHELL **by David G. Gordon, Nancy E. Blanton, and Terry Y. Nosho (2001)**
This is a wonderful book that devotes a lot of attention to the foundation of the Northwest region's oyster industry, complete with many historic photos and illustrations. It helps paint a rich picture of why oysters matter so much in this area. A second edition was released in 2023.

CONSIDER THE OYSTER **by Mary Frances Kennedy Fisher (1941)**
This small and enchanting book is doubly magnificent. The topic is a beloved one to begin with. And it is studied through the prism of M. F. K. Fisher's wholly unique writing style that is enlightening, opinionated, poetic, inspiring, and funny all at once.

MEET PARIS OYSTER: A LOVE AFFAIR WITH THE PERFECT FOOD **by Mireille Guiliano (2014)**
This story is woven in and around a tiny oyster bar in Paris, so it has a clearly Francophile perspective. But there is plenty of general discussion about the delights of eating oysters. And it will make sure you put Huitrerie Régis on a wish list for upcoming travel to France; I highly recommend it.

WEB & OTHER DIGITAL

THE OYSTER GUIDE
This is the digital companion to Rowan Jacobsen's *A Geography of Oysters.*
OysterGuide.com

OYSTERATER
Another oyster-focused site from Rowan Jacobsen, here the oyster-loving community can learn about and rate a few hundred oysters, find oyster bars, and build a personal list of favorite oysters and oyster bars along the way.
Oysterater.com

WILLAPA BAY DOCUMENTARIES
Filmmaker Keith A. Cox and his team have produced a series of documentary videos highlighting Willapa Bay's oyster industry in the southwest corner of Washington State. You'll be able to view some videos directly on the website and others are available for purchase. Wonderful character comes through, with the interviews of many oyster growers and fascinating glimpses of the work they do.
StonyPix.com

IN A HALF SHELL

Julie Qiu shares her exploration of oyster connoisseurship in this site to help make enjoying oysters as easy as possible, even for the novice. Her focus includes practical information such as shucking how-tos and visits to oyster farms and oyster bars. There are also links to interviews she has done with oyster pros around the world.
InAHalfShell.com

ORGANIZATIONS

PUGET SOUND RESTORATION FUND

Though their mission is about more than just oysters, the work of the PSRF supports many projects and activities related to oyster habitats and restoration. Among them are rebuilding Olympia oyster populations and engaging oyster-supporters through shellfish farms.
RestorationFund.org

PACIFIC COAST SHELLFISH GROWERS ASSOCIATION

PCSGA is a trade organization supporting the growers in the industry, but the site also includes consumer information about restoration initiatives, species, growers in the region, events, and more.
PCSGA.org

OYSTER SHOPPING GUIDE

TAYLOR SHELLFISH FARMS

Oysters shucked, in-shell, and Ekone smoked oysters, plus kits and other seafood

TaylorShellfishFarms.com

HAMA HAMA OYSTER COMPANY

Oysters shucked, in-shell, and smoked, plus other seafood

HamaHamaOysters.com

GOOSE POINT OYSTERS

Oysters shucked, in-shell, and smoked

GoosePoint.com

HOG ISLAND OYSTERS

Oysters in-shell, plus kits and other seafood

HogIslandOysters.com

ACKNOWLEDGMENTS

MANY FOLKS IN THE oyster business were generous with their time and expertise, including Bill Taylor, Jeff Pearson, and "Oyster Bill" Whitbeck, among others at Taylor Shellfish Farms; Lissa James Monberg at Hama Hama Oyster Company; John Finger, Terry Sawyer, George Curth, and Brenna Schlagenhauf at Hog Island Oyster Co.; and Greg Dale at Coast Seafoods.

Margaret Pilaro Barrett, executive director of the Pacific Coast Shellfish Growers Association and Betsy Peabody, executive director of the Puget Sound Restoration Fund provided a wealth of information and perspective that I found invaluable. Many others working in or with the oyster industry contributed input as well, including Jerrod Davis, Director of the Office of Environmental Health & Safety, Washington State Department of Health; Roberta Stevenson, executive director of British Columbia Shellfish Growers Association; Alex Manderson, shellfish specialist with the Oregon Department of Agriculture Food Safety and Animal Health Program; and Laura Hoberecht, PhD, Aquaculture Coordinator for NOAA National Marine Fisheries Service.

I gained valuable insight about the biology of oysters and their role in our local ecology from Dr. Jennifer Ruesink, professor, University of Washington Department of Biology.

It was a pleasure to spend time talking with Portland chef Cory Schreiber to learn more about his family's role in Oregon's oyster history.

Many friends and colleagues lent me their taste buds and their opinions in the course of testing recipes, slurping oysters, and generally contemplating the most delicious ways to enjoy them. Particular thanks to Susan Volland, Jake Kosseff, Kathy Casey, and Robert Hess. And to Cathy Sander and Vanessa Ruedebusch for help with testing recipes.

Huge thanks to the Hogensons for loaning me their cozy island home for the perfect writing retreat.

Thanks to Gary Luke at Sasquatch Books for the nudge to write this book; it has been a particularly wonderful and delicious adventure. And what a pleasure to work with such a talent as photographer Jim Henkens, who lent marvelous visual perspective to the story of Pacific Coast oysters.

And finally, special thanks to Jon Rowley, who I've known since I was a little spat of a food writer. I would not venture to guess how many oysters I've consumed in his presence. But sitting on top of that pile of discarded shells we'd have a nice view of the waters where oysters are such an important part of our Northwest seascape. As the inimitable R. W. Apple titled an article he wrote about Jon in the *New York Times*, "The Oyster is his World." And so many of us benefit from him sharing that oyster-loving world with us.

INDEX

Note: Photographs are indicated by *italics*.

CONVERSIONS

VOLUME

UNITED STATES	METRIC	IMPERIAL
¼ tsp.	1.25 mL	
½ tsp.	2.5 mL	
1 tsp.	5 mL	
½ Tbsp.	7.5 mL	
1 Tbsp.	15 mL	
⅛ c.	30 mL	1 fl. oz.
¼ c.	60 mL	2 fl. oz.
⅓ c.	80 mL	2.5 fl. oz.
½ c.	120 mL	4 fl. oz.
1 c.	230 mL	8 fl. oz.
2 c. (1 pt.)	460 mL	16 fl. oz.
1 qt.	1 L	32 fl. oz.

LENGTH

UNITED STATES	METRIC
⅛ in.	3 mm
¼ in.	6 mm
½ in.	1.25 cm
1 in.	2.5 cm
1 ft.	30 cm

WEIGHT

AVOIRDUPOIS	METRIC
¼ oz.	7 g
½ oz.	15 g
1 oz.	30 g
2 oz.	60 g
3 oz.	90 g
4 oz.	115 g
5 oz.	150 g
6 oz.	175 g
7 oz.	200 g
8 oz. (½ lb.)	225 g
9 oz.	250 g
10 oz.	300 g
11 oz.	325 g
12 oz.	350 g
13 oz.	375 g
14 oz.	400 g
15 oz.	425 g
16 oz. (1 lb.)	450 g
1½ lb.	750 g
2 lb.	900 g
2¼ lb.	1 kg
3 lb.	1.4 kg
4 lb.	1.8 kg

TEMPERATURE

OVEN MARK	FAHRENHEIT	CELSIUS	GAS
Very cool	250–275	120–135	½–1
Cool	300	150	2
Warm	325	165	3
Moderate	350	175	4
Moderately hot	375	190	5
Fairly hot	400	200	6
Hot	425	220	7
Very hot	450	230	8
Very hot	475	245	9

For ease of use, conversions have been rounded.

SHELLS

ABOUT THE AUTHOR

CYNTHIA NIMS is a lifelong Northwesterner who reveled in growing up surrounded by great food—both in her mother's kitchen and exploring the region with her family, whether eating grilled oysters on a San Juan Island beach or huckleberry pancakes while backpacking in the Olympic Mountains. After graduating from the University of Puget Sound, having majored in mathematics and French literature, Cynthia followed her dreams and went to France to study cooking at La Varenne Ecole de Cuisine. There, she received the Grand Diplôme d'Etudes Culinaires and worked on numerous cookbooks with the school's president, Anne Willan, including *Great Cooks and Their Recipes, Château Cuisine,* and ten in the *Look & Cook* series.

The author of over a dozen cookbooks, Cynthia's most recent is *Shellfish*, with *Salty Snacks* and *Gourmet Game Night* among other books she has written. In her magazine work, Cynthia has served as editor of *Simply Seafood* and food editor of *Seattle Magazine*, in addition to contributing to *Cooking Light, Coastal Living, Alaska Airlines* magazine, and other publications. She is an active member of the International Association of Culinary Professionals (for which she served as president of the board) and Les Dames d'Escoffier. Her website is MonAppetit.com and her newsletters, *Seafood Savvy* and *Long Live the Recipe Box*, are available on Substack. Cynthia and her husband live in Seattle.

Printed in China

SASQUATCH BOOKS with colophon is a registered trademark of Blue Star Press, LLC

Part of *Essential Shellfish Collection*, published 2025.
ISBN: 978-1-63217-635-6
Not for Individual Sale

29 28 27 26 25 9 8 7 6 5 4 3 2 1

The authorized representative in the EU for product safety and compliance is Authorised Rep Compliance Ltd., Ground Floor, 71 Lower Baggot Street, Dublin D02 P593, Ireland. www.arccompliance.com

Editor: Gary Luke
Production editor: Em Gale
Photographs: Jim Henkens
Cover art: Molly Reeder
Design: Anna Goldstein
Copyeditor: Michelle Hope Anderson

Sasquatch Books
1325 Fourth Avenue, Suite 1025
Seattle, WA 98101

SasquatchBooks.com

MIX
Paper | Supporting responsible forestry
FSC® C188448

SHELLFISH

SHELLFISH

Recipes with the Fresh Taste of the Sea

CYNTHIA NIMS

Photography by Jim Henkens

SASQUATCH BOOKS | SEATTLE

To all the seafood fanatics in my life: those I've had the good fortune to learn from, be inspired by, travel with, and—above all—sit alongside for countless fabulous meals over the years. Here's to much more of the same.

CONTENTS

INTRODUCTION

AT A COOKBOOK SIGNING YEARS AGO, a gentleman walked up to my table, glanced at the cover of my book, and said, more or less, "Why would anyone need a crab cookbook? All you have to do is steam it and eat it!" I don't recall how I responded in that moment, but I've thought often about that remark and how—at a basic level—he was absolutely right. When shellfish is at its best, the less you do, the better. Steam, grill, or pan-fry with minimal accoutrements, and you've got an unparalleled feast.

So why did I sit down to write this book, knowing that to be true? For the simple fact that we're not all lucky enough to have the comfort level with shellfish to simply wing it when the opportunity presents itself. In light of that, this book covers some basics of sourcing and handling seven types of shellfish, and a selection of recipes to showcase each with a range of techniques and ingredients. Plus, I'm certain that even those who have an abundance of fresh-from-the-water shellfish to cook like to change things up now and again. You know what they say about variety.

I'm a lifelong Northwesterner who was fortunate to land a great magazine editing gig right out of culinary school. By the time my stint at *Simply Seafood* magazine was done, I had traveled to Kodiak Island in Alaska; Veracruz, Mexico; and Hawaii—among other fabulous destinations—for stories about outstanding seafood. I also interacted with an array of inspiring seafood experts, including many amazing chefs. I ate it *all* up, literally and figuratively.

In the years since that job, I've had countless shellfish adventures large and small, close to home and far afield—from slurping oysters on a Puget Sound beach late-night in midwinter to procuring littleneck clams at the source while on Virginia's Eastern Shore, to enjoying enormous shrimp and gooseneck barnacles at a sixty-plus-year-old restaurant in Lisbon. I've eaten so very many great meals, both dining out and home-cooked, featuring outstanding shellfish. It has all contributed to perspectives about, and an enduring enthusiasm for, cooking shellfish that I'll be sharing with you here. Of my many thoughts about shellfish, three themes rise to the top.

First, with each bite, we have a chance to appreciate just how distinctly delicious each type of shellfish is. Exploring the range of flavors and forms among the shellfish clan is a worthy pursuit. In our kitchens, this can mean branching out from the shellfish we're most familiar with to try new things. Venture to ask about selections you're not familiar with at the seafood counter and give them a try. If you've only tried a favorite shellfish fried in the past, give it a go grilled next time. When traveling, order a different type of shellfish you don't see at home, for both the pleasure of trying something new and adding another layer of local experience to the trip.

Second, the options for cooking (or not cooking, as the case may be) shellfish are seemingly endless. Shellfish can be dressed up or served casually, they work with most any cooking technique, they can be in-shell or not, they can be perfect for a weeknight supper or for a special occasion. With basic building blocks of cooking technique and familiarity with handling different types of shellfish, your shellfish repertoire will know no bounds.

Third, and I think most importantly, shellfish are naturally evocative creatures. From the way they look to how and where they grow to regions and cultures where they've been rooted for many generations, they are undeniably delicious little storytellers. We benefit from taking a moment to consider that story. It can be simply a matter of going from generic "clams" or "shrimp" to learning of different species and where they come from, maybe how they were caught or raised. I contend that a little backstory can make the dining experience more delectable, more memorable, richer.

While "family" has a specific taxonomic meaning in the scientific world, for the purposes of this book, I think of each chapter as a family of shellfish. The shellfish covered here fall into two groups: crustaceans (crab, shrimp, and lobster) and bivalves (clams, mussels, oysters, and scallops).

Within these chapters, I focus on shellfish species that I expect are likely to be available to most readers across the United States. Some others that you might come across—either occasionally in a specialty store or in narrower regional availability—will get a brief nod. I also offer shopping and storing tips, general cooking approaches, and a handful of recipes to exemplify some of that shellfish's delicious and varied possibilities.

Each of these families are worthy of their own spotlight, and there are books that showcase them individually. Including a couple of my own: one about oysters, another featuring crab. This collection covers more shellfish in smaller bites to fuel the general enjoyment of cooking shellfish at home and a broad appreciation for shellfish overall.

SHELLFISH BASICS

IT'S BEEN INTERESTING TO HEAR FRIENDS remark now and then that though they eat shellfish in restaurants pretty regularly, they seldom cook shellfish at home (echoing a national habit I've seen referenced a few times: many leave seafood cooking to the professionals). When they do prepare shellfish at home, it's often just one or two types, those they feel most confident cooking, likely from simple repetition if nothing else.

I can imagine the vicious cycle that traps some home cooks: cooking shellfish seems intimidating, so they don't buy it very often to cook at home, so they don't have a chance to get more comfortable with cooking shellfish, so they rarely buy shellfish to cook at home, and so on. If that sounds familiar, I hope to help break that cycle, with information and encouragement to make the prospect seem a bit less daunting. The recipes include a number of ideal entry-level preparations for first-time shellfish cooks.

Whether it's an initial introduction or a refresher, this chapter includes some tips for buying shellfish, an overview of ideal shellfish-cooking techniques, and discussion of some of my favorite ingredients to pair with shellfish. And when it comes to sourcing shellfish, take some comfort in knowing that living far from a coastline does not leave you out of the fun.

As noted earlier, preparing a great shellfish meal can be as easy as finding high-quality shellfish and cooking it simply, minimally adorned. At least as a starting point, beyond which there are endless possibilities for specific dishes to create. Your shellfish-cooking repertoire will grow quickly by applying different cooking techniques and incorporating flavors that can range from mellower citrus and herbal to bolder spicy and piquant.

TIPS FOR FINDING THE BEST

First off, I want to dispel the idea that access to great shellfish is limited to those of us who can smell the briny sea air from our front doors. Top-quality seafood shops—and well-stocked seafood counters within grocery stores—can be found across the country. Shellfish travel quite well, whether to a local store or even to your doorstep, with direct fisher- or farmer-to-consumer options. It might take a bit of work if you're not already familiar with shopping options near you. But it'll be worth the effort.

You will find shellfish sold in a range of forms, from live to frozen. Tips for selecting them vary with the species, and this is covered in more detail in the following chapters. Here are some general things to keep in mind.

A pretty seafood case doesn't necessarily mean better-quality shellfish, but it's one indication of care being taken with the product. Shellfish should be on or in ice or otherwise clearly well chilled. There may even be tanks holding live crab, oysters, or lobster. Ask questions if anything's unclear: what species it is, where it's from, if it's been previously frozen (not a bad thing at all, just something to know). If the person helping you doesn't have the answer and doesn't offer to find out for you, in my mind that leaves a big question mark. And I might move on to find something else for dinner.

FRESH
SMALL
LOCAL
KING
SALMON
14.99 POUND
STAINABLY RAISED
WHOLE
COOKED
DUNGENESS
CRABS
WILD
COLOSSAL
BLACK
TIGER
PRAWNS
FRESH
WILD
JUMBO
GRILLING
SEA
SCALLOPS
JUMBO
WILD
GRILLING
LOBSTER
TAILS

I dislike the term "fishy" in the context of what poor quality seafood smells like, as if smelling of fish is inherently undesirable. Good fish, and shellfish, should smell of the ocean at high tide: brisk, clean, a little briny; sometimes I find it has little aroma at all. Skip shellfish that has an aroma that is sour, funky, ammonia-like, or otherwise off.

"Fresh" is a squishy concept. Does it mean "never frozen"? Or "currently not in a frozen state"? Or "out of the water for less than a day"? It's hard to know without clarification from whoever's using the term. Ultimately, quality is the overriding goal. Frozen is preferable to a "fresh" piece of shellfish that's been lingering in the case a bit too long.

Done well, freezing preserves the quality of the shellfish shortly after harvest—sometimes done within a matter of hours. Commercial operations do this freezing at far lower temperatures than our home freezers can attain. Buying shellfish frozen makes many varieties available year-round and gives you some leeway before needing to cook it.

Any ice crystals on the surface should be very tiny, if visible at all; larger crystals (like you might see on ice cream that's hung around in the freezer too long) can indicate less-than-ideal handling. And avoid frozen shellfish with dry, opaque patches that can indicate freezer burn. If you see something in the case that's noted as previously frozen and you like the idea of having some to hold for cooking down the line, it's worth asking if they have some still frozen that you can buy.

Be sure to plan ahead and allow time for frozen shellfish to thaw slowly in the refrigerator overnight; it's the best way to preserve the quality of the shellfish. I like to do so in a colander set over a bowl so the shellfish aren't soaking in the water released as they thaw.

Your shellfish need to stay good and cold on the way home. If it's a warm day or the trip home's not a quick one, plan ahead and take along a cooler with frozen gel packs, or ask at the seafood counter if they can give you a bag of ice to tuck alongside the shellfish. Be sure any shellfish you buy frozen stays frozen, getting it into the freezer as soon as possible. Don't try to refreeze thawed frozen shellfish: the quality will be significantly reduced.

COOKING SHELLFISH

I have designed the recipes here to be as versatile as possible, allowing you to use varieties of shellfish available to you. So I call for "medium clams" or "crabmeat" or "large shrimp" for the most part, rather than specific species, with just a few exceptions.

The beauty of shellfish, which you'll see expressed here often, is how easy it is to cook. I know there can be a lingering intimidation factor, not wanting to mess up that lovely, sometimes pricey, shellfish you brought home. But I believe you'll

Shellfish Tags

As part of the National Shellfish Sanitation Program, a number of federal and state agencies in the United States participate in close monitoring of shellfish habitats and other efforts that work to ensure a safe shellfish eating experience. One part of this program requires that shipments of live clams, mussels, oysters, and scallops in their shells are accompanied by tags with details including the species and the location and date of harvest. These tags are to accompany the shellfish from harvest to the store. Retailers should be able to produce the tag associated with those items upon request.

find shellfish to be a little more forgiving than you might have thought. And for the most part, shellfish cook quickly; so as long as it's not a more elaborate preparation, dinner can be on the table lickety-split.

Techniques

With a pot, some heat, and a bit of liquid, steaming is a go-to technique for shellfish. You can use water, wine, beer, or hard cider, with or without herbs, garlic, other aromatic elements. This is ideal for clams and mussels (tossed in the pot directly) as well as crab, lobster, and shrimp (perched on a basket or rack above the steaming liquids).

Boiling crab and lobster is another option, but I much prefer steaming. It takes far less time to bring a couple of inches of water to a boil than it does a full pot. And you don't have to worry about just the right amount of water: enough to be sure the shellfish will be submerged but not too much to risk overflow when they're added to the pot.

All these shellfish are outstanding grilling options too. Oysters in their shells, pre-shucked or not. Clams and mussels in a foil pouch or cast-iron pan, or directly on the grill if large enough. Crab and lobster grilled in their shells; scallops and shrimp threaded on skewers.

Baking and roasting are great all-season techniques that, like grilling, work well with shellfish in or out of their shells. And these methods can be just as easy: shellfish plus a bit of seasoning and a good dose of heat is all it takes.

There are many ways to fry, from a light stir-fry to more indulgent deep-frying. In between is frying in a shallow layer of oil, the quintessential expression of which, for me, is pan-fried oysters. Less oil and a hotter pan make way for searing, an ideal option for large sea scallops.

And cooking isn't even required for some shellfish. Just check out the offerings at your favorite oyster bar to know how beloved is the simplicity of an oyster slurped from its freshly shucked shell. East Coasters love their half-shell raw clams too. Scallops and shrimp appear in ceviche and similar preparations that are essentially raw, with lime juice or other acidic elements transforming—but not cooking—the flesh.

If you end up with leftover cooked shellfish after a meal, it should hold well for a day or two in the fridge. In the case of clams and mussels, take the meats from the shells. If you have the steaming liquid, strain it and store the meats in that liquid; otherwise just store as is, covered. Cooked crab, shrimp, and lobster meat should be stored in an airtight container; I prefer to take them out of the shell before storing so that they are ready to use the next day.

There are so many great options for those leftovers. In fact, many recipes here use cooked shellfish, so you'll find lots of inspiration for using leftover shellfish, whether on mini pizzas, in hearty salads, or in a dip for chips. Beyond those, think about embellishing some of your favorite recipes. Lobster quesadillas? Crab mac and cheese? Mussels tossed in curried vegetables? So many possibilities.

Getting Ready

The fancy-sounding French phrase *mise en place* (*meez ahn plahss*) is one of the best habits to develop when cooking. It simply means to put things in their place—more specifically, to account for and set up everything needed for a recipe before you dive in to begin cooking. I'd argue that it also includes carefully reading the whole recipe—not just a glance at ingredients for your shopping list and checking the cooking time to plan your schedule.

An important aspect of mise en place is addressing details mentioned in the ingredient list, such as cleaning and slicing leeks. When it comes time to add leeks to the skillet, they'll be ready to go, rather than needing to halt the cooking process so you can prep them at that moment. Or, oops, those eggs were supposed to be hard-cooked? Similarly, reading through the instructions ahead of time helps avoid surprises, such as a "set aside to cool" that throws off your timing. Taking the extra time for advanced preparation of the recipe makes the cooking process as smooth and uninterrupted as possible once you get under way.

Equipment

For the most part, cooking shellfish requires little in the way of specialty kitchen equipment. One exception would be an oyster knife for shucking oysters. I don't advise attempting that with any other knife. Good oyster knives are designed to be sturdy enough to withstand the pressure needed to pry apart the shells, with just enough of an edge to facilitate severing the adductor muscle from the shells, not sharp like our kitchen knives. There are lots of beautiful oyster knives to choose from these days. The workhorse in my collection is a style pro shuckers use, with a long, slender blade. This is the type you'll often find available from oyster farms when you're buying a dozen or two of their delicious product. They typically have a sturdy plastic handle with a bit of texture to help ensure a good grip even when your hand's a bit wet. Shucking isn't complicated but does require care: go slow and easy to get the hang of it (see page 90).

Another less-common item is an extra-large two-part steamer made for steaming seafood—particularly useful when a few or more live lobster or crab are on the menu. The bottom portion holds the liquids used for steaming, the deep top portion has a perforated base that allows steam to rise through the shellfish for cooking. I don't use the one I have all that often (and no recipe in this book relies on one), but it is handy when the occasion calls for it. Otherwise, I use a collapsible steamer basket in the bottom of my largest stock pot, usually big enough for a couple of whole crab or lobster at a time. If you don't have a pot quite that large, you can steam in batches, planning dinner time accordingly.

Long-handled tongs are helpful for maneuvering shellfish—particularly whole crab and lobster—in and out of their steaming pots, as well as handling shellfish on the grill. (Those may be two different sets of tongs.)

To get meat out of crab and lobster shells, there are crackers and mallets made for the purpose, plus slender picks and seafood forks to help extract the meat. A small pair of kitchen shears (some are made with shellfish in mind) can be helpful too, particularly with lobster and king and snow crab legs, cutting the length of the shell to easily expose the meat.

Shellfish Safety

Consuming raw or undercooked shellfish may increase your risk of foodborne illnesses, particularly for those who are pregnant or nursing, the very young, the very old, and those with compromised immune systems and other health issues. Safety guidelines from the United States Department of Agriculture list the safe internal temperature for cooked shellfish to be 145 degrees F.

It may seem wasteful to toss out clams, mussels, and oysters that have broken shells or shells that don't completely close when tapped. But if live in-shell shellfish expire before being cooked they begin to spoil quickly; it's just not worth the chance, in my opinion.

Otherwise, you probably have most of the equipment needed to accomplish a lot of great shellfish cooking already. A medium pot gets a lot of use, particularly for steaming clams and mussels; that pot could be a saucepan, Dutch oven, or similar vessel of 5- to 6-quart capacity or so. And a small, sturdy scrub brush to clean shells comes in handy too.

Ingredients

Not only are shellfish versatile in terms of cooking techniques, they play well with plenty of other ingredients also. Here are some items that I turn to most often when cooking shellfish:

- Citrus, of course: it can be tempting to finish every dish with a spritz of lemon—the bright acidity is such a perfect complement to shellfish. Lemon, grapefruit, and other citrus get good play here.
- That acidic element comes in other forms too: vinegar is an easy choice; capers, tomatoes, and yogurt also bring contrasting acidity.
- Bright, aromatic flavors of fresh herbs, ginger, and garlic are well suited to shellfish; and while a number of onion types are used throughout the recipes, I find myself reaching for green onions and leeks often.
- Peppery and piquant flavors complement shellfish well, showing up with ingredients such as horseradish, chiles, peppery greens, wasabi.
- Butter (which I love dearly) is a particularly great partner for shellfish, whether for cooking—in a skillet or spooned on top before grilling—or as a finishing touch at the table in the form of a sauce or topping.

Save Your Shells

A number of the recipes call for Shellfish Stock (page 183), whether as one of a few optional ingredients or—as in the case of Lobster and Artichoke Stew (page 151)—more of a key component. So your first assignment, should you accept it, is to cook some meals starting with in-shell shrimp, crab, and/or lobster. Rinse and save the shells, tucking them in an airtight container for the freezer if not using them right away, so you can accumulate what you need with other shells later. Or just make a smaller batch, using however many shells you have. You'll be very happy to later have portions of shellfish stock to pull from the freezer for future recipes.

SUSTAINABILITY

There is a simple fact that no matter how seemingly mundane or ubiquitous a type of shellfish may be, every piece we purchase came from some stretch of water in some particular part of the globe. Contemplating where it came from and considering how it was caught or raised can help us make more thoughtful choices at the seafood counter. Even if only to become more aware that we *have* choices.

It is possible that, without even trying, you've been buying more shellfish that's considered sustainable than you were ten or fifteen years ago. There is so much more attention now on sustainability, with increasing consumer interest in knowing more about the food we eat, and rising demand for transparency as to where and how it was grown/harvested/produced. Seafood is a prime category for that interest.

A number of factors are considered regarding the sustainability of a particular seafood. These criteria include the specific species, how healthy its population is, the location of the harvest, how it was harvested or grown, and the impact on other species. These variables explain why few seafoods have a blanket thumbs-up or thumbs-down status with sustainability-focused organizations. It may be that a seafood caught in one region is an ideal choice, while the same species from another region is less so. And some seafoods may meet a number of sustainability criteria, but fall short on a couple others, getting a mixed review of sorts.

Broadly, buying from fisheries in the United States is considered a good starting point, given programs and regulations in place that set a foundation for sustainability standards. The majority of the seafood we consume in the United

States, however, is imported, and the practices of related fisheries cover the gamut from sustainable—some certified as such—to troubling.

There seem to be more and more programs and organizations with a global scope helping to draw attention to, and improve, the overall sustainability of seafood harvesting around the world, not to mention ongoing research and technological advances. As a consumer (even as a writer!) it can be hard to keep track of the latest considerations in this very dynamic industry. You can dig in to do your own research if it's of interest, and ask questions of those supplying the seafood to you. Working with seafood on a daily basis, they may have insights to share.

Some seafood markets, and seafood departments within larger stores, make clear their focus on sustainable products, whether stating those commitments on in-store displays, on their website, or through other channels. And signage in the display case or information shared elsewhere may cite a specific reference to sustainability, perhaps MSC (Marine Stewardship Council) or BAP (Best Aquaculture Practices) certification, a Monterey Bay Aquarium Seafood Watch rating, or a designation from other organizations associated with monitoring sustainability practices.

It may not be feasible to choose the most sustainable shellfish on every trip to the market. I try but don't hit it 100 percent of the time. Making even a brief mental connection between the shellfish we cook and where it came from adds to an overall appreciation of the sources of the shellfish we eat. And it's a step that works toward assuring those shellfish populations thrive for generations to come.

CLAMS

This is one easy-going family of shellfish. Clams take little work to prep, and all you need is a pot, some heat, maybe a splash of wine or beer, and ten minutes or so to get dinner on the table. I imagine this ease is partly why clams have ranked among the top ten seafoods consumed in the United States for a number of years. That's a lot of steamed clams, pots of chowder, and countless other ways that clams are enjoyed.

The hard-shell clam varieties most commonly seen in stores are Manila clams from the West Coast and those known also as quahogs from the East Coast. Manila clams vary in size somewhat, but not nearly as much as do East Coast clams, which warrant a range of size grades. The smallest of them, littleneck, is on par with larger Manila clams. Going up from there, bigger grades include middleneck, cherrystone, and chowder. Having eaten mostly Manila clams for so many years, I was startled one day when my neighborhood grocery store in Seattle had huge East Coast clams in the case. A shopper next to me was giddy at the prospect of taking some home to cook. I couldn't get over the fact that just four clams weighed nearly one and a quarter pounds. I steamed, chopped, and stuffed them for a new-to-me treat.

There are a number of other clams you may see that have limited regional and seasonal availability. West Coast examples include the Pacific littleneck, a different species from the East Coast's, and the strikingly outsize geoduck (*gooey-duck*) clam, which can weigh as much as ten pounds (typically harvested at one to two pounds or so). Any clam that's steamed might be thought of as a "steamer," but in New England it references a specific species, also known as soft-shell clams. They have thinner (not really "soft") shells, primarily enjoyed simply steamed or breaded and fried. Different enough from hard-shell clams, they're not interchangeable in the recipes here.

Both coasts have a razor clam as well: the East Coast's version is more narrow and long, the West Coast's a bit shorter with an elongated oval shape. Mahogany and savory are among other clam types you might see on occasion.

While some clam harvesting today remains wild, most of what we see in stores has been farm-raised, which results in rather steady availability throughout the year.

SHOPPING AND STORING

Manila clams are generally sold by the pound, either bulk or in mesh bags of a preset weight. Littleneck clams and other East Coast hard-shell clams may be sold by the pound or by the piece, either bulk or in set quantities by the bag.

Clams you buy fresh in the shell are alive and need to stay alive until you cook them. It's best to get them home and in the fridge as quickly as you can. If it's a warm day or it'll be a while before you get home, ask for a small bag of ice at the seafood counter to accompany your shellfish. Or plan ahead and have a cooler with frozen gel packs in the car.

Transfer the clams to a large bowl when you get home. I usually put them in a colander set inside the bowl to hold them above any liquid that accumulates. Top the clams with a damp, but not sopping wet, kitchen towel. The clams need air to survive, so don't cover the bowl any more than that.

Don't be tempted to store clams in water. Keeping them moist is one thing, but they will perish if submerged in fresh water for too long. If the towel dries out, dampen it again. It's ideal to cook clams the same day you buy them, but stored well, they should hold for a day or two.

CLEANING

Clams should be cleaned just before cooking. To do so, put them in a sturdy colander and shake them vigorously under cold running water for a minute or two. If you still feel grit or sand on the shells, pull out a brush to scrub them. You can always do a test: scrub a couple of shells and see if there's a visible difference in grit being removed.

To Purge, or Not

After cooking lots of clams for many years, I've rarely encountered a batch that needed purging, but it's still a practice I see mentioned now and then. As I understand it, most clams sold commercially are purged before they get to us, though perhaps there still are exceptions. Purging encourages the clams to pass water through their system and expel any sandy grit they may still contain. You can steam open a couple of the ones you brought home and do a quick test. If you encounter some grit, put the remaining clams in a big bowl with cold salted water to generously cover and refrigerate for 20 to 30 minutes. Drain well, scrub the shells, and continue with the recipe, discarding any clams that don't close completely after the soak.

As you're cleaning the clams, discard any with broken shells. Also make sure the shells are tightly closed: tap any gaping clams on the counter to see that they close completely. If not, discard them.

COOKING

Clams are the perfect casual meal that can be on the table in no time, with a salad alongside and obligatory bread to help soak up the flavorful liquids. From simple wine and garlic to citrus and herb accents to zesty chile-tomato mixtures, the steaming components have countless potential variations. Beyond that classic preparation, clams can be grilled, roasted, and sautéed in the shell, with many possibilities out of the shell. Among recipes here are steamed clams, clam-topped pizzas, clams stuffed for baking, and a rather classic chowder.

Manilas are on the smaller end of the scale, perfect for steaming to serve in the shell, and the cooked meats can be used whole in soups, pastas, and such. Larger East Coast hard-shell clams are also versatile, with smaller clams used for simpler steamed recipes, and the meats of larger clams often chopped to use in recipes such as chowders, fritters, and stuffed clams.

One thing about the different varieties of clams I noticed while testing is that the East Coast hard-shell clams had heavier shells than did the Manilas. So one pound of littlenecks usually produced a little less meat than a pound of Manila clams. The amount of clam meat you end up with in these recipes may vary depending on which clam you use.

Clam Chowder with Petite Peas

MAKES 4 TO 6 SERVINGS

2½ to 3 pounds small to medium live hard-shell clams, well rinsed (see page 17)

1½ cups water

About 2 cups clam juice (see page 22), Shellfish Stock (page 183), or water

¼ cup unsalted butter

1 large leek, trimmed, cleaned and thinly sliced (about 1½ cups)

1 large carrot, cut into ¼-inch dice (about 1 cup)

2 stalks celery, thinly sliced (about 3/4 cup)

2 tablespoons all-purpose flour

1½ teaspoons minced fresh thyme, or ½ teaspoon dried thyme

6 ounces red new potatoes, scrubbed and cut into ½-inch dice

As much as I love bacon and often include it in chowders, this version skips it to emphasize the briny-sweet flavor of the clams. This is a lighter style of chowder, just moderately thickened with a bit of flour. If you want to keep some of the clams in their shells for serving, feel free. How about enjoying another classic alongside: grilled cheese?

Put the clams and water in a medium pot, set the pot over medium-high heat, and cover. After 2 to 3 minutes, gently stir the clams with a large slotted spoon. Cover the pot and continue cooking, stirring once or twice more, until all, or mostly all, of the clams have opened, 2 to 5 minutes longer. Use the slotted spoon to transfer the opened clams to a large bowl. Continue cooking any remaining clams for 1 to 2 minutes, but discard any not opened after that time. If the liquids boil vigorously at any point, reduce the heat a bit.

Pour the cooking liquids from the pot through a small fine-mesh sieve into a 4-cup measuring cup, leaving behind any grit in the bottom of the pot. When the clams are cool enough to handle, remove the meats. Add the liquids from the bottom of the bowl to those from the pot. Add enough clam juice to make 4 cups.

In the same pot (washed) or another soup pot, melt the butter over medium heat. Add the leek, carrot, and celery and cook, stirring occasionally, until tender (the carrot may not be fully tender), 5 to 7 minutes. Sprinkle the flour into the pot and cook for 2 minutes, stirring frequently to evenly

CONTINUED

1 cup thawed frozen petite peas

1 cup half-and-half

Kosher salt and freshly ground black pepper

distribute with the vegetables. Stir in the clam juice mixture and thyme, then add the potatoes. Simmer gently, stirring occasionally, until the potatoes are tender, 12 to 15 minutes; reduce the heat if needed to keep the liquid from boiling. The chowder will thicken a bit as it cooks.

While the chowder is simmering, chop the clams, though small clams can be used as is if you like.

Once the potatoes are tender, reduce the heat to medium-low and add the clams, peas, and half-and-half. Simmer gently until heated through, 3 to 5 minutes, taking care to avoid boiling or it may curdle a bit (still perfectly fine). Season to taste with salt and pepper, then ladle the chowder into individual bowls and serve right away.

Clam Juice

Also known as clam broth and clam nectar, this is essentially a by-product of cooking clams, capturing the briny essence they give off. If the recipe you're making doesn't need all—if any—of the cooking liquid left in the pot after steaming clams, it's a shame to toss it out. Strain the liquid through a small fine-mesh sieve, leaving any grit behind in the bottom of the pot. Let cool completely, then store in an airtight container and refrigerate for a couple of days, or freeze for a few months. The clam juice is ideal in Clam Chowder with Petite Peas (page 21), other seafood soups or stews, seafood risotto, and other places where its distinct briny sea flavor would be a welcome addition. Commercial clam juice is a good shortcut. Sometimes I'll mix clam juice with water to temper the strength of its flavor depending on the use.

Hard-Cider Steamed Clams

Beer is a common steaming partner for clams and mussels—always a solid choice. With a growing selection of great hard ciders available, it just gives us more options to play with. For cooking, I prefer to stick with simpler types of hard cider that are on the dry side.

MAKES 2 TO 4 SERVINGS

8 green onions, trimmed

2 tablespoons mild olive oil

2 cloves garlic, minced or pressed

1 bay leaf, preferably fresh, broken or torn in half

3 pounds small to medium live hard-shell clams, well rinsed (see page 17)

1 cup dry hard cider

Sliced baguette or other bread, for serving

Slice the white and light-green parts of the green onions to cook with the clams. Thinly slice enough of the green tops to measure about ¼ cup and set aside to use as a garnish.

Heat the oil in a medium pot over medium heat. Add the white and light-green parts of the green onions, garlic, and bay leaf and cook, stirring occasionally, until the green onion is tender, 2 to 3 minutes. Add the clams and hard cider, increase the heat to medium-high, and cover. After 2 to 3 minutes, gently stir the clams with a large slotted spoon. Cover the pot and continue cooking, stirring once or twice more, until all, or mostly all, of the clams have opened, 2 to 5 minutes longer. If the liquids boil vigorously at any point, reduce the heat a bit.

Scoop the clams and cooking liquids into shallow bowls, discarding any clams that did not open (along with the bay leaf) and leaving any grit behind in the bottom of the pot. Scatter the sliced green onion tops over the clams and serve right away, with bread alongside.

Steamed Clams with a Frenzy of Herbs

This "frenzy" describes a generous addition of tender herbs to the pot, an array more varied in the height of summer, when herbs flourish in our gardens. It's easy to go through a pound or more of clams per person when this dish is served as a meal with crusty bread and a favorite salad alongside. Depending on your appetite and how this is served (lunch, appetizer, lighter meal), the amount per person can vary.

MAKES 2 TO 4 SERVINGS

1¼ cups loosely packed tender fresh herbs, divided (see note)

3 tablespoons unsalted butter

⅓ cup thinly sliced shallot

1 tablespoon finely chopped rosemary (optional)

3 pounds small to medium live hard-shell clams, well rinsed (see page 17)

½ cup dry white wine or water

Sliced baguette or other bread, for serving

Toss together the tender herbs in a small bowl.

Melt the butter in a medium pot over medium heat. Add the shallot and rosemary and cook, stirring occasionally, until the shallot is tender and lightly browned, 2 to 3 minutes. Add the clams and wine, cover, and increase the heat to medium-high. After 2 to 3 minutes, add 1 cup of the herbs and gently stir the clams with a large slotted spoon. Cover and continue cooking, stirring once or twice more, until all, or mostly all, of the clams have opened, 2 to 5 minutes longer. If the liquids boil vigorously at any point, reduce the heat a bit.

Scoop the clams, herbs, and cooking liquids into shallow bowls, discarding any clams that did not open and leaving any grit behind in the bottom of the pot. Top with the remaining herbs and serve right away, with bread alongside.

CONTINUED

NOTE: Herbs I've used include chives, thyme, shiso, tarragon, bronze fennel, parsley, cilantro, and basil. Select just three or four for this dish, but if you don't have a selection on hand, don't feel obligated to purchase multiple bundles. "Frenzy" could just as well be a whole lot of parsley—an herb I don't think gets nearly enough opportunity to shine on its own. (Have you tried parsley pesto? See page 173.) Small tender leaves can remain whole, larger leaves should be chopped or thinly sliced, and chives cut into about ½-inch lengths. Rosemary is a great addition too, but it gets some sauté time with the shallot to temper its stronger flavor a bit.

Grilled Clam Pouches with Bay Leaf and Butter

MAKES 4 SERVINGS

2 pounds small to medium live hard-shell clams, well rinsed (see page 17)

4 tablespoons unsalted butter, divided

8 fresh bay leaves, divided

Sliced baguette or other bread, for serving

Fresh bay leaves really stand out in this preparation; dried leaves won't offer as much fragrant flavor. A rosemary or thyme sprig in each packet, or a couple of fresh sage leaves, can be used in place of fresh bay. And you can't go wrong with just butter and clams on the grill either. I use 12-inch-wide aluminum foil; you can use larger and/or heavy-duty foil if you like.

The packets make a good serving vessel perched on a plate for casual dining. You can instead transfer the clams and buttery cooking juices to shallow bowls. These lighter portions are ideal as an appetizer, followed perhaps by other items destined for the grill while it's hot.

Preheat an outdoor grill for medium-high direct heat.

Cut 8 pieces of aluminum foil about 12 inches long and arrange them on the counter stacked in pairs, for making 4 packets.

Put 1 tablespoon of butter in the center of each foil packet. Fold or tear each bay leaf in half, which helps release its aromatic character, and put 2 leaves on or alongside the butter for each packet. Divide the clams evenly among the pouches, mounding them on top of the butter and bay and leaving a few inches of foil around.

CONTINUED

GRILLED CLAM POUCHES WITH BAY LEAF AND BUTTER, CONTINUED

Draw the four corners of the foil up over the clams to meet in the center and crimp together along the edges, where the sides of the foil meet, so the packet is well sealed. The goal is to create pouches that will hold in the steam for cooking and preserve the flavorful cooking juices that result.

Set the foil packets on the grill, cover, and cook for about 10 to 12 minutes for small clams, 12 to 15 for medium. Partly open a packet to see if all the clams have opened, being careful to avoid the escaping steam; if not, reseal and cook for another 2 to 3 minutes.

Set each pouch on an individual plate and fold down the foil edges, creating a rustic bowl of sorts to hold the flavorful cooking liquids. Or carefully transfer the contents to shallow bowls. Serve right away, with bread alongside, discarding any clams that did not open.

NOTE: This recipe works well in the oven too. Preheat the oven to 475 degrees F. Use a broad, shallow vessel, such as a large cast-iron skillet or a 12-inch gratin dish or similar baking dish. Add the butter pieces and bay leaves to the dish and put in the oven until the butter has melted. Take the dish from the oven, add the clams in a relatively even layer, and return the dish to the oven. Roast until all, or mostly all, of the clams have opened, 12 to 15 minutes. Spoon the clams into individual shallow bowls, discarding any that did not open, then carefully pour the buttery cooking liquids over the top.

Stuffed Clams with Pork Rinds

MAKES 6 TO 8 SERVINGS

36 medium live hard-shell clams (about 2½ pounds), well rinsed (see page 17)

½ cup dry white wine or water

2 teaspoons mild olive oil

½ cup finely chopped celery

½ cup finely chopped green onions, white and light-green parts

½ teaspoon minced garlic

1 cup finely chopped pork rinds

Freshly ground black pepper

The interesting combination of clams and pork shows up in some delicious guises, such as a traditional Portuguese stew (*porco à alentejana*). And there's that bacon that often finds its way into a pot of clam chowder. Here the pork element is a bit more subtle, taking the form of crisp pork rinds that stand in for the bread crumbs sometimes used for stuffed clams. You may see a number of flavor options in the snack aisle; the traditional unflavored rinds will be best here.

Because of variances in meat-to-shell ratios of clams, the amount of chopped clams in your filling can vary as well. Adjust as needed, which could mean using less filling per shell, or filling fewer of the shells.

Preheat the oven to 400 degrees F.

Put the clams and wine in a medium pot, set the pot over medium-high heat, and cover. After 2 to 3 minutes, gently stir the clams with a large slotted spoon. Cover the pot and continue cooking, stirring once or twice more, until all, or mostly all, of the clams have opened, 2 to 5 minutes longer. Use the slotted spoon to transfer the opened clams to a large bowl. Continue cooking any remaining clams for 1 to 2 minutes, but discard any not opened after that time. If the liquids boil vigorously at any point, reduce the heat a bit.

CONTINUED

Pour the cooking liquids from the pot through a small fine-mesh sieve into a small bowl, leaving behind any grit in the bottom of the pot. When the clams are cool enough to handle, remove the meats and reserve half of each shell. Wash these shell halves and dry them well. Add the liquids from the bottom of the bowl to those from the pot. Coarsely chop the clams; you should have about ½ cup—more is even better, with less you may fill fewer shells.

Heat the oil in a medium skillet over medium heat. Add the celery, green onions, and garlic and cook, stirring occasionally, until tender, 2 to 3 minutes. Take the skillet from the heat and add the pork rinds, clam meats, ¼ cup of the reserved clam juice, and a few grindings of black pepper. Stir to mix and evenly incorporate the clams. The pork rinds will absorb much of the liquid, and the mixture should be moist but not soupy; if it's a bit on the dry side, add more clam juice a tablespoon at a time.

Spoon the clam filling into the cleaned shells (as many as you have filling for) and set them on a rimmed baking sheet. Bake the clams until the juices bubble at the edges and the tops are lightly browned, 5 to 7 minutes. Use tongs to transfer the clams to a serving platter or individual plates and serve.

Clam Puttanesca Mini Pizzas

MAKES 4 SERVINGS

About 1 pound prepared pizza dough, thawed if frozen

2 pounds small to medium live hard-shell clams, well rinsed (see page 17)

¼ cup water

All-purpose flour, for forming dough

2 medium tomatoes (about 12 ounces), seeded and finely chopped (see page 74)

¼ cup finely chopped green olives

3 tablespoons finely chopped fresh flat-leaf parsley

2 tablespoons drained capers

1 anchovy fillet, finely chopped

1 teaspoon chopped garlic

⅛ teaspoon dried red pepper flakes

1 tablespoon mild or extra-virgin olive oil

The bold flavors of classic puttanesca pair well with sweet, briny clams; here the two are perched on pizza dough in snack-size portions. Use a favorite homemade pizza dough recipe, or look for prepared dough, which may be available frozen at your grocery store. Pull out your pizza stone, if you've got one, and use according to manufacturer's instructions. Caesar salad would be a great accompaniment.

Preheat the oven to 475 degrees F. Line a rimmed baking sheet with parchment paper or a silicone baking mat.

Cut the pizza dough into 4 equal pieces, form each into a ball, and cover with a kitchen towel to rest while cooking the clams.

Put the clams and water in a medium pot, set the pot over medium-high heat, and cover. After 2 to 3 minutes, gently stir the clams with a large slotted spoon. Cover the pot and continue cooking until all, or mostly all, of the clams have opened, 2 to 5 minutes longer. Use the slotted spoon to transfer the opened clams to a large bowl. Continue cooking any remaining clams for 1 to 2 minutes, but discard any not opened after that time. If the liquids boil vigorously at any point, reduce the heat a bit. When the clams are cool enough to handle, remove the meats.

CONTINUED

CLAM PUTTANESCA MINI PIZZAS, CONTINUED

Working on a lightly floured surface, flatten each round of dough with your fingers, then use a rolling pin to roll them into roughly 6-inch rounds. If the dough begins springing back quite a lot, let that piece rest while rolling out other rounds; after a few minutes it should be easier to roll out again. Lightly dust the dough with more flour as needed, but avoid overdoing it. Set the dough rounds on the prepared baking sheet, covered with a kitchen towel.

Combine the tomatoes, olives, parsley, capers, anchovy, garlic, and pepper flakes in a small bowl, tossing well with a fork to evenly mix. The anchovy pieces in particular tend to clump; break them up as best you can.

Brush each dough round with some oil, leaving about ½ inch bare around the edges. Scatter the clams over each pizza and top with the puttanesca mixture, spreading it out evenly.

Bake until the dough is puffed and browned on the edges and the topping is sizzling, 8 to 12 minutes. Use a spatula to transfer the pizzas to individual plates and serve.

Open-Faced Clam and Quick-Pickled Carrot Sandwiches

MAKES 6 TO 8 SERVINGS

1½ teaspoons caraway seeds

¼ cup red wine vinegar

¾ teaspoon kosher salt, plus more if needed

2 pounds small live hard-shell clams, well rinsed (see page 17)

¼ cup dry white wine or water

1 cup coarsely grated carrot (about 1 medium carrot)

¼ cup very thinly sliced red onion

2 tablespoons coarsely chopped fresh flat-leaf parsley

4 tablespoons salted butter, at room temperature (see note)

4 large slices dense pumpernickel or other dense rye bread

With inspiration from the open-faced sandwiches of Scandinavia, this recipe has an interesting blend of flavors: briny, rich, sweet, vinegary, and bright. The bread I use comes in dense rectangular slices with lots of whole grain, not a typical sandwich bread. Other similarly dense dark bread can be used. Or serve the clam-carrot mixture on a cracker-like option, such as rye crispbread, with or without the spread of butter. Note that the clams and carrots sit in the refrigerator for at least an hour before serving.

Put the caraway seeds in a small, dry skillet and toast over medium heat, stirring or gently tossing frequently, until just a bit darker in color and aromatic, 1 to 2 minutes. Transfer the seeds to a small plate or dish to avoid over-toasting and set aside to cool.

Combine the vinegar and salt in a medium bowl, stirring until the salt dissolves. Set aside.

Put the clams and wine in a medium pot, set the pot over medium-high heat, and cover. After 2 to 3 minutes, gently stir the clams with a large slotted spoon. Cover the pot and continue cooking, stirring once or twice more, until all, or mostly all, of the clams have opened, 2 to 5 minutes longer. Use the slotted spoon to transfer the opened clams to a large bowl. Continue cooking any remaining clams for

NOTE: For this recipe, I prefer salted butter for accentuating the flavors of the other ingredients. If you only have unsalted butter, simply stir a good pinch of kosher salt into it.

1 to 2 minutes, but discard any not opened after that time. If the liquids boil vigorously at any point, reduce the heat a bit.

When the clams are cool enough to handle, remove the meats. Small clams can be used as is, otherwise coarsely chop the clams. Add the clams to the vinegar. Pour the cooking liquids from the pot through a small fine-mesh sieve into a small bowl, leaving behind any grit in the bottom of the pot. Add the liquids from the bottom of the large bowl to those from the pot.

Add ¼ cup of the clam cooking liquids to the clam and vinegar mixture; remaining liquids can be saved for another use (see page 22). Stir to mix, then add the carrot, onion, and 1 teaspoon of the caraway seeds, tossing gently to evenly mix. Cover and refrigerate for 1 to 2 hours.

Put the parsley on a cutting board and top it with the remaining ½ teaspoon of the caraway seeds, then finely chop them together. This will garnish the sandwiches.

Spread the butter on the bread and cut the bread into roughly 3-inch pieces—triangles, squares, or rectangles, depending on the shape of bread used.

Drain the clams and carrots in a fine-mesh sieve and set the sieve over a bowl to continue draining while assembling the sandwiches. Spoon some of the clam and carrot mixture onto each piece of bread, spreading it out relatively evenly. Top with a generous pinch of the parsley-caraway mixture and serve.

MUSSELS

THE LEGENDARY NORTHWEST GASTRONOME James Beard noted in his 1972 classic *James Beard's American Cookery* that mussels "remain the most neglected of all our shellfish." It's perhaps understandable that they were overlooked for so long; those clusters of dark shells that accumulate on pier pilings and rocks are not all that appealing at first glance. Though it's a shame it took so long for mussels to become more broadly loved in the United States. All those years we could have been taking inspiration from Spanish paella and the *moules frites* (steamed mussels with fries) of Belgium.

The blue mussel is a prolific species found throughout the North Atlantic. In the United States, this mussel is harvested in the wild and farm-raised primarily in New England. The shells can be so darkly colored as to look more black than blue. On the West Coast, the transplanted Mediterranean mussel is grown by many aquaculture operations, and the native Pacific blue mussel is in limited production as well.

These three varieties of mussels are similar enough in appearance, with an elongated teardrop shape slightly angled on one side, that they can be difficult to distinguish with an untrained eye. In the kitchen, they're fully interchangeable.

Although there may be slight variations with different species and regions, mussels are generally available year-round.

SHOPPING AND STORING

Mussels are generally sold by the pound. You may see them in bulk, so you can buy a specific amount, or in bags of a set quantity. Because mussels have thinner shells than clams, it's not uncommon to get home and find some with broken shells. Consider buying a few more mussels than needed in the recipe to account for that.

Mussels purchased in the shell are alive and need to stay alive until you cook them. If it's a hot day or your trip home from the store will be a long one, ask at the seafood counter for a bag of ice to accompany the mussels. Or plan ahead and put a cooler with some frozen gel packs in the car.

When you get home, transfer the mussels to a large bowl. I put the mussels first in a colander, then set that in the bowl so the mussels sit above any water that accumulates in the bottom of the bowl. Cover the mussels with a damp, but not sopping wet, kitchen towel to keep them moist until needed. Don't cover the bowl any more than that; the mussels need air to survive. And don't be tempted to store the mussels in water or top them with ice, as they can expire in fresh water.

CLEANING

Mussels should be cleaned just before cooking. If you see the tough, stringy byssal thread, or beard, with which mussels attach themselves to their home base, it needs to be removed. It can be a little tricky to get a good grip with bare fingers: try grabbing it using a paper towel, tugging gently to remove the beard from the mussel. For anything else attached to the shell, such as other strands of the beard or a stray barnacle, scrape them away with a scrub brush or the back of a small knife.

Rinse the debearded mussels well by tossing gently in a colander under cold running water. As you clean the mussels, discard any with broken shells. If any shells are gaping, tap the mussel on the counter: if its shell does not close firmly, discard that mussel as well.

COOKING

Cooking mussels follows pretty much the same principles, and versatility, as cooking clams. Casual, quick, easy, and with plenty of room for variation to suit your tastes. The liquid used to steam open mussels can be water, wine, beer, or hard cider. I prefer crisp, dry options, any hint of acidity a bonus. And as with any time you cook with these potable ingredients, choose something of a quality you'll want to drink alongside as well: a little for the pot, a little for you and your guests.

Beyond steaming, mussels in the shell are great roasted, grilled, sautéed, and stewed. The cooked meats have countless possibilities, from a tapas-like nibbles to pasta dishes to substantial salads with grains and vegetables.

Steamed Mussels with Kimchi and Daikon

MAKES 2 TO 4 SERVINGS

¾ cup kimchi

4 ounces daikon radish, peeled and julienned (about 1 cup)

½ cup dry white wine or water

3 pounds live mussels, scrubbed and debearded (see page 41)

4 green onions, white and green portions thinly sliced

Sliced baguette or other bread, for serving

Steamed mussels can be exquisitely simple, with little more than a splash of wine added to the pot. But they take well to bold flavors too. The crunch of both kimchi and daikon add contrast to the tender meat as well. You may see a number of kimchi varieties available; I used the more common cabbage version for this recipe. This is great for a light supper with a salad and/or roasted vegetables alongside.

Coarsely chop any larger pieces of kimchi; smaller bite-size pieces can be used as is. Put the kimchi, daikon, and wine in a medium pot and add the mussels. Set the pot over medium-high heat and cover. After 2 to 3 minutes, gently stir the mussels with a large slotted spoon. Cover the pot and continue cooking, stirring once or twice more, until all, or mostly all, of the mussels have opened, 2 to 4 minutes longer.

Scoop the mussels into shallow bowls, discarding any that did not open, and distribute the kimchi, daikon, and cooking liquids evenly among the bowls, leaving any grit behind in the pot. Scatter the green onion over and serve right away with bread alongside.

Mussels with Mustard and Mustard Greens

MAKES 2 TO 4 SERVINGS

3 tablespoons unsalted butter

½ cup finely chopped shallot or yellow onion

½ cup dry white wine or water

2 tablespoons Dijon mustard

¼ teaspoon kosher salt

Freshly ground black pepper

3 pounds live mussels, scrubbed and debearded (see page 41)

4 cups loosely packed mustard greens, tough stems removed and larger leaves torn

This slight variation on the steaming technique cooks mussels in a pot with a bit of liquid, but does so without adding the lid. You can use other braising greens if you like, but stick to those that will wilt quickly, such as spinach, baby kale, or chard. To round out a dinner, serve the mussels with fried or roasted potatoes.

Melt the butter in a medium pot over medium heat. Add the shallot and cook, stirring, until tender and aromatic, 2 to 3 minutes. Stir in the wine, mustard, salt, and a few grindings of black pepper, then add the mussels. Increase the heat to medium-high and cook, stirring often, until all, or mostly all, of the mussels have opened, 5 to 8 minutes.

Add the greens to the pot and stir gently into the mussels so the greens wilt, 1 to 2 minutes. Scoop the mussels and greens into shallow bowls, discarding any mussels that did not open. Pour the cooking liquids over the mussels, leaving any grit behind in the pot, and serve right away.

Mussel Stew with Winter Squash and Green Curry

MAKES 4 SERVINGS

About 1 pound delicata, butternut, or kabocha squash

2 tablespoons mild olive oil

1 large or 2 small leeks, trimmed, cleaned, and cut into ¼-inch slices (about 1½ cups)

2 medium carrots, cut into ¼-inch slices (about 1 cup)

2 tablespoons green curry paste

1½ cups Shellfish Stock (page 183) or clam juice (see page 22)

½ cup full-fat or lite canned coconut milk

¼ teaspoon kosher salt

2½ pounds live mussels, scrubbed and debearded (see page 41)

Chopped fresh cilantro or flat-leaf parsley, for serving

The earthy sweetness of winter squash is a great complement to mussels, and their vivid color is striking against the dark shells in this quick stew inspired by flavors of Southeast Asia. Delicata squash is a favorite for its small size and skin thin enough to not require peeling. Other winter squash can be used, their thicker skin peeled before using.

Cut the delicata in half lengthwise and scoop out the seeds. Halve each piece lengthwise again, then cut across into ¾-inch slices. Other winter squash should be peeled and seeded, then cut into about ¾-inch cubes.

Heat the oil in a medium pot over medium heat. Add the leek and carrots and cook, stirring occasionally, until the leek is tender, 3 to 4 minutes. Add the curry paste and cook for 1 minute, stirring constantly to evenly coat the vegetables. Stir in the stock, coconut milk, and salt, then add the squash. Stir to incorporate and bring just to a low boil, then cover and simmer over medium-low heat until the squash is nearly tender (less firm than when raw but the tip of a knife still meets some resistance), about 5 to 10 minutes depending on the type used.

Add the mussels and increase the heat to medium-high. Cook uncovered, stirring occasionally and gently until all, or mostly all, of the mussels have opened, 5 to 8 minutes.

Scoop the stew into shallow bowls, discarding any mussels that did not open. Sprinkle with cilantro, and serve right away.

Mussels Roasted with Potatoes and Chiles

MAKES 2 MAIN COURSE SERVINGS
or 6 appetizer servings

12 ounces fingerling or other small potatoes, scrubbed

2 to 3 medium jalapeños, trimmed and cut into ¼-inch slices (seeded if you like)

2 tablespoons mild olive oil

¼ teaspoon kosher salt

Freshly ground black pepper

2½ pounds live mussels, scrubbed and debearded (see page 41)

When they're available, small fingerling potatoes are perfect for this recipe. Otherwise small red or white potatoes work well, cut into smaller pieces as needed for even cooking. To temper the heat of the chiles, you can remove the seeds from the slices. You can also use a milder chile instead, such as Anaheim. This can be served in small portions as a sort of tapas offering with drinks, or for two as a main course with sautéed zucchini or another green vegetable alongside.

Preheat the oven to 475 degrees F.

Depending on the size and shape of the potatoes you're using, cut them into pieces as needed: larger fingerlings in half lengthwise and/or across into pieces about 1½ inches long; round potatoes in half or quarters. Small fingerlings or little "nugget" potatoes can be cooked as is.

Put the potatoes in a steamer rack in a medium saucepan set above a couple of inches of water. Cover, bring the water to a boil, and steam until the potatoes are about half cooked: a paring knife should pierce with a little resistance, 7 to 10 minutes. Remove the potatoes from the steamer and set aside to cool and dry.

CONTINUED

Combine the potatoes and jalapeño slices in a 9-by-13-inch baking dish and drizzle the oil over, then add the salt and a few grindings of black pepper. Gently toss well so the vegetables are evenly coated in oil. Spread them in a relatively even layer and roast until the potatoes are partly browned and the jalapeños are mostly tender, 10 to 12 minutes.

Remove the baking dish from the oven and add the mussels in a relatively even layer. Return the baking dish to the oven and roast until the mussels have opened, 6 to 8 minutes.

Scoop the mussels (discarding any that did not open), potatoes, and jalapeños into shallow bowls, spoon the cooking liquids over, and serve right away.

Crostini with Mussels in Romesco Sauce

MAKES 6 TO 8 SERVINGS

1 medium red bell pepper

1 small tomato (about 5 ounces), halved

⅓ cup slivered almonds, toasted

2 tablespoons sherry vinegar or red wine vinegar, plus more to taste

1½ teaspoons chopped garlic

¼ teaspoon kosher salt

¼ teaspoon dried red pepper flakes

24 slices baguette or similar-size bread slices

1 to 2 tablespoons mild olive oil

2 pounds live mussels, scrubbed and debearded (see page 41)

¼ cup water

2 teaspoons fresh thyme or oregano leaves

Romesco is a versatile sauce with roasted pepper, tomato, almonds, garlic, and a little chile heat that pairs well with seafood. Here, steamed mussels are tossed in a quick version of the sauce and used as a topping for toasted baguette. Other sliced bread can be used as well, cut into pieces easy enough to manage in a couple of bites.

The red pepper and tomato can be pretty wet after roasting, so I dry them before continuing to avoid a watery sauce. If, after sitting, the sauce has excess liquid collecting at the edges, you can drain it off before serving.

Preheat the broiler and set the oven rack 5 to 6 inches below the element.

Put the whole bell pepper and tomato halves (cut side down) on a rimmed baking sheet lined with aluminum foil and broil, turning the pepper occasionally (the tomato halves just stay as is), until the pepper is tender and the skin blackens, 12 to 15 minutes. Put the pepper in a bowl and cover securely with plastic wrap. Transfer the tomato halves to a small plate; set both aside to cool. Set the oven temperature to 400 degrees F and return the oven rack to the center.

When the pepper is cool, peel away and discard the skin, then remove the core and seeds. When the tomato is cool, peel away and discard the skin, then scoop out and discard the seeds. Dry both with a paper towel to draw off excess liquid, then chop the pepper and tomato and put them in a food processor. Add the almonds, vinegar, garlic, salt, and pepper flakes and pulse until finely chopped and well blended but not quite a smooth purée; I like to leave a little texture to this sauce. Taste for seasoning, adding more salt if needed. Transfer the romesco to a medium serving bowl and set aside.

Lightly brush one side of each baguette slice with some of the oil and arrange the slices on a rimmed baking sheet. Bake until lightly toasted, 3 to 5 minutes. Transfer to a wire rack to cool.

Put the mussels and water in a medium pot, set the pot over medium-high heat, and cover. After 2 to 3 minutes, gently stir the mussels with a large slotted spoon. Cover the pot and continue cooking, stirring once or twice more, until all, or mostly all, of the mussels have opened, 2 to 4 minutes longer. Use the slotted spoon to transfer the opened mussels to a large bowl. Continue cooking any remaining mussels for 1 to 2 minutes, but discard any not opened after that time. If the liquids boil vigorously at any point, reduce the heat a bit.

When the mussels are cool enough to handle, remove the meats and scatter them on paper towels to drain. Add the mussels and thyme to the romesco sauce and stir to evenly mix. Serve with the toasted bread alongside, each guest topping their own crostini with a mussel or two and a bit of sauce.

Mussel and Chickpea Salad

MAKES 4 TO 6 SERVINGS

3 tablespoons red wine vinegar

¼ teaspoon kosher salt

Freshly ground black pepper

⅓ cup extra-virgin or mild olive oil

3 tablespoons finely chopped fresh flat-leaf parsley, basil, and/or chives

2 pounds live mussels, scrubbed and debearded (see page 41)

¼ cup water

1 (15-ounce) can chickpeas, rinsed and well drained

1 medium zucchini, diced (about 1½ cups)

Flavorful and hearty, this salad can stand alone as a light meal or serve with warmed pita bread and tzatziki. It can be made a day ahead and refrigerated; the flavor will be best if it sits at room temperature a bit before serving, stirred well to reincorporate the dressing that settles to the bottom of the bowl. The salad could also travel well for a picnic, kept cold en route.

Whisk together the vinegar and salt with a couple of grindings of black pepper in a large bowl until the salt is dissolved. Whisk in the oil, then add the herbs. Set the dressing aside.

Put the mussels and water in a medium pot, set the pot over medium-high heat, and cover. After 2 to 3 minutes, gently stir the mussels with a large slotted spoon. Cover the pot and continue cooking, stirring once or twice more, until all, or mostly all, of the mussels have opened, 2 to 5 minutes longer. Use the slotted spoon to transfer the opened mussels to a large bowl. Continue cooking any remaining mussels for 1 to 2 minutes, but discard any not opened after that time. If the liquids boil vigorously at any point, reduce the heat a bit.

1 cup moderately packed thinly sliced spinach (about 1 ounce)

½ cup crumbled feta cheese (about 2 ounces)

¼ cup slivered sun-dried tomato, oil-packed or rehydrated dry

When the mussels have cooled, remove the meats and add them to the bowl with the dressing. Add the chickpeas, zucchini, spinach, feta, and sun-dried tomato and toss gently to evenly mix and coat with the dressing. Taste for seasoning, adding more salt or pepper to taste.

Spoon the salad into individual bowls and serve right away. Or cover the salad and refrigerate until ready to serve, up to a day later, letting it sit at room temperature for 15 to 20 minutes before serving.

Pan-Fried Mussel and Sage Bites

MAKES 4 TO 6 SERVINGS

5 tablespoons mild olive oil, divided, plus more if needed

24 medium fresh sage leaves (see note) plus 2 teaspoons finely chopped fresh sage

24 large live mussels (about 1½ pounds), scrubbed and debearded (see page 41)

¼ cup water

1 medium lemon

4 tablespoons all-purpose flour, divided, plus more if needed

½ teaspoon kosher salt

Freshly ground black pepper

A perfect snack for your next cocktail party or game-night gathering, this isn't a complicated recipe but it does take a bit of time—mussels are steamed and the meats tossed in seasoned flour to pan-fry. You can steam the mussels, store them in their cooking liquids in the refrigerator, and make the seasoned flour an hour or two ahead. Then finish things off just before serving. Fancy picks that have a frilly top or other fun accent are great, or simple round toothpicks work just as well. This recipe has larger mussels in mind, though you may not have a choice when shopping. Smaller mussels may need more flour to thoroughly coat them, and you might want to get more than twenty-four.

Heat 2 tablespoons of the oil in a small skillet over medium heat. Add the sage leaves and cook until just lightly crisp, stirring occasionally with a fork to ensure they cook evenly, 1 to 2 minutes; they shouldn't brown much. With the fork, lift out the leaves to a paper towel to drain. When just cool enough to handle, pierce each leaf onto a small serving pick about ¾ inch from the end; fully cooled crisp leaves are harder to pierce without breaking.

CONTINUED

Put the mussels and water in a medium pot, set the pot over medium-high heat, and cover. After 2 to 3 minutes, gently stir the mussels with a large slotted spoon. Cover the pot and continue cooking, stirring once or twice more, until all, or mostly all, of the mussels have opened, 2 to 4 minutes longer. Use the slotted spoon to transfer the opened mussels to a large bowl. Continue cooking any remaining mussels for 1 to 2 minutes, but discard any not opened after that time. If the liquids boil vigorously at any point, reduce the heat a bit.

Pour the cooking liquids from the pot through a small fine-mesh sieve into a medium bowl, leaving behind any grit in the bottom of the pot. When the mussels are cool enough to handle, remove the meats and put them in the bowl with the cooking liquids.

Finely grate enough zest from the lemon to measure 2 teaspoons. Cut the lemon into 8 wedges and set aside for serving.

Combine 3 tablespoons of the flour, the lemon zest, finely chopped sage, salt, and a few grindings of pepper in a mini processor and pulse for about a minute to incorporate the zest and sage well with the flour. Put the flour in a large bowl. (If you don't have a mini processor, just stir them all together well in a large bowl, carefully breaking up any clusters of the zest.)

NOTE: Don't fret if you don't have enough sage leaves for every mussel, you can either cut larger leaves in half, or include the leaves on half the mussels instead of all of them. The mussels are delicious without that crisp embellishment on top, so you can skip the fried sage leaf garnish as well.

Drain the mussels in a sieve and add them still damp to the flour, tossing with a fork to quickly and evenly coat in the flour. Add the remaining tablespoon of flour and toss to coat. If the mussels become a little sticky while sitting, add another tablespoon or so of flour and toss. Too much extra flour diminishes the lemon-sage flavors; the goal is just enough to keep the mussels from sticking to each other, and flouring them in stages helps ensure an even coating.

Heat a medium heavy skillet, preferably cast iron, over medium heat. When hot, add the remaining 3 tablespoons oil and heat for a few moments. Add about half of the mussels (less if necessary to avoid crowding), gently shaking off any excess flour if needed. Spread them out evenly and cook until nicely browned on one side, about 2 minutes. Turn and brown well on the second side. Scoop out to a plate and repeat with the remaining mussels, adding more oil to the skillet if needed.

Arrange the mussels on a serving plate and pierce each with a sage-leaf-studded pick—ideally the sage leaf will be resting on the surface of the mussel. Arrange the lemon wedges around for squeezing, and serve right away.

SCALLOPS

One of the most interesting things about scallops—to me, at least—is that they are so mobile relative to their fellow bivalves. In their natural states, oysters sit rather still on a beach, clams burrow into sand, and mussels cling to rocks and pilings. But not scallops. They live free, scooting around the sea floor, locomoting with the opening and closing of their shells. (Apparently, while young, they're quite the impressive swimmers, and become a bit less mobile as they get older.) The adductor muscle that facilitates the shell action is the same thing that we sever in an oyster to remove it from its shell. The scallop's version is much larger relative to that of other bivalves, and is usually the only part of the scallop that we eat.

The Atlantic sea scallop is the most abundant variety available in the United States. They are generally found from Maine as far south as North Carolina, though most of the harvest comes from Massachusetts. Alaska waters are home to the weathervane scallop, which is harvested in smaller volumes than are the Atlantic scallops. Weathervane scallops are available in the same range of sizes as are Atlantic sea scallops and can be used interchangeably for them in recipes.

The smaller bay scallop is found in roughly the same area as the Atlantic sea scallop, though at harvest levels that are a small fraction of those for sea scallops. Nantucket bay scallops are a treat to enjoy when possible.

Among other scallops that are worth enjoying when available are the small pink, or "singing," scallops from the Pacific Northwest, so named because of their pretty pink shells and someone's interpretation that the shells opening and closing made it look as though they were singing their way through the water. These are small and often cooked and served in their shells, akin to clams or mussels.

Scallops are mostly a wild product, at least in terms of the domestic supply. Fishing for Atlantic sea scallops occurs throughout the year, with peak harvest usually spring into early summer, available fresh and frozen. Alaska weathervane scallops are fished primarily in summer, with most of the catch frozen at sea, offering consistent availability through the year. Bay scallops have a limited season over the winter months in the United States, with frozen bay scallops available year round.

SHOPPING AND STORING

Most sea scallops are shucked at sea; just the luscious meat comes to shore. You won't often see a sea scallop sold in its shell, though on occasion in specialty markets.

Scallops are generally white in color, but there are natural variances that can include ivory, light beige, and even pale orange. The aroma should be fresh and clean, no hints of ammonia or other sharp or sour smells.

Scallops should look moist and glisten. While dry-pack scallops have less moisture than other scallops, no scallop should look dried out. Frozen scallops should not have any exposed, dry-looking patches, which can indicate freezer burn.

"Dry-pack" may not be the most evocative of descriptions, but is a characteristic worth seeking out when buying scallops. This "dry" indicates that the scallops were not treated with sodium tripolyphosphate, an additive that helps scallops retain moisture. The benefit of using dry-pack scallops is that they will give off a minimum amount of water, if any, during cooking. Extra water impedes the browning of a good sear in the skillet and can dilute sauces and otherwise alter the intended outcome of a recipe. When it's particularly advantageous to use dry-pack scallops, I've noted this in the recipe. If not using dry-pack scallops, take extra care to dry them well before cooking to minimize excess liquid.

Sea scallops and weathervane scallops are frequently sold with a size indication of some kind. It may be general, such as "medium" or "jumbo." Or it may echo industry-standard size grading, such as "U-10" or "30/40," referencing how many scallops (on average) will be in one pound: under 10 for the former, and 30 to 40 for the latter. It's the same idea behind the size grades often listed for shrimp; the larger the number, the smaller the scallop.

Fresh scallops should be stored, well wrapped, in the refrigerator. As long as the packaging they came home in is in good shape, just store them as is. It should be okay to hold them a day before cooking, but the sooner you cook them the better they'll be—my usual mantra with all shellfish. If you bought still-frozen scallops, get them in the freezer right away to avoid any premature thaw. Don't try to refreeze a scallop that has thawed.

CLEANING

There may be a little side muscle at the edge of your scallops (if not removed during processing), a tough piece that should be removed before cooking. It peels away easily with your fingers. Otherwise scallops don't generally need cleaning before use, only the briefest of rinses under cold water. Just ensure that scallops are well dried before cooking, particularly before searing or pan-frying.

COOKING

This is one shellfish in this collection that you'll rarely see sold in its shell, so recipes here use just the shucked meat. Still, scallops are quite versatile.

The simplest way to experience the best a large scallop has to offer is a quick sear in a hot skillet until richly browned on each side, just a matter of minutes. You'll see here a couple of recipes with seared scallops, plus others that serve them raw, baked, sautéed, and grilled. It's always good to avoid overcooking shellfish, and with scallops it's a bit more imperative as they become rubbery and less flavorful if cooked too long.

For many recipes, any size of scallop can be used, keeping in mind that smaller scallops will cook more quickly. Bay scallops and smaller sea and weathervane scallops are ideal in sautés, soups, pastas, salads, and similar dishes mixed with other ingredients. Big scallops—those weighing an ounce or more each—are perfect for the elegant presentation of a seared scallop. And they're ideal for the grill too, with less risk of overcooking.

FRESH
WILD
JUMBO
GRILLING
SEA
SCALLOPS

Sautéed Scallops with Ginger-Rosé Sauce

MAKES 4 SERVINGS

1 to 1½ pounds bay scallops or small sea scallops

5 tablespoons unsalted butter, divided

6 green onions, white and light-green portions cut into ½-inch pieces on the bias

2 tablespoons julienned fresh ginger (from about a 1-inch piece of peeled ginger)

⅓ cup dry rosé wine

¼ teaspoon kosher salt

Cooked jasmine rice or other long grain rice, for serving

Simple sautés like this are often finished with a splash of white wine, but for this one I grabbed a bottle of rosé instead. Rosé wines can range from bone dry to rather fruity. I recommend one toward the dry end, perfect to sip alongside as well. This is a great recipe for bay scallops or smaller sea scallops. If you use larger sea scallops, add a minute or two more cooking time, depending on how large they are. In place of rice, the scallops could be served with sautéed greens.

Remove and discard the tough little side muscle if it's present on any of the scallops. Drain the scallops on paper towels, with a piece of paper towel pressed on top if they're particularly wet; set aside.

Cut 3 tablespoons of the butter into 3 to 4 pieces and put it in the refrigerator to chill.

Melt the remaining 2 tablespoons butter in a large skillet over medium heat. Add the scallops and cook, stirring occasionally, until evenly opaque on the surface and just a touch of translucence remains at the center when cut into, 3 to 5 minutes. Use a slotted spoon to scoop the scallops onto a plate and set aside.

Add the green onions and ginger to the skillet and cook, stirring often, until tender and aromatic, 2 to 3 minutes. Add the rosé and increase the heat to medium-high, simmering the liquid until reduced by about half and stirring to lift up flavorful bits stuck to the bottom of the skillet, 2 to 3 minutes.

Take the skillet from the heat and add the chilled butter, stirring or swirling gently so the butter melts creamily into the pan liquids, creating a simple sauce. Set the skillet over low heat, add the scallops and salt, and warm gently, stirring, for about 1 minute. Taste for seasoning, adding more salt if needed.

Spoon the scallops and sauce over rice on individual plates, and serve right away.

Sea Scallops with Apple-Celery Root Slaw

MAKES 4 SERVINGS

1 to 1¼ pounds large sea scallops

1 tablespoon mild olive oil

For the apple-celery root slaw

3 tablespoons extra-virgin olive oil

2 tablespoons cider vinegar

2 teaspoons Dijon mustard

¼ teaspoon kosher salt

Freshly ground black pepper

1 small tart apple (about 6 ounces), cored and julienned

¼ trimmed celery root (about 4 ounces), julienned (see note)

Celery root, also known as celeriac, has hints of the more common celery stalks' flavor, though with added earthiness and firmer texture. Extra can be used as you might other root vegetables: roasted, in a soup, paired with potatoes in a gratin. If you're unable to find celery root, a few tender inner stalks of celery, thinly sliced, can be used instead. To get the best sear on these scallops, try to find dry-pack scallops. An arugula salad would be a great accompaniment.

Remove and discard the tough little side muscle if it's present on any of the scallops. Drain the scallops on paper towels, with a piece of paper towel pressed on top if they're particularly wet; set aside.

For the slaw, combine the extra-virgin olive oil, vinegar, mustard, salt, and a few grindings of pepper in a medium bowl and mix with a fork until well blended. Spoon 2 tablespoons into a small dish and set aside for drizzling at the end.

Add the apple and celery root to the bowl with the remaining dressing and toss lightly to evenly mix. Arrange the slaw in an even layer in the center of individual plates and set aside while cooking the scallops.

Heat a large heavy skillet (cast iron is ideal) over medium-high heat. Season the scallops lightly with salt and pepper.

Working quickly but carefully, add the mild olive oil to the skillet and gently swirl to coat the bottom. Use tongs to add the scallops and cook undisturbed until well browned, 1½ to 2 minutes. Turn the scallops and cook until browned on the second side, about 2 minutes longer; they should be a bit translucent at the center.

Arrange the scallops on top of the slaw, drizzle the reserved dressing over them, and serve right away.

NOTE: If you've never cooked with celery root, it may look daunting. Unlike turnips or carrots that have a relatively thin, smooth skin to peel away, that of celery root is thicker and often embedded with fine little root ends.

Using a chef's knife rather than a peeler, start by cutting away the top end, where you may see remnants of the stalks. Set the root then on its side and carefully cut away the rooty bits from the other bulbous end of the root, which will probably take a number of cuts at various angles, until you have a relatively even rounded surface of the off-white flesh exposed around that base. (To make quicker work of this, you can simply lop off a larger piece of the base to remove all that rooty stuff at once, but I find that cuts away too much flesh with it.) Now set the root with the flat top side down on the cutting board and use the knife to cut away the skin remaining around the sides of the celery root.

Grilled Sea Scallops and Radicchio with Caesar Sauce

MAKES 4 SERVINGS

For the Caesar sauce

¼ cup freshly grated Parmesan cheese

2 cloves garlic, chopped

¼ cup freshly squeezed lemon juice (from about 2 small lemons), plus more to taste

¼ cup mayonnaise

2 anchovy fillets, chopped

¼ teaspoon Worcestershire sauce

¼ cup mild olive oil

Freshly ground black pepper

16 large sea scallops (about 1 pound)

1 large head radicchio (about 12 ounces)

3 tablespoons mild olive oil, divided, plus more if needed

Kosher salt and freshly ground black pepper

Parmesan shavings, for serving

This is an ideal recipe for large sea or weathervane scallops, a bit less worry about overcooking on the hot grill. The slight bitterness of radicchio—which is tempered a bit with cooking—is a delicious complement to their sweet flavor. Since the scallops and radicchio don't need much grilling time, consider having other things, such as vegetables or flatbread, ready to grill for serving alongside. If the radicchio heads you find are small, you can use two and cut each in quarters, rather than eighths. For the Parmesan shavings, use a vegetable peeler to shave long thin strips of the cheese.

If using bamboo skewers, soak eight 8- to 10-inch bamboo skewers in cold water for at least 20 minutes to limit charring on the grill.

To make the Caesar sauce, combine the Parmesan and garlic in a food processor (a mini processor is ideal) and pulse a few times to more finely mince and blend. Add the lemon juice, mayonnaise, anchovy, and Worcestershire sauce and blend until smooth, scraping down the sides a couple of times.

Add the oil and a few grindings of black pepper and process again until smooth and well blended. Taste for seasoning, adding more lemon juice to taste (salt is likely not needed, but add to your taste). Transfer the dressing to a small bowl and set aside (the dressing can be made a few hours ahead and stored, covered, in the refrigerator).

CONTINUED

GRILLED SEA SCALLOPS AND RADICCHIO WITH CAESAR SAUCE, CONTINUED

NOTE: Scallops on a single skewer tend to spin around when you try to maneuver them, making it tricky to turn them over on the grill. Threading 2 bamboo skewers through the scallops, one either side of center, holds them securely for turning. Line up the 4 scallops for each portion and thread the skewers through them at the same time.

Remove and discard the tough little side muscle if it's present on any of the scallops. Drain the scallops on paper towels, with a piece of paper towel pressed on top if they're particularly wet; set aside.

Preheat an outdoor grill for direct medium-high heat.

Peel away and discard any torn or blemished outer leaves from the radicchio. Cut the head in half through the midpoint of the core to help hold the layers of leaves together. Cut each half into 4 wedges, also cutting through the core. Set the radicchio wedges on a plate or tray and brush 2 tablespoons of the oil over them, on both sides. Sprinkle them lightly with salt and pepper.

Thread the scallops onto the skewers, 4 at a time (see note). Brush the scallops with the remaining tablespoon olive oil and lightly season with salt and pepper.

Grill the radicchio wedges until nicely browned and tender, 1 to 2 minutes per side (turn more often, if needed, to avoid too much char; a bit on the edges is fine). Remove the radicchio and grill the scallops until lightly browned and just a bit translucent at the center, about 2 minutes per side.

Arrange the radicchio wedges on individual plates, lean the skewers of scallops on top (or remove scallops from skewers and place on the radicchio), and drizzle generously with the Caesar sauce. Scatter Parmesan shavings over and serve right away.

Avocado with Scallop Salsa

MAKES 4 SERVINGS

4 ounces sea scallops or bay scallops

¼ cup freshly squeezed lime juice (from about 2 medium limes)

½ cup finely diced and seeded tomato (see note)

¼ cup finely diced sweet onion

2 tablespoons finely chopped fresh cilantro or flat-leaf parsley

1 tablespoon minced jalapeño

¼ teaspoon Tabasco or other hot sauce, plus more to taste

¼ teaspoon kosher salt

2 ripe avocados, halved, pitted, and peeled

Tortilla chips, for serving (optional)

This idea started as homemade salsa made fabulous by adding scallops—upgrading your basic chips-and-salsa option for happy hour. The salsa—much like a ceviche—tops avocado with the chips on the side. As an alternative, you could dice the avocado to add to the scallops for a more classic chips-and-salsa scenario. Note that while the citrus juice alters the scallops flesh, making it opaque and a bit firmer after sitting, these scallops remain raw.

Remove and discard the tough little side muscle if it's present on any of the scallops. Cut the scallops into roughly ½-inch dice. Combine the scallops and lime juice in a small bowl, stir, and refrigerate for 30 minutes.

Toss together the tomato, onion, cilantro, jalapeño, Tabasco, and salt in a medium bowl. Use a slotted spoon to scoop the scallop pieces from the lime juice and add them to the bowl with the tomato mixture. Toss gently to mix, and taste for seasoning, adding more Tabasco or salt if needed. You can drizzle in a tablespoon or so of the lime juice for extra flavor, but avoid making the mixture too wet.

Set each avocado half cut side up on an individual plate and spoon the scallop salsa into the cavity where the pit was; it's fine if some spills onto the plate. Serve with chips alongside.

NOTE: Set the tomato upright on a cutting board and cut the thicker outer shell of flesh away from the core in broad strips following the curve of the tomato. Scrape off any bits of seed and cut the strips of flesh, as needed. The core can be used in a sauce, soup, or other preparation.

Seared Scallops with Capers and Lemon

MAKES 2 MAIN COURSE SERVINGS *or 4 to 8 appetizer servings*

8 large sea scallops (1 to 1½ ounces each)

Kosher salt and freshly ground black pepper

1 tablespoon mild olive oil

2 tablespoons unsalted butter

¼ cup freshly squeezed lemon juice (from about 2 small lemons)

2 tablespoons capers (preferably smaller nonpareil), drained

This quick recipe is perfect for a celebratory dinner. It's an ideal time to seek out luxuriously large scallops, and dry-pack scallops help ensure a good sear. I also recommend warming the plates to hold the warmth of the scallops while the pan sauce is finished. As a light main course, serve them with pasta or a potato gratin. For a multicourse dinner, serve one or two scallops per serving.

Remove and discard the tough little side muscle if it's present on any of the scallops. Drain the scallops on paper towels, with a piece of paper towel pressed on top if they're particularly wet; set aside.

Heat a large heavy skillet (cast iron is ideal) over medium-high heat. Season the scallops lightly with salt and pepper.

Working quickly but carefully, add the oil to the skillet and gently swirl to coat the bottom. Use tongs to add the scallops and cook undisturbed until well browned, 1½ to 2 minutes. Turn the scallops and cook until browned on the second side, about 2 minutes longer; they should be a bit translucent at the center. Transfer the scallops immediately to warmed plates to avoid overcooking from sitting in the hot skillet any longer than needed.

Reduce the heat to medium, add the butter to the skillet, and stir a bit with the tongs to help it melt quickly. Add the lemon juice and capers and cook just until the lemon juice has reduced a bit, stirring to lift up cooked bits from the bottom of the skillet, about 1 minute. Spoon the sauce over the scallops and serve right away.

Bay Scallop Salad with Citrus and Radishes

MAKES 2 TO 4 SERVINGS

12 ounces bay scallops or small sea scallops

1 small grapefruit

1 small navel orange

1 small lime

1 cup thinly sliced radishes (about half a large bunch)

1 tablespoon mild olive oil

2 tablespoons extra-virgin olive oil, or more mild olive oil

½ teaspoon kosher salt

Freshly ground black pepper

1 tablespoon chopped fresh chives, or ½ cup coarsely chopped arugula, for serving

In this salad, citrus segments are tossed with crisp, peppery radishes and topped with warm scallops and a simple dressing that's assembled right in the skillet. I like the brisk flavor of the lime segments contrasting with the sweeter fruits and scallops, but if that sounds too tart to you, feel free to use a bit more orange or grapefruit, or simply leave the lime out. This is an ideal lunchtime option, served with sliced baguette, or a first course for a dinner party. Serving two at dinner, consider adding a light pasta or roasted cauliflower alongside.

Remove and discard the tough little side muscle if it's present on any of the scallops. Drain the scallops on paper towels, with a piece of paper towel pressed on top if they're particularly wet; set aside.

Cut the segments from the grapefruit, orange, and lime (see sidebar), collecting them together in a medium bowl. Strain the juice from the segments and set aside, and return the segments to the same bowl. If any segments are quite large, you can break them in half. Add the radishes to the citrus segments and toss gently to mix. Arrange the salad on individual plates, leaving excess juice behind in the bowl so the salads aren't too wet. Spread the salad out a bit as a bed for the scallops.

CONTINUED

Heat the mild olive oil in a medium skillet over medium heat. Add the scallops and cook, stirring occasionally, until evenly opaque on the surface and just a touch of translucence remains at the center, 3 to 5 minutes. Take the skillet from the heat and use a slotted spoon to scoop the scallops onto the citrus salad on the plates.

Add 3 tablespoons of the reserved citrus juice, the extra-virgin olive oil, salt, and a couple of grindings of black pepper to the skillet. Warm over medium-low heat and stir to evenly blend and incorporate the flavorful bits stuck to the bottom of the skillet, 1 to 2 minutes; the dressing will reduce a bit too. Drizzle this over the scallops and citrus, scatter the chives over, and serve right away.

Segmenting Citrus Fruit

To segment citrus fruits, use a paring knife or small serrated knife to cut both ends from the fruit, just to the flesh. Set the fruit upright on a cutting board and use the knife to cut away the peel and pith (the white part under the peel), following the curve of the fruit. Try not to cut away too much of the flesh with the peel.

Working over a medium bowl to catch the juice, hold the peeled fruit in your hand and carefully slide the knife blade down one side of a section, separating it from the membrane. Cut down the other side of the same section and let it fall into the bowl. (Pick out and discard any seeds as you go.) Continue for the remaining sections, turning back the flaps of the membrane like the pages of a book. Squeeze the juice from the membrane core into the bowl and discard the core.

Scallops Baked with Rice and Green Olives

MAKES 4 SERVINGS

1 pound bay scallops or small sea scallops

3 tablespoons mild olive oil, divided, plus more for the dish

¼ cup finely chopped yellow onion

½ cup long grain white rice

¾ teaspoon kosher salt, divided

1 cup Shellfish Stock (page 183), fish stock, or water

1 cup (about 3 ounces) pitted green olives, halved lengthwise

½ cup diced red bell pepper

¼ cup slivered almonds, toasted

1 teaspoon smoked paprika, sweet or hot

Lemon wedges, for serving

If you don't already have a tin of smoked paprika on your shelf, you'll enjoy adding it to the mix of your spice collection. With just a few shakes, it adds earthy-robust flavor—with some heat, if you choose the hot version—to anything from toasted nuts to roasted chicken. Here it adds its character to a Spanish-influenced blend of bell pepper, almonds, green olives, and rice baked with scallops. I think the smaller-size scallops work better here, but you can use large sea scallops if you like, adding a couple of minutes of cooking time. Serve with sautéed garlicky green beans or another favorite green vegetable.

Remove and discard the tough little side muscle if it's present on any of the scallops. Drain the scallops on paper towels, with a piece of paper towel pressed on top if they're particularly wet; set aside.

Preheat the oven to 425 degrees F. Lightly oil a 12-inch gratin dish or similar shallow baking dish.

Heat 1 tablespoon of the oil in a small skillet over medium heat. Add the onion and cook, stirring occasionally, until tender, 2 to 3 minutes. Stir in the rice and ½ teaspoon of the salt and cook, stirring, until the rice smells lightly toasty, 2 to 3 minutes.

CONTINUED

Transfer the rice to the gratin dish, add the stock, and spread the rice out relatively evenly. Cover the dish with aluminum foil and bake until the liquid is absorbed and the rice is nearly tender, 15 to 18 minutes.

While the rice is cooking, combine the scallops, olives, bell pepper, almonds, paprika, remaining 2 tablespoons oil, and remaining ¼ teaspoon salt in a medium bowl. Use a rubber spatula to stir and mix them together well.

When the rice is ready, remove the dish from the oven (leaving the oven on) and carefully remove the foil, avoiding the steam that escapes. Add the scallop mixture to the rice, scraping out the seasoned oil from the bowl as well, and gently mix with the rice, then spread things out relatively evenly. Return the dish to the oven, uncovered, and bake until the scallops are just barely cooked through (only slightly translucent at the center when cut into), 8 to 10 minutes for bay scallops, 10 to 12 minutes for small sea scallops.

Scoop the scallops and rice onto individual plates and serve right away, with lemon wedges alongside for squeezing.

OYSTER
SHELLS
ONLY

OYSTERS

Every one of these shellfish has its charms, its history, its fan base of devotees that eagerly extol its virtues. But by my estimation, oysters manage to draw the most boisterous enthusiasm. The explosion of oysters bars across the country is just one testament to that, as are oyster festivals, shucking championships, slurp-offs, and countless other places where oyster fans congregate.

An oyster's striking character is evident from first glance at the rugged, cupped shell that blends in beautifully with its natural environment of rocky beaches and tide flats. Sometimes the shells even carry evidence of that environment, with small barnacles or tufts of seaweed clinging to them. And some are extravagantly fluted, almost (but not quite) too pretty to shuck.

Inside is the most wondrous of little virtual vacations, transporting you to the body of water where the oyster lived. Oysters are filter-feeders, drawing many gallons of water through their shells each day to collect nutrients. The characteristics of that water contribute to the flavor and texture of the oyster. This taste of place, or "meroir," if you will, is one of the most compelling aspects that draw oyster lovers. And it makes sitting down to slurp a few different types such a treat. There's no better way to appreciate their distinct character than to taste them side by side.

Once an oyster is cooked, nuances are less evident. Which brings up a dividing line for some oyster eaters: those who only eat them raw, others who only eat them cooked. Though there are plenty of people like me who happily consume them whichever way they're served. (Sure, I'll acknowledge, too, those who have not yet worked up the courage to try an oyster at all.)

The two oyster varieties most widely available in the United States are the native Eastern oyster found from Texas to Maine and points north, and the Pacific oyster, which was introduced in the early twentieth century from Japan, found from California (and points south) to Alaska. You'll rarely see them sold by the species name, however. Instead they'll usually have a name indicating the body of water they came from, or perhaps a branded name that still traces back to a particular region or grower. This is because of those aforementioned variances in character that come from the oyster's habitat. Those two species take on an incredible array of guises, and flavors, based on locale.

A few other oysters you may come across include the Kumamoto oyster, another transplant from Japan that is particularly popular as a slurping oyster—you may see it more in oyster bars than in seafood markets. Same for the West Coast's only native oyster, the tiny Olympia oyster, with bold flavor that is also prized for enjoying raw. The fifth species is another transplant, this from across the Atlantic instead: The European flat oyster was introduced to Maine in the 1950s, where it sometimes goes by Belon, a French river renowned for flat oysters. Over time a population began to sustain itself naturally in the state—available in quite small volumes, the European flat is a specialty oyster. It is sometimes available from a few farming operations on the West Coast as well.

Though there is some wild harvest of oysters, most of what we buy will have been farm-raised, which means a ready supply from most growing regions throughout the year. Aficionados will indulge a bit more over winter and into early spring, when colder waters mean oysters are at their crispest, most plump, and most flavorful.

You may see oysters referred to as "tumbled." There are a few ways that process is done, but basically it's a way growers manage the oyster's growth so that it develops a deeper cup and plumper meat.

SHOPPING AND STORING

Oysters in their shells must be alive up to the point that you cook or shuck them. It's most common to buy oysters in the shell by the piece rather than by weight. Another option for oysters is pre-shucked in jars or tubs. They come in various sizes, both in terms of the container itself (8 ounces to 16 ounces or more) and the size of the oysters inside (see page 103). I love this option for cooked oyster recipes, perfect for pan-fried and baked preparations. But not for slurping raw; save that pleasure for freshly shucked oysters.

Oyster shells are less susceptible to breakage than are clam and mussel shells, and they tend to gape less as well. You should still confirm that the oysters you buy have unbroken shells that are firmly closed—or that shut tightly when tapped. One extra test I apply is to tap two oysters together: it should sound like knocking two rocks together, a dull, solid sound. If an oyster sounds hollow, it will have lost a lot of its liquor that keeps it in prime form; I skip these oysters.

Get the oysters home and in the refrigerator as soon as you're able. If it's a warm day or the trip home not quick, ask for a bag of ice at the seafood counter to keep your oysters chilled in transit, or plan ahead and take along a cooler with a couple of frozen gel packs. Once home, I transfer the oysters to a colander set inside a bowl to catch any drips. Cover the oysters with a damp, not sopping wet, towel to keep them moist. Don't cover the bowl any more than that to ensure they get the air they need to survive.

It's important that the oysters not sit in water, so don't be tempted to add ice or water to the bowl. If you have a lot of oysters, or if they're quite large, it may be easier to store them in a broad deep pan, like a roasting pan.

CLEANING

How much cleaning your in-shell oysters will need can vary. Those with smoother shells may harbor little in the way of sand or grit, needing just a quick rinse under cold running water. Those with more fluted or otherwise elaborate shells may need a touch of scrubbing. If you plan to serve them in the shell, cleaning the shells ensures a tidier presentation and avoids grit getting inside the oyster. If you'll be using just the oyster meat, it still pays to briefly toss the oysters under cold running water.

COOKING

To some, oysters never, or rarely, require any cooking. Nor any other ingredients, honestly. For devotees, the liquor that surrounds it in the shell is all the adornment a slurped oyster needs. Otherwise, a squeeze of lemon, splash of mignonette, or dash of hot sauce are some ways to accent the raw briny treat.

Cooked in the shell, oysters are perfect on the grill. It can be as simple as putting the whole cleaned oysters directly on the grill (cupped side down) and cooking until they pop open. I prefer grilling oysters shucked, though, because it's easier to monitor the progress and you can add a flavor accent, such as seasoned butter, that cooks with the oyster. Shucked oysters also bake beautifully.

Out of the shell, I think one of the perfect options is pan-fried oysters. Pick your coating—flour, cracker crumbs, cornmeal, and beyond—and cook until nicely browned. It's hard to go wrong. Shucked oysters shine too, in stews, in gratins, deep-fried, and poached.

Shucking Oysters

If you have a heavy-duty shucking glove, here's the time to use it. Otherwise a thick kitchen towel works great too. You're protecting your hand from not only any potential slip of the shucking knife, but also from the often-sharp edges of the oyster shell. Fold the towel lengthwise in thirds on the counter, producing a few layers of thickness. Set the oyster on the towel near one end, with its cupped side down and pointed hinge end facing your dominant hand. Fold the rest of the towel up and over the oyster, holding the oyster down toward the rounded end with your nondominant hand and leaving the hinge still exposed.

1 Firmly grasp a good oyster knife (page 8) and use the tip to wedge carefully between the oyster halves at the hinge. Sometimes this is easy, and sometimes it takes determination. Keep at it and you will find the hinge gives and the knife tip will slip between the shells. The trick is to have just the tip of the knife slip in, rather than barging in with the whole blade. The latter is not a catastrophe, but it often means the oyster meat will be a bit marred.

2 Once the blade tip has slipped in, twist the knife handle to pry apart the shells.

3 Run the blade of the knife flat against the top shell of the oyster, separating the adductor muscle. To give you an idea of where to direct your efforts, the muscle is in roughly the top-right quarter portion of the oyster relative to the hinge.

4 Lift off and discard the top shell and gently slide the knife blade under the oyster as well, to slice through the other end of the adductor muscle and fully separate the oyster.

5 If serving the oysters on the half shell, arrange them on ice. Otherwise, proceed as directed for the recipe.

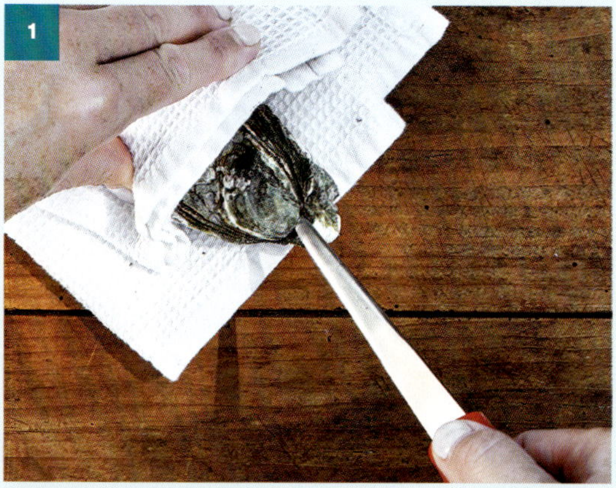
1

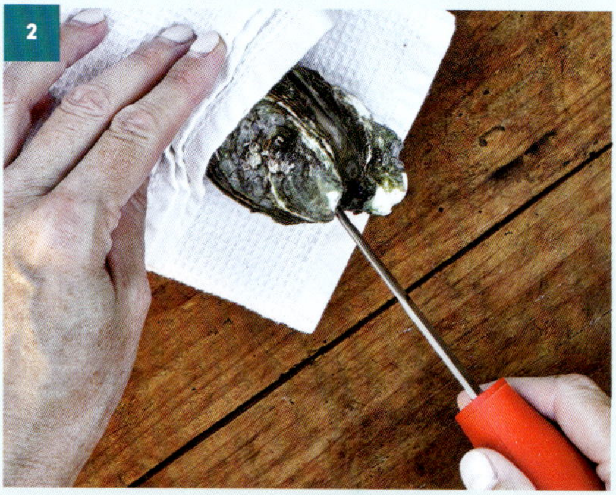
2

3

4

5

Half-Shell Oysters with Cucumber Mignonette

MAKES 2 DOZEN OYSTERS AND A SCANT ½ CUP MIGNONETTE

1 small English cucumber, peeled, or regular cucumber, peeled and seeded (about 12 ounces)

3 tablespoons Champagne or white wine vinegar

1 teaspoon minced shallot

Freshly ground black pepper

24 small to medium live oysters, shells well rinsed

How many servings do you get from a dozen half-shell oysters? It's something of a trick question. For some, one or two raw oysters is plenty in one sitting, for others a dozen might be just the warm-up. So consider your audience and plan accordingly. You should have enough cucumber to make a double batch of mignonette, doubling the other ingredients as well.

Coarsely grate about half of the cucumber and put it in a fine-mesh sieve set over a small bowl. Squeeze the cucumber in your hand to extract enough juice to measure 3 tablespoons. Mince enough of the remaining cucumber to measure 1 tablespoon. Save the remaining cucumber for another use, or just snack away.

In a small ramekin or other small serving dish, combine the cucumber juice, minced cucumber, vinegar, shallot, and a few grindings of black pepper and stir to mix. Refrigerate until ready to serve, up to 2 hours ahead.

Arrange crushed ice or rock salt on a rimmed serving tray (see sidebar). Shuck the oysters (see page 90) and nestle them into the ice, leaving room in the center for the mignonette, or simply serve the mignonette alongside. Have a small spoon in the mignonette so a drizzle can be added to each oyster just before slurping.

Serving Half-Shell Oysters

Perching oysters on ice for serving accomplishes two goals: keeping the oysters chilled and providing something for shells to nestle into so they don't tip and lose their liquor. Chunky ice cubes aren't much help; crushed ice is much more amenable to the task. Choose a tray or platter with a rim to contain the ice-melt, even if that's just a baking sheet. Guests will be more focused on the beautiful oysters than what they're served in.

In a pinch, rock salt can be used, accomplishing just the second benefit of the ice. Be sure you're shucking and serving these oysters right away so they are at their coldest.

Oysters Baked with Horseradish Bread Crumbs

MAKES 2 MAIN COURSE SERVINGS
or 4 to 6 appetizer servings

1 cup fresh bread crumbs (see note) or panko crumbs

12 medium live oysters, shells well rinsed

3 tablespoons finely grated fresh horseradish, or 2 tablespoons prepared horseradish

3 tablespoons unsalted butter, melted

½ teaspoon kosher salt

Freshly ground black pepper

Freshly made and lightly toasted bread crumbs have a texture both light and crisp, ideal for this use. As a shortcut, panko crumbs are a decent substitute; they won't need the toasting step. For an extra punch of horseradish, grate a bit more over the oysters just before serving, if you're using fresh. Braised or steamed greens with lemon will round out these oysters as a main-course offering; they're also great as an appetizer. For an out-of-shell option, you could use jarred oysters (see page 103) and bake them in a shallow, buttered baking dish with the crumb mixture spread evenly on top; they'll need 15 to 18 minutes baking time.

Preheat the oven to 400 degrees F. Line a rimmed baking sheet with rock salt or cut a piece of aluminum foil twice as long as the baking sheet and crumple it to evenly cover the bottom of the baking sheet, which will help the oyster shells sit evenly.

Put the fresh bread crumbs in a small baking pan, like a cake pan or pie pan. Lightly toast them in the oven, 5 to 7 minutes, stirring two or three times. The crumbs need not brown evenly, just a bit of color is good. Set aside to cool. Leave the oven set at 400 degrees F.

CONTINUED

Shuck the oysters (see page 90). Pour off excess liquor so it won't make the crumb topping too soggy, and nestle the oysters into the rock salt or foil so that they sit evenly.

If using fresh horseradish, combine it with the bread crumbs in a small bowl and toss well with a fork to mix. Drizzle the butter over, add the salt and few grindings of black pepper, and toss well to mix. If using prepared horseradish, stir it together with the melted butter in a small bowl, then add the bread crumbs, salt, and pepper and toss well to mix.

Top the oysters with the bread crumbs, spreading to evenly cover each oyster. Bake until the oysters are plump, crumbs browned, and juices around the edges bubbling, 8 to 10 minutes. Use tongs to transfer the oysters to individual plates, perching them as evenly as you're able. Serve right away.

NOTE: One to two slices of regular white sandwich bread should be plenty for the 1 cup bread crumbs here; extra crumbs can be saved for another use. Tear each bread slice into 5 or 6 pieces and pulse them in a food processor to a relatively even texture of fine crumbs. (I don't bother removing the crusts; seems a waste unless you have another use for them.) The fresh crumbs can be used as is for some recipes, but in this case, they'll be toasted a bit for the best texture as an oyster topping.

Grilled Oysters Marinière

MAKES 2 TO 4 SERVINGS

4 tablespoons unsalted butter, at room temperature

2 tablespoons minced shallot

2 tablespoons minced fresh flat-leaf parsley

½ teaspoon minced fresh thyme (lemon or traditional)

¼ teaspoon kosher salt

12 medium to large live oysters, shells well rinsed

2 tablespoons dry white wine, divided (optional)

I'm mixing things up a bit with this combination of wine, shallot, butter, and herbs that is often used for steaming mussels. The flavors apply beautifully to grilled oysters as well. If you happen to have lemon thyme available, this is a great time to use it. It's easy enough to skip the wine if you prefer; they're delicious either way. Add crusty bread and coleslaw or another favorite salad to make this a meal for two. It's simple to double, if you'd like to grill a couple dozen oysters instead.

One small trick with grilling oysters is that the cupped shells (some more deeply cupped than others) take some care to perch evenly on the grill grate. It's a technique worth lots of practice, even after you get it down!

Combine the butter, shallot, parsley, thyme, and salt in a small bowl and stir well to thoroughly blend.

Preheat an outdoor grill for direct medium-high heat.

Shuck the oysters (see page 90). A little oyster liquor is fine, but pour off excess if there is quite a lot in some of the shells. Arrange the oysters on a tray perched as evenly as you can manage.

Spoon a generous teaspoon of the butter mixture onto each oyster and add about ½ teaspoon of wine to each shell. Use long-handled tongs to transfer the oysters to the preheated grill, perching the shells as evenly as you're able. Grill until the oysters are plump, their edges curled, and buttery juices bubbling, 6 to 9 minutes. Use the tongs to carefully transfer oysters to a platter or individual plates, preserving as much of the flavorful liquids in the shell as you can en route.

Cornmeal-Fried Oysters with Pickled-Pepper Tartar Sauce

MAKES 2 MAIN COURSE SERVINGS
or 4 to 6 appetizer servings

For the pickled-pepper tartar sauce

¾ cup mayonnaise

3 to 4 tablespoons finely chopped pickled peppers

2 tablespoons finely chopped fresh flat-leaf parsley or chives

2 tablespoons finely chopped green onion, white and light-green portions

1 tablespoon white wine vinegar or freshly squeezed lemon juice

¼ teaspoon kosher salt

1¼ cups fine cornmeal, plus more for sprinkling

1 teaspoon kosher salt

½ teaspoon freshly ground black pepper

→

Pan-fried oysters rank as one of my all-time favorite preparations for the lovely bivalves. There are lots of options for the coating; here, I use cornmeal to add a bit of nutty-crunchy character. The tartar sauce uses pickled peppers in place of dill pickles, with flavor as potentially varied—and spicy—as the type of pepper you use. Pepperoncini are a great option, and I love using Mama Lil's peppers as well. A cucumber-tomato salad would complement the rich oysters well.

To make the tartar sauce, combine the mayonnaise, pickled peppers, parsley, green onion, vinegar, and salt in a small bowl and stir well to mix. Taste for seasoning, adding more pickled peppers or salt if needed, though keep in mind that flavors will develop a bit over time. Cover and refrigerate until ready to serve. (The sauce can be made a day ahead.)

Preheat the oven to 200 degrees F. Set an oblong wire rack on a rimmed baking sheet. Sprinkle a thin layer of cornmeal across the bottom of another rimmed baking sheet or tray.

Combine the cornmeal, salt, and pepper in a medium bowl and stir with a fork to combine. Add a few of the oysters to the cornmeal and toss with the fork to evenly coat. Pat to remove excess cornmeal from the oysters and set them, not touching each other, on the baking sheet sprinkled with cornmeal. Continue coating the remaining oysters.

24 medium freshly shucked (see page 90) or jarred oysters (see page 103)

Vegetable or other neutral oil, for cooking

Heat about ¼ inch of oil in a large heavy skillet, such as cast iron, over medium-high heat.

When the oil is heated, carefully add 6 to 8 of the oysters without crowding them (cook fewer if needed) and cook until nicely browned, about 3 minutes; if the oysters are browning too quickly, reduce the heat to medium. Note that the oysters may spatter as they give off liquid while frying. Turn the oysters and brown on the second side, 2 to 3 minutes longer. Transfer the oysters to the baking sheet with the wire rack and keep warm in the oven while frying the remaining oysters. Add a bit more oil to the skillet and allow to reheat as needed between batches.

Arrange the fried oysters on individual plates, add a generous dollop of the tartar sauce alongside, and serve right away, passing extra tartar sauce separately.

Jarred Oysters

By jarred oysters, I mean those that are sold shucked and available in the seafood case in jars or tubs. Sizes vary, both for the container (8 ounces to 16 ounces or more) and for the oysters inside. I find extra-small to be consistently available and an ideal size for most recipes, really more of a medium-size oyster in general terms. This size is a good choice for use in these recipes.

There are also smaller “yearling” oysters and larger “small,” sometimes “medium,” size as well, the latter being actually quite large. East Coast and Gulf oysters can be sold by different grades, from smaller “standard” up to larger “count” oysters.

Note that the exact number of oysters you’ll get from a jar is not certain. By very rough average, I’ve found a 10-ounce jar or tub of extra-small Pacific oysters may have about 10 oysters, sometimes 8 or fewer, sometimes 12. You can save any extra oysters for another preparation the next day; simply toss with seasoned cornmeal or flour to pan-fry. Or the Baked Oysters with Bacon and Eggs (page 104), using just 4 oysters, is a great option.

Baked Oysters with Bacon and Eggs

MAKES 4 SERVINGS

6 slices bacon, not thick-cut

4 large eggs

2 tablespoons half-and-half or whole milk

2 tablespoons finely chopped chives or green onion tops

Kosher salt and freshly ground black pepper

4 small freshly shucked (see page 90) or jarred oysters (see page 103), well drained

Toast, for serving

Perfect for breakfast or brunch, this recipe can just as well swing into lunch or even dinnertime, with green salad and fried potatoes alongside. I find the bacon often prevents the egg from sticking to the ramekin, so you may be able to turn these out for serving if you'd like. Some oysters in your jar may be smaller than others, in which case you can double up a couple of smaller oysters. Extra oysters from the container will be great in Cornmeal-Fried Oysters (page 101).

The oysters are going to give off a bit of liquid as they cook, which can be easy to mistake for uncooked egg. Do your best to test for doneness in the cooked egg; the texture should be firm when pressed as well.

Preheat the oven to 450 degrees F. Line a rimmed baking sheet with aluminum foil. Lightly butter 4 ramekins of about ½-cup volume.

Lay the bacon on the prepared baking sheet and bake until it has given off a good bit of its fat, 4 to 6 minutes. Turn the pieces over and continue baking until just lightly browned, but not crisp, about 5 minutes longer. Transfer the bacon to paper towels to drain. Reduce the oven temperature to 375 degrees F.

When the bacon is cool, line the inside edge of each ramekin with 1 piece of the bacon, upright against the sides, with the ends of the bacon overlapping if needed. Cut the remaining pieces of bacon in half crosswise and lay a piece on the bottom of each ramekin, with the ends coming up the sides. Set the ramekins on a baking sheet.

Lightly beat the eggs in a medium bowl, then add the half-and-half and chives with a good pinch of salt and a few grindings of pepper.

Add 1 oyster to each ramekin, then pour in the egg mixture to reach just below the rim of the ramekins. Bake until the eggs puff up nicely and are cooked through (a knife inserted into the cooked egg, rather than the oyster, will come out clean), 15 to 20 minutes.

Transfer the ramekins to individual plates and serve right away, with toast alongside.

Oysters à la Falafel in Pita

MAKES 4 SERVINGS

For the oysters

12 medium freshly shucked (see page 90) or jarred oysters (see page 103)

1 cup chickpea flour

¼ cup finely chopped fresh flat-leaf parsley

½ teaspoon ground cumin

½ teaspoon kosher salt

¼ teaspoon garlic powder

Pinch dried red pepper flakes or freshly ground black pepper

⅔ cup water, plus more if needed

The nutty-herbal-spiced character of falafel becomes a coating for fried oysters in this recipe. They're served on warm pita bread, with bright, crisp vegetables and a zippy tahini drizzle. The pita can be halved, filling each pouch, or served whole as a wrap. Or skip the pita, simply serving the oysters on a bed of the vegetables, drizzled with sauce. Add a cucumber-yogurt salad or roasted vegetables alongside to make for a more substantial meal.

Look for chickpea flour, also known as garbanzo bean flour, with other specialty flours or other Mediterranean ingredients.

Preheat the oven to 200 degrees F. Set an oblong wire rack on a rimmed baking sheet.

To prepare the oysters, first drain the oysters on paper towels, with another piece of paper towel pressed on top.

Use a fork to stir together the chickpea flour, parsley, cumin, salt, garlic powder, and pepper flakes in a medium bowl. Add the water in a slow stream, stirring constantly to form a smooth batter. This will be a rather thick batter, but if it's a bit too thick to easily coat the oysters, stir in another 1 to 2 tablespoons water.

For the tahini sauce

¼ cup plain whole-milk or low-fat yogurt

3 tablespoons freshly squeezed lemon juice, plus more if needed

2 tablespoons tahini

¼ teaspoon kosher salt

Vegetable oil or other neutral oil, for frying

½ cup finely shredded red cabbage

½ cup grated carrot

½ cup finely chopped cucumber

2 to 4 pita breads, warmed

To make the tahini sauce, stir together the yogurt, lemon juice, tahini, and salt in a small bowl until smooth. The sauce should be thin enough to drizzle, stir in extra lemon juice or a bit of water if needed.

Add enough oil to a large heavy skillet (cast iron is ideal) so it is about ¼ inch deep. Heat the oil over medium-high heat.

Drop a few oysters into the batter and turn them with the fork to evenly coat. Lift out one oyster at a time, allowing excess batter to drip off, and carefully add it to the skillet. Repeat with a few more oysters, careful to not crowd them in the skillet to ensure even cooking. Cook until nicely browned on one side, 3 to 4 minutes, reducing the heat a bit if the oysters are browning too quickly. Note that the oysters may spatter as they give off liquid while frying. Gently turn the oysters and cook until browned on the second side, 2 to 3 minutes longer. Transfer the fried oysters to the baking sheet and keep warm in the oven. Continue with the remaining oysters, adding a bit more oil to the skillet if needed.

To serve, distribute the red cabbage, carrot, and cucumber evenly among the pita breads (on top for a wrap, or in the pouch if halved) and top with the fried oysters. Drizzle some of the tahini sauce over and serve right away, passing extra sauce separately.

Smoked Oyster Dip

MAKES ABOUT 2 CUPS

8 ounces cream cheese, at room temperature

½ cup sour cream

3 to 4 ounces smoked oysters, finely chopped (see note)

¼ cup finely chopped green onion, white and green parts

1 teaspoon finely grated lemon zest

2 tablespoons freshly squeezed lemon juice

½ teaspoon Worcestershire sauce

½ teaspoon kosher salt

A few dashes Tabasco sauce or other hot sauce

Thick-cut potato chips, pita chips, or crackers, for serving

This simple dip can be made with other shellfish. Consider other smoked options—such as clams or mussels—or cooked shrimp, clams, or crabmeat, adding a bit more of these if you like since they're milder than the smoked options. The flavor will be best if made a couple of hours ahead, and the dip holds well for a couple of days in the refrigerator. If the smoked oysters you're using are packed in oil, drain them on paper towels before using.

In a medium bowl, combine the cream cheese and sour cream and stir with a rubber spatula until well blended and smooth. If the cream cheese still shows some lumps, let it sit for a bit longer to fully soften.

Add the smoked oysters, green onion, lemon zest, lemon juice, Worcestershire sauce, salt, and Tabasco. Stir gently to mix well, then taste for seasoning, adding more salt to taste. Transfer the dip to a serving bowl, cover, and refrigerate until ready to serve, preferably for at least 2 hours.

Serve the dip with potato chips alongside.

NOTE: You may see smoked oysters with various flavors; I think the classic smoked oyster works best here. Package and can sizes vary, ideally you'll have about 1 cup chopped to use, though a 3-ounce can may leave you shy. I found it was still tasty at that amount; it's up to you if you want to open a second can.

SHRIMP

I WON'T BE SURPRISED if this is the section of the book that most folks turn to first. Of all the shellfish in the sea, shrimp are without a doubt the most loved: easy to cook, mild in flavor, and extremely versatile, both in terms of potential cooking methods and flavor combinations. It's the number one seafood consumed in the United States, and has been in that spot for some time.

Shrimp are so ubiquitous that it can be easy to take their supply for granted, and think that a shrimp is a shrimp is a shrimp. But there are distinctions to look for, with regard to species and provenance in particular. Add questions of sustainability to the mix—which are particularly varied with this globally produced shellfish—and the consumer has a number of things to consider with shrimp.

The most common species of larger shrimp harvested in the United States are white, brown, and pink shrimp, the first two in the greatest volumes. These shrimp are caught primarily in the Gulf of Mexico. The range for commercial harvest of the shrimp wraps around Florida and continues up the Atlantic coast as far as North Carolina.

Tiny little pink shrimp found on the West Coast are a different species from the Gulf pink shrimp. These shrimp are sold cooked and peeled, and can go by a number of names including bay shrimp or salad shrimp. Found from British Columbia to Southern California, the bulk of harvest is off the coast of Oregon. Thus another of their possible names, Oregon pink shrimp. These are sometimes referred to as cold-water shrimp, in contrast to those from the warmer waters of the Gulf.

Regional and seasonal shrimp varieties you may come across include spot prawns from Alaska and the Pacific Northwest and royal red shrimp from the Gulf. I've been fortunate to enjoy the former more than a few times, and have yet to get a taste of the latter. It's on my list.

White, brown, and pink shrimp are harvested year-round, though harvest is at lower volumes through the first few months of the year, and are available fresh and frozen. Oregon's pink shrimp season runs April through October, when fresh shrimp can be found, with frozen product readily available year-round as well.

SHOPPING AND STORING

Shrimp are found in an array of forms. Head-on shrimp are something of a specialty item; most will be just the tail meat. These shrimp might be sold as is with the full shell intact. Or there may be a slit the length of the shell, which allows the vein to be removed in advance and makes the shell easier for you to peel away. Or the shrimp may have been peeled and deveined, with or without the last bit of fan-tipped tail still intact.

So should you buy shrimp with the shell on or off? For a simple shrimp boil or when cooking shrimp for another use, shell-on offers maximum flavor and helps keep the shrimp moist. Even if

I'll be cooking the shrimp peeled, I prefer buying shrimp shell-on so I've got shells for making either a quick shrimp stock (see page 184) or batch of Shellfish Stock (page 183).

Sometimes shrimp are just sold as "shrimp," with little detail beyond perhaps confirming that it is raw or cooked, peeled or not. A general size, such a small or jumbo, may be noted, if not the more specific size grades used by the industry, such as "26/30" or "U-15". These sizes indicate how many shrimp—more or less—it takes to make a pound, with the U meaning "under." So for these examples, 26 to 30 shrimp per pound, and 15 or fewer shrimp per pound. The smaller the number, the bigger the shrimp.

As long as there's no excess liquid in the packaging for the shrimp you brought home, it should be fine to store them as is in the refrigerator for a day or two. Though the sooner you cook them, the better they'll be. Frozen shrimp should go into the freezer as quickly as you can manage to avoid any premature thaw, unless you intend to thaw right away to use soon. Otherwise, plan ahead to thaw overnight in the refrigerator. Don't refreeze thawed shrimp; it won't do the quality any favors.

CLEANING

The "vein" referenced in the "peel and devein" step of preparing shrimp is the digestive tract that runs along the back of the shrimp. It's more visible in some shrimp than others, often dark gray or black. It's easy enough to remove if it hasn't been already. Use the tip of a small knife to make a shallow slit along the back of the peeled shrimp, open the slit, and pull out the vein to discard. Otherwise, shrimp need little in the way of cleaning: I just given them a quick toss in a colander under cold running water and dry thoroughly before cooking.

COOKING

Shrimp are one of the easiest shellfish for home cooks to rely on. For the recipes I've included here, you'll see them grilled, deep-fried (how could I not!), marinated, sautéed, as a decadent sandwich, and baked a couple of ways. This is just a small drop in the bucket of potential options for enjoying this popular shellfish.

When I call for "peeled" shrimp in recipes, it's usually up to you if you want to leave the last bit of tail intact. Where it definitely needs to be removed, I'll point that out. When using peeled shrimp, it's worth taking the time to confirm there are no lingering bits of shell before cooking.

Shrimp Tails

I'm not against the pleasing aesthetics of leaving tails on the otherwise-peeled shrimp for recipes that serve the shrimp whole—they add some visual appeal and can serve as a handy little holder for eating the shrimp with your fingers. When a dish requires silverware, it becomes a bit messy navigating the tails, so I tend to remove them before cooking in those cases.

Sautéed Shrimp with Garlic and Crisp Rosemary

MAKES 4 TO 6 SERVINGS

¼ cup unsalted butter

2 tablespoons fresh whole rosemary leaves

3 cloves garlic, thinly sliced

1½ pounds large shrimp, peeled, deveined, and rinsed

Kosher salt and freshly ground black pepper

½ cup dry white wine, shrimp stock (see page 184), or Shellfish Stock (page 183)

2 tablespoons freshly squeezed lemon juice

One of the simplest and most delicious preparations for shrimp is a quick sauté in a hot skillet, with many possibilities for embellishment. I opt here for the aromatic combination of garlic and rosemary, the latter cooked until crisp.

Melt the butter in a large skillet over medium heat. Add the rosemary and cook, stirring occasionally with a fork, until the rosemary is lightly crisped, aromatic, and just beginning to lightly brown, about 2 minutes (too brown and it becomes a tad bitter). Note that the butter will brown as it cooks, which is a good thing, adding a bit of nutty flavor as well. Take the skillet from the heat and use the fork to lift out the rosemary onto a small plate, allowing excess butter to drip back into the skillet. Set the rosemary aside to cool.

Return the skillet to medium heat and add the garlic. Cook, stirring often with a wooden spoon, until aromatic, 30 to 60 seconds. Add the shrimp with a good pinch of salt and a few grindings of black pepper and cook, stirring occasionally, until the shrimp are evenly opaque on the surface, 2 to 3 minutes. Add the wine and simmer over medium-high heat until the sauce is reduced by about half and the shrimp are just cooked through (opaque through the thickest part), 3 to 4 minutes longer. Take the skillet from the heat, stir in the lemon juice, taste the sauce for seasoning, and add more salt or pepper to taste.

Spoon the shrimp and sauce onto individual plates, sprinkle the crisp rosemary over, and serve right away.

CIRO'
Azienda Agricola
Ciro Marina

Grilled Shrimp on Lentil-Arugula Salad

MAKES 4 SERVINGS

For the vinaigrette

3 tablespoons white wine vinegar

2 teaspoons Dijon mustard

¼ teaspoon kosher salt

Freshly ground black pepper

⅓ cup extra-virgin olive oil or mild olive oil

1 pound medium to large shrimp, peeled, deveined, and rinsed

1 teaspoon kosher salt

1 bay leaf, preferably fresh

1 clove garlic

¾ cup green or black lentils, rinsed

4 cups loosely packed arugula (about 3 ounces)

¼ cup thinly sliced green onion (white and green parts), or 2 tablespoons chopped fresh chives

Since shrimp don't need much time on the grill, consider planning to cook something else on the grill while it's hot. Maybe skewers of mushrooms and zucchini to serve alongside, and pieces of rustic bread brushed with olive oil to grill-toast. I always have French green lentils on hand, occasionally black "beluga" or "caviar" lentils, so named for their small, nearly round shape reminiscent of caviar. Both hold their shape well when cooked, great for countless uses. Regular green or brown lentils are good too; they just may get a tad softer. The vinaigrette gets double duty here: part used to marinate the shrimp, the rest for dressing the salad.

If using bamboo skewers, soak four 8- to 10-inch bamboo skewers in cold water for at least 20 minutes to limit charring on the grill.

To make the vinaigrette, whisk together the vinegar, mustard, salt, and a couple of grindings of pepper in a large bowl until the salt is dissolved, then whisk in the oil.

Put the shrimp in a medium bowl. Rewhisk the vinaigrette to blend, and drizzle about half of it over the shrimp. Toss the shrimp to evenly coat, cover the bowl, and refrigerate while cooking the lentils.

CONTINUED

Half-fill a medium saucepan with water and add the salt, bay leaf, and whole garlic clove. Bring the water to a boil over high heat. Add the lentils, reduce the heat to medium-low, and simmer uncovered until the lentils are just tender, 18 to 22 minutes. Drain the lentils, discarding the bay leaf but reserving the garlic with the lentils. Set aside to cool (I set the strainer over the pan the lentils cooked in to allow excess water to drain away as they sit).

Preheat an outdoor grill for direct medium-high heat.

Lift the garlic clove from the cooked lentils, flicking any clinging lentils back with the others (if the garlic has fallen apart and mixed with the lentils, leave it as is). Add the soft garlic to the remaining vinaigrette and mash with a fork to blend. Add the cooled lentils and stir to evenly coat. Add the arugula and green onion and toss to mix, then arrange the salad on individual plates, slightly mounded in the center.

Thread the marinated shrimp onto 4 skewers, catching the tail and broad end of each to form a C as they go on the skewers. Grill the shrimp until just opaque through the thickest part, 2 to 3 minutes per side.

Lean a skewer of shrimp against each salad, or remove the shrimp from the skewers to perch on the salad, and serve right away.

Harissa-Roasted Shrimp, Carrots, and Radishes

MAKES 4 SERVINGS

12 ounces small to medium carrots, trimmed

2 bunches radishes, trimmed

¼ cup mild olive oil, plus more if needed

1 to 2 tablespoons harissa

¾ teaspoon ground cumin

½ teaspoon ground coriander

½ teaspoon kosher salt

1½ pounds medium to large shrimp, peeled, deveined, and rinsed

Shrimp get colorful and flavorful accents from carrots and radishes, which are sometimes available in hues beyond their classic orange and red. If you happen to find extra-small carrots—finger-slender and about 4 inches long or less—they can be roasted whole. The harissa I use is the paste type, a staple in my fridge. It comes in varying styles, including varying degrees of heat, so use more or less to suit your taste. You can find it in powdered form as well. Either will work, though an extra drizzle of olive oil may be needed if using powder. This could be served with, or over, couscous or orzo.

Preheat the oven to 450 degrees F.

Cut larger carrots into 3- to 4-inch lengths, and then cut in half or quarters so they're not much more than ½ inch wide; extra-small carrots can be used as is. Small radishes can be cooked as is; medium or large radishes should be halved or quartered.

Combine the oil, harissa, cumin, coriander, and salt in a large bowl and use a rubber spatula to evenly mix the seasonings. Add the shrimp, carrots, and radishes and toss to evenly coat. If using dried harissa and the coating is a bit sparse, add another 1 or 2 tablespoons oil and toss again.

CONTINUED

Transfer the shrimp and vegetables to a rimmed baking sheet (see sidebar), spreading them out in an even layer with the shrimp toward the center and the vegetables around the edge. Use the spatula to get all the flavorful oil from the bowl onto the shrimp and vegetables. Roast until the carrots and radishes are just tender and the shrimp are opaque through the thickest part, 10 to 12 minutes.

Transfer the shrimp and vegetables to individual plates and serve right away.

Sheet Pan Cooking

The beauty of sheet pan cooking is the convenience of tossing things on the pan to roast together. The only trick is managing the components so they're done at the same time. In this case, carrots a bit too big may be crunchy when the shrimp are done, or the shrimp dry and tough if cooked longer to accommodate the carrots. Bigger shrimp give you more leeway; if you're using smaller shrimp or just want a bit of insurance, you can roast the vegetables for 5 minutes or so first, then add the shrimp at the center of the pan, in which case they'll cook a minute or two more quickly because the pan's preheated. In the long run, a slightly crunchy carrot or radish is better than an overcooked shrimp.

Fried Shrimp, Lemon, and Herbs

MAKES 4 SERVINGS

1 small lemon

1¼ pounds medium shrimp, peeled, deveined, and rinsed

Vegetable oil, for frying

¾ cup all-purpose flour

½ cup cornstarch

1 teaspoon kosher salt

1 cup cold water, plus more if needed

2 handfuls (about 2 cups loosely packed) large flat fresh herb leaves, such as basil, shiso, flat-leaf parsley, and/or sage, rinsed and well dried

Given how big a fan base both shrimp and fried foods have, it's little wonder that fried shrimp are so popular. Here they are accompanied by thinly sliced lemon and tufts of fresh herbs—both of which also are lightly battered and quickly fried. I love these shrimp as is, but if you want a sauce alongside, consider the Pickled-Pepper Tartar Sauce (page 101). Shrimp with the tail on or off—it's up to you. If you have a deep fryer, of course here's the time to use it, following the manufacturer's instructions. A green salad or coleslaw will be perfect alongside.

Preheat the oven to 200 degrees F. Set an oblong wire rack on a rimmed baking sheet.

Trim the ends from the lemon and cut it into slices about ⅛ inch thick, removing any seeds you encounter along the way. Dry the shrimp well on paper towels.

Heat about 2 inches of oil in a medium heavy pot (the oil should come no more than halfway up the sides of the pot) over medium heat to 375 degrees F.

While the oil heats, make the batter. Use a fork to stir together the flour, cornstarch, and salt in a medium bowl. Add the water gradually, blending to make a smooth batter. It should be thin enough to delicately coat the shrimp. If it's a bit too thick, stir in another 1 to 2 tablespoons water.

CONTINUED

Drop 5 or 6 shrimp into the batter and stir to coat. Lift them out one by one with the fork or tongs, allowing excess batter to drip off, then gently add them to the hot oil. Fry the shrimp until lightly browned, 3 to 4 minutes. Scoop them out with a slotted spoon, transfer to the prepared baking sheet, and keep warm in the oven. Continue to coat and fry the shrimp in batches, allowing the oil to reheat between batches as needed.

Add about a quarter of the herbs to the batter, coating well with the batter. Lift the leaves out one by one, allowing excess batter to drip off, and gently add to the oil. Fry each batch until crisp, 1 to 2 minutes. Add the fried herbs to the baking sheet with the shrimp. Cook the lemon slices in the same way, in two batches. Arrange the shrimp, lemon, and herbs on individual plates and serve right away.

Marinated Shrimp with Sweet Onions

I've rejiggered one of my mom's favorite recipes from a 1950s *Better Homes & Gardens* cookbook (see sidebar) for this preparation that's perfect as the first course for a dinner party, cocktail party, or buffet dinner spread. Since the shrimp cook so quickly, I simmer the spices a bit to impart more flavor before adding the shrimp. The shrimp need to marinate for at least 8 hours, and up to 24 hours, so plan accordingly. This is a great do-ahead recipe.

MAKES 8 TO 10 SERVINGS

3 tablespoons pickling spice

½ cup moderately packed celery leaves

1 tablespoon plus 1 teaspoon kosher salt, divided

2 pounds medium to large shrimp, preferably shell-on, rinsed

1 small sweet onion (about 12 ounces), cut into ¼-inch rounds and separated into rings

6 bay leaves, preferably fresh

⅔ cup white wine vinegar

½ cup mild olive oil

2 tablespoons capers and their juice

2 teaspoons celery seed

Tabasco or other hot sauce

Watercress, frisée, and/or arugula, for serving

Cut a double layer of cheesecloth about 6 inches square. Put the pickling spice in the center, draw up the edges, and secure the packet with a piece of kitchen string. Put the spice packet, celery leaves, and 1 tablespoon of the salt in a medium pot half filled with water. Bring the water to a boil over medium-high heat and simmer for 10 minutes, pressing the spice packet down into the water now and then if it's floating at the surface. Carefully add the shrimp and simmer until opaque through the thickest part (lift one out with a slotted spoon and cut into it to check), 6 to 8 minutes. If the water boils at any point, reduce the heat a bit. Drain the shrimp, discarding the spice packet and celery leaves. When cool enough to handle, peel and devein the shrimp, unless they already have been.

CONTINUED

Put the shrimp, onion, and bay leaves in a 9-by-13-inch baking dish or similar deep dish, or in a large resealable plastic bag or other container. Stir together the vinegar, oil, capers and juice, celery seed, remaining 1 teaspoon of salt, and a few dashes of Tabasco (or to taste). Pour this evenly over the shrimp, cover or close the container, and refrigerate for at least 8 hours, and up to 24 hours, before serving. Gently stir or toss things around a few times to ensure even seasoning while they marinate.

To serve, arrange the greens on a serving platter or individual plates. Spoon the shrimp and onion onto the greens with just enough marinade to lightly coat; use a slotted spoon to retrieve any capers from the remaining marinade to scatter over.

Nostalgia & Shrimp

"Shell and devein and carry on," my mom wrote many years ago on the inside of a 1960s booklet with shellfish recipes produced by the Washington Department of Fisheries. It was part of her instructions related not to a recipe in that booklet but to one she said was a "favorite shrimp hors d'oeuvre which I've made dozens of times." She credited it to *Better Homes & Gardens New Cookbook*, her 1953 copy of which I have. Turning to that page, I see she wrote "The Greatest" in broad felt pen alongside the recipe, with a penciled note about having added mushrooms on occasion. My sister recalls this being a frequent element on a buffet spread, served in a shallow bowl with cocktail sauce alongside for those who might wish to dip.

Shrimp-Stuffed Eggplant with Sesame

MAKES 2 TO 4 SERVINGS

4 Chinese or Japanese eggplants (about 8 ounces each)

2 tablespoons mild olive oil, plus more for drizzling

½ cup finely chopped shallot or onion

1 teaspoon minced or pressed garlic

12 ounces shrimp, peeled (tails too), deveined, rinsed, and chopped

4 tablespoons finely chopped fresh cilantro, divided

1 tablespoon finely chopped fresh mint

2 teaspoons toasted sesame oil

½ teaspoon kosher salt

1 tablespoon lightly toasted sesame seeds

Chinese and Japanese eggplants are long and slender, smaller than the more common globe eggplant. Try to pick four that are of about the same size (length and width), for even cooking and portion sizes. Those that are straight or just slightly curved will be easiest to work with. Don't be tempted to chop the shrimp in a food processor; you want distinct small pieces rather than a near purée. This is delicious with sautéed bok choy or broccoli alongside, and steamed rice if you wish.

Preheat the oven to 400 degrees F. Line a rimmed baking sheet with aluminum foil.

Trim the stem ends from the eggplants so what remains is more or less 7 inches long. Cut the top quarter or so of the eggplant off, "top" being relative: however the eggplant sits most naturally on the counter, determine the top from that position. Eggplant pieces that have been cut away can be saved for another use.

Use the tip of a small knife to score the flesh about ¼ inch in from the skin and about 1 inch deep, then use a spoon to scoop out this flesh, making a cavity for the shrimp mixture. Finely chop the scooped-out eggplant flesh.

Drizzle oil on the foil and set the eggplant shells cut side down on the baking sheet. Bake until the sides are tender (the tip of a sharp knife should meet little resistance), 10 to 15 minutes. Take the baking sheet from the oven and let cool while preparing the filling. Keep the oven set at 400 degrees F.

Heat the oil in a medium skillet over medium heat. Add the shallot, garlic, and chopped eggplant and cook, stirring often, until they are tender and turning golden, about 5 minutes. Transfer the mixture to a medium bowl and let cool. Stirring occasionally will help it cool a bit more quickly.

Add the chopped shrimp to the cooled shallot mixture along with 3 tablespoons of the cilantro, the mint, sesame oil, and salt and stir well to evenly blend. When the eggplants are cool enough to handle, turn them over and spoon the shrimp mixture into the cavities, pressing it in gently and mounding slightly. Sprinkle the sesame seeds over. Return the eggplants to the baking sheet and bake until the shrimp is cooked through (fully opaque when you peek into the center of the filling), about 20 minutes.

Transfer the eggplants to individual plates, scatter the remaining 1 tablespoon of cilantro over, and serve right away.

Shrimp Salad with Garlic Bread

MAKES 4 SERVINGS

1¼ pounds small to medium shrimp in their shells, rinsed

2½ cups shrimp stock (see page 184), Shellfish Stock (page 183), or water

⅓ cup mayonnaise, plus more if needed

¼ cup finely chopped sweet onion

2 tablespoons minced fresh chives

¼ teaspoon kosher salt

Freshly ground black pepper

For the garlic bread

6-inch piece French bread

¼ cup unsalted butter, at room temperature

1 tablespoon minced fresh chives

2 cloves garlic, minced or pressed

¼ teaspoon kosher salt

It's tempting to say, for the first step of this recipe, "Get yourself to Charleston, South Carolina, and buy some shrimp at Shem Creek." That was the starting point when I first made this shrimp salad, using cooked shrimp and garlic bread left over from a shrimp boil while on vacation there with friends. If you have shellfish or shrimp stock in the freezer, add extra flavor by cooking the shrimp in that instead of water. The cooking liquids are then reduced to create a flavorful addition to the shrimp salad. The shrimp can be cooked and the reduction made the day ahead, both covered and refrigerated.

Put the shrimp in a medium saucepan and add enough stock to just cover the shrimp completely (if you don't have enough stock, add water as needed). Bring the stock to a low boil over medium-high heat, then reduce the heat to medium and simmer, stirring a couple of times to ensure even cooking, until the shrimp are opaque through the thickest part (lift one out with a slotted spoon and cut into it to check), about 4 to 7 minutes. Drain the shrimp, reserving the cooking liquids. Wash out the pan to use again.

When the shrimp are cool enough to handle, peel them (tails included) and set the meat aside. Put the shells in the medium saucepan and add 2 cups of the reserved cooking liquids, which should cover the shells about halfway. Bring just to a boil over medium-high heat, then reduce

NOTE: For a shortcut, start with cooked shrimp, even little bay shrimp, and skip the simmering and reduction steps. You'll still have a very good shrimp salad. A broader, softer style of French bread, rather than a classic baguette, is best for the garlic bread.

the heat to medium and simmer until quite aromatic and the liquids have reduced by about half, 10 to 15 minutes, stirring occasionally. Take the pan from the heat and strain the liquid, discard the shells, and return the liquid to the pan. Set the pan over medium heat and simmer until the liquids reduce to a volume of about 3 tablespoons, 15 to 20 minutes. The final stage of reduction can go quickly, so keep a close eye on things and reduce the heat if needed toward the end to avoid burning. Scrape the reduction into a small bowl and let cool completely.

Devein the shrimp if needed, then coarsely chop the meat and put it in a medium bowl. Add the cooled shrimp reduction, mayonnaise, onion, chives, salt, and a couple grindings of black pepper and stir well to mix. Cover and refrigerate until ready to serve.

Preheat the oven to 450 degrees F.

To make the garlic bread, halve the bread horizontally, then cut each half into 2 pieces. Use a small rubber spatula to stir together the butter, chives, garlic, and salt in a small bowl until smooth and well blended, then spread it evenly on the bread. Set the bread on a rimmed baking sheet and bake until aromatic and just lightly browned at the edges, 5 to 7 minutes.

Spoon the shrimp salad onto individual plates, with the garlic bread alongside. Or spoon the shrimp directly onto the garlic bread and serve as a decadent open-faced sandwich.

LOBSTER

Other shellfish have their moments to shine in fancy presentations, but lobster seems most naturally suited to a sense of elegance. Consider its reputation as an entrée of choice for celebratory occasions and romantic dinners. Though for those who live near the home waters of those lobster, they are equally—if even more passionately—associated with casual summertime meals outdoors with ice-cold beverages. Perhaps that makes lobster a bit of a chameleon, able to admirably adapt to its environment, with guests in shorts and flip-flops for a shoreside feast or dressed to the nines for a fancy dinner with Champagne. And lobster are suited to countless options in between.

The species we see most often is the cold-water American lobster, with a long narrow carapace, fan-tipped tail, antennae, and big claws that make its eight other legs look particularly spindly. One claw is a bit bigger, the "crusher" claw; the more slender one called the "pincher." These lobster have a range of mottled deep purple-green-blue-russet color tones when alive, turning a vivid orange-red when cooked. American lobster are found from North Carolina as far north as Newfoundland; the bulk of the US harvest is from the waters off Maine.

Other lobster species are found in warmer waters to the south, on both sides of the country. Spiny lobster are distinct from American lobster, having large tails and no claws, just oversized antennae. Florida, and points south, is prime harvest area for Caribbean spiny lobster, while on the West Coast, the California spiny lobster is caught primarily in, unsurprisingly, California waters.

These lobster are all wild harvest. American lobster are harvested year-round, peak season being July into November, when a greater supply generally results in lower prices. Other times of year, prices are more variable. The warm-water lobster are harvested most of fall and winter. Frozen offerings of lobster, particularly in tail form, can be found year-round.

SHOPPING AND STORING

It's important that whole uncooked lobster be alive up until they're cooked. When buying live lobster, choose from among the livelier of the bunch. The range in size for American lobster is roughly 1¼ pounds up to 4 pounds, though 3 pounds and up are less common.

Raw American lobster tails are a quite convenient and widely available option year-round, in sizes from about 4 ounces up to 8 ounces or more. Spiny lobster tails are also versatile (seldom found in whole live form), though I see them less frequently in stores.

Cooked lobster meat may be available either in bulk in the seafood case, or prepackaged in containers. Also, you may see tails, meat, or other forms of lobster in the freezer section as well.

Live lobster manage rather well out of water in the right conditions, though you should plan to cook the lobster the same day you buy them. Store lobster in a container large enough to hold them comfortably, such as an oblong baking dish or large broad bowl. Top the lobster with a damp, not sopping wet, kitchen towel to keep it moist. Don't enclose the dish any more than that; the lobster need air to survive. Don't be tempted to store live lobster in water or with ice, as fresh water kills them.

Lobster tails and meat should be well wrapped and stored in the refrigerator until needed. If purchased in a frozen state, get them into your freezer as soon as possible after getting home to avoid any premature thawing. Plan ahead to thaw slowly in the refrigerator before using.

CLEANING

Whole lobster and lobster tails in the shell should require little cleaning before cooking, perhaps just a quick rinse under cold running water.

COOKING

When cooking live lobster, the change in shell color to vivid orange-red isn't the sole indicator for doneness; the meat may still be a bit undercooked at that point. To verify doneness after the suggested cooking time, lift the lobster from the pot and carefully (with pot holders) twist open where the tail meets the carapace and check the meat, which should be opaque white, no longer translucent.

I prefer steaming over boiling for a few reasons, which I discuss more on page 6. It means cooking for a couple of minutes longer, but it's a minor time adjustment for what I find to be a much easier process. These whole lobster are perfect to enjoy as is—with melted butter or a light sauce. They can be grilled or roasted as well.

Lobster tails can be grilled, roasted, or steamed, whether to serve as is, or to use the cooked meat in another dish. Cooked lobster meat, like cooked crabmeat, is quite versatile. Recipes using it here include a light stew, a sandwich, and a flavorful salad. Those handsome lobster have quite sharp points on their shells, so take care when handling them to avoid puncturing yourself.

Portioning Cooked Lobster

NOTE: If you will use the body for Shellfish Stock (page 183) or wish to pick extra bits of meat from the body, lift away the top shell (carapace), then remove and discard the viscera, including the greenish tomalley. Rinse well under cold water. There is a bit of meat in the small walking legs as well, which you can pick if you like.

These steps can be followed if you are picking the meat from a cooked lobster for another use. If preparing the lobster to be served right away, how much advance prep you do depends on the setting: for a casual meal, diners can do this work themselves. Otherwise you can go through some or all of the process before serving so that eating is a bit less messy at the table.

1. Holding the lobster body in one hand and tail in the other, twist gently to separate the two.
2. Remove the front clawed legs from the body by bending them back where they meet the body. Separate the front legs into two sections, Use crab crackers or a small mallet to lightly crack the shell of the smaller knuckle joints, removing those nuggets.
3. For each claw, bend backward and remove the movable part from the claw, which should come out with a thin membrane attached.
4. Use crab crackers or a small mallet to lightly crack the claw shell, pulling the shell apart to remove the large piece of meat.
5. For the tail, use kitchen shears to cut through the membrane on the bottom, and pull the sides apart to remove the tail meat in one piece.
6. Use the tip of a small knife to make a slit in the top of the tail, then lift out and discard the vein.

1
2
3
4
5
6

Grilled Lobster Tails and Summer Squash with Gremolata Butter

MAKES 4 SERVINGS

For the gremolata butter

1 large lemon

6 tablespoons unsalted butter, at room temperature

2 tablespoons finely chopped fresh flat-leaf parsley

¼ teaspoon minced or pressed garlic

¼ teaspoon kosher salt

1 pound summer squash (zucchini, yellow squash, and/or pattypan squash)

2 tablespoons mild olive oil, divided, plus more if needed

Kosher salt

4 lobster tails, 5 to 8 ounces each

Such a treat to pull from the grill, these lobster tails get slathered with a butter that's blended with the gremolata trio of parsley, garlic, and lemon zest. While the grill's hot, consider cooking other things as well—thick slices of sweet onion, ears of corn—whether to serve alongside or to have on hand for other uses.

For the gremolata butter, finely grate enough zest from the lemon to measure 1 teaspoon. Stir together the butter, parsley, lemon zest, garlic, and salt in a small bowl until smooth and well blended. Cut the lemon into 4 wedges; set the butter and lemon aside.

Preheat an outdoor grill for direct medium-high heat. If using bamboo skewers, soak four 8- to 10-inch skewers in cold water for at least 20 minutes to limit charring on the grill.

Trim the stem ends from the squash. Cut zucchini or yellow squash across into 1-inch pieces. Larger pattypan can be cut into halves or quarters; small pattypan or other mini squash can be grilled whole (no skewer needed). Put the squash in a large bowl, drizzle 1 tablespoon of the oil over, and season with a good pinch of salt. Toss well to evenly coat. Thread the squash pieces onto the skewers, leaving a bit of space between them to help with even cooking; I find skewering from edge to edge, rather than through the center, ensures easier handling on the grill.

CONTINUED

GRILLED LOBSTER TAILS AND SUMMER SQUASH WITH GREMOLATA BUTTER, CONTINUED

NOTE: Standard zucchini and yellow squash can be found year-round, while summertime offerings may include small zucchini, pattypan squash, and other varieties—mix and match as inspired by what's available.

Set one of the lobster tails shell side up on the cutting board, its tail pointed away from you. Use the tip of a chef's knife to pierce the tail where it tapers to the narrow point just before the fanned end. Take care to avoid your fingers while lowering the blade down the length of the tail to cut it about three-quarters of the way through the meat. Bend the two shell halves apart a bit to expose more of the meat, avoiding those sharp bits on the shell. Remove and discard any visible vein running the length of the meat. Repeat with the remaining tails.

Brush the lobster meat and shell with the remaining tablespoon oil. Season the meat lightly with salt.

Grill the squash skewers until tender and nicely browned, 6 to 10 minutes, using long-handled tongs to turn them every couple of minutes to avoid excessive char. Transfer the skewers to a serving platter and cover with aluminum foil to keep warm. (Or if there is room on your grill, move the skewers to the edge, away from direct heat, to stay warm while grilling the lobster.)

Add the lobster tails to the grill, meat side down to begin with. Cook until the meat is just lightly browned, about 3 minutes. Use the tongs to turn the tails and continue cooking until the flesh is opaque through the thickest part, 3 to 6 minutes longer, depending on the size of the tails.

Transfer the lobster tails to individual plates and spread some of the gremolata butter on the meat. Add the grilled squash alongside (removed from the skewers if you like) and the lemon wedges, and serve right away. Pass extra gremolata butter separately for folks to dab on their squash and lobster.

Steamed Lobster with Orange-Fennel Sauce

MAKES 2 SERVINGS

2 live lobster, about 1½ pounds each

2 tablespoons kosher salt

For the orange-fennel sauce

¾ cup freshly squeezed orange juice (from about 2 medium oranges)

¼ cup finely chopped fennel bulb

2 tablespoons minced shallot

2 tablespoons white wine vinegar

½ cup (1 stick) unsalted butter, cut into 8 pieces and refrigerated

1 tablespoon chopped fennel fronds (optional)

½ teaspoon finely grated orange zest

½ teaspoon kosher salt

Steamed lobster with simple melted butter is perfectly sublime; this recipe just embellishes things. The flavors of orange and fennel, with a touch of vinegar, meld beautifully in this silky butter sauce for dipping. Look for a fennel bulb that has tender green fronds to use as a pretty and flavorful addition to the sauce. Extra fennel bulb can be thinly sliced to use in a green salad to serve alongside the lobster. Instead of using live lobster, you could use lobster tails instead, following the instructions on page 150 for cooking.

Lay the lobster on a tray and put them in the freezer for 15 to 20 minutes (not longer) to sedate them. (This can make handling the lobster a bit easier but if you don't have freezer space for it, you can omit this step.)

For the sauce, combine the orange juice, fennel bulb, shallot, and vinegar in a medium heavy saucepan. Bring the juice to a boil over medium-high heat and cook until reduced by about two-thirds, 3 to 5 minutes. Reduce the heat to medium-low and add 2 pieces of the cold butter. Whisk gently and constantly until the butter has creamily melted into the sauce, then add 2 more pieces of the butter and repeat. Continue incorporating the remaining butter in the same way, then whisk in the fennel fronds, orange zest, and salt. Scrape the sauce into a small heatproof bowl and set it over a small pan of warm, not boiling, water to keep warm until ready to serve.

CONTINUED

NOTE: If your lobster are smaller or larger than the 1½ pounds called for here, adjust cooking time as needed, about 2 minutes more or less per ¼ pound difference in weight.

Put a couple of inches of water in the bottom of a steamer pot or a large pot with collapsible steamer basket. Add the salt, cover the pot, and bring to a boil over high heat. Carefully add the lobster, cover, reduce the heat to medium-high, and steam for 15 minutes, or a couple of minutes more or less based on the size of your lobster (see note). (The meat of the tail should be no longer translucent when the body and tail are separated.)

Use tongs to transfer the steamed lobster to a rimmed tray to drain and cool just enough to handle. Serve the lobster as is, or partially portion it first, following steps as noted on page 138.

Arrange the lobster on individual plates, pour the sauce into 2 ramekins or other small dishes, and serve alongside for dipping. Have a bowl available for discarded shells.

Basil, Lobster, and Tomato Sandwiches

MAKES 4 SERVINGS

12 ounces cooked lobster meat (see page 150)

¼ cup mayonnaise

8 slices sandwich bread, lightly toasted

About 1 pound vine-ripened tomatoes, cored and sliced

Flaky sea salt or kosher salt and freshly ground black pepper

8 to 12 large fresh basil leaves

Here's a different kind of BLT—but like the original (of which I am an ardent fan), a beacon of simplicity. And it is at its best when the common ingredient, tomatoes, are in prime, peak-of-season form. For other times, I have an all-season alternative (see note). This is an ideal time to go nostalgic and choose old-school sandwich bread. Serve with some extra-fancy potato chips.

For lobster tail meat, remove the vein if needed and cut the meat lengthwise into slices about ¼ inch thick. Claw meat can be used as is or halved horizontally if large. Other meat that is in bite-size pieces can be used as is. Discard any bits of shell or cartilage you come across.

Spread the mayonnaise on 4 of the bread slices and top with the tomato slices, seasoning to taste with salt and pepper. Lay the basil leaves evenly over the tomatoes and arrange the lobster evenly over the basil. Top the sandwiches with the remaining slices of bread and serve right away.

NOTE: When fresh tomatoes aren't at their most flavorful, you can use the sun-dried variety and mix the components rather than layer them. Coarsely chop the lobster meat and stir it together with ⅓ cup mayonnaise, 2 tablespoons finely chopped fresh basil, and 2 tablespoons finely chopped sun-dried tomatoes (oil-packed or rehydrated dry) with salt and pepper to taste. Add a bit more mayonnaise if it's a little dry. Spread onto 4 slices of the bread, add butter lettuce or romaine, top with the remaining bread, and serve.

Bloody Mary Lobster Cocktail

MAKES 4 SERVINGS

¼ cup tomato juice

2 tablespoons minced celery

1 tablespoon freshly squeezed lemon juice

1 teaspoon horseradish, freshly grated or prepared

¼ teaspoon Worcestershire sauce

⅛ teaspoon celery seed

Kosher salt

8 ounces cooked lobster meat (see page 150)

1 large or 2 small heads Belgian endive, cored and thinly sliced (about 1 cup lightly packed)

Lemon wedges, for serving

This recipe is assembled much like a classic shellfish cocktail, though the sauce is a bit different. In addition to having a couple of extra ingredients often identified with Bloody Marys, this lobster cocktail has a much lighter consistency, using tomato juice instead of thicker and sweeter ketchup or chili sauce. All the better to let the lobster be the star. In place of endive, you could use about a cup of shredded romaine or other lettuce to serve as the base for the cocktails.

Stir together the tomato juice, celery, lemon juice, horseradish, Worcestershire sauce, and celery seed in a medium bowl. Taste for seasoning, adding salt to taste if needed (the tomato juice may provide enough salt).

Remove the vein from the lobster tail meat if needed. Cut the tail across into thin slices, and cut other lobster meat into about ½-inch dice; discard any bits of shell or cartilage you come across.

Put the endive in small individual serving dishes, spreading it out evenly. Arrange the lobster over the endive, spooning the Bloody Mary mixture over. Tuck a lemon wedge along one edge of each cocktail and serve right away.

Cooked Lobster Meat

When a recipe calls for cooked lobster meat, you have a few options:

- Purchase it as cooked meat, if you can find it (either at the seafood market or online).
- Buy raw lobster tails and cook them yourself, planning on roughly 50 percent yield of cooked meat from the raw tails (e.g., 1 pound of tails produce about 8 ounces of cooked meat). Steam 4-ounce tails for about 8 minutes; add a minute or so more for each extra ounce. (Insert a skewer through the center of the meat before cooking if you'd like the tails to be straight, rather than curled, when removed.) Or bake at 350 degrees F for 12 to 15 minutes. With either technique, the meat should be opaque through the center of the thickest part.
- Steam a whole live lobster as described on page 143 and pick the meat as noted on page 138. The yield of meat varies quite a lot, for a range of reasons, but can be in the 20 to 25 percent range. So for 8 ounces of meat, you'd want to start with two 1¼-pound lobsters.

NOTE: The yield of meat you'll get from a whole lobster will vary with the season and the size, not to mention the skills and patience of the picker. In rough terms this yield can be in the 20 to 25 percent ballpark. So if you start with a 1½-pound lobster, you may get 5 to 6 ounces of cooked meat from its shells. For 8 ounces of meat, you'd want to start with two 1¼-pound lobsters. For lobster tails, my meat-to-shell ratios varied in testing but were broadly in the 50 percent range: a 6-ounce tail should give you about 3 ounces of cooked meat.

Lobster and Artichoke Stew

This light and quick-cooking stew calls to mind the classic oyster stew, like the kind my mom made when I was a kid—oysters, milk, butter—which my dad loved and I wouldn't get near. Shellfish stock adds distinct character, but a good fish stock works well too. As a light meal for two, serve with sliced baguette and romaine salad alongside. In smaller cups, this can be served as a first course.

MAKES 2 TO 4 SERVINGS

8 ounces cooked lobster meat (see page 150)

1 cup thawed frozen or top-quality canned quartered artichoke hearts (see note)

2 tablespoons unsalted butter, plus more for serving

½ cup thinly sliced leek

2 cups Shellfish Stock (page 183) or fish stock

1 cup half-and-half

½ teaspoon minced fresh tarragon or thyme

¼ teaspoon kosher salt

Freshly ground black pepper

NOTE: If using frozen artichoke hearts, lay them on double-layer paper towels to thaw and drain. For canned artichoke hearts, you'll need about half of a 14-ounce can. Rinse them under cold water and drain well on paper towels.

Remove the vein from the lobster tail meat if needed. Cut the tail across into thin slices, and claw meat into 3 or 4 pieces; knuckle meat can be used as is. Discard any bits of shell or cartilage you come across.

If the artichoke pieces are much wider than 1 inch, cut them in half, through the bottom core so the pieces mostly hold together.

Melt the butter in a medium saucepan over medium heat. Add the leek and cook, stirring occasionally, until tender, 3 to 5 minutes. The leek should not brown; reduce the heat if needed. Stir in the stock and half-and-half and cook for about 5 minutes, bringing the liquid to a low simmer. Reduce the heat to medium-low and add the lobster, artichoke pieces, tarragon, salt, and a couple of grindings of pepper. Cook to warm everything through and meld the flavors, about 5 minutes.

Ladle the stew into shallow bowls, top each with a dab of butter (about a teaspoon, or to your taste), and serve right away.

Lobster Gribiche Salad

MAKES 4 SERVINGS

8 ounces cooked lobster meat (see page 150)

3 tablespoons white wine vinegar

2 teaspoons Dijon mustard

¼ teaspoon kosher salt

Freshly ground black pepper

¼ cup extra-virgin olive oil or mild olive oil

3 large eggs, hard-cooked and cooled (see page 180)

¼ cup coarsely grated or chopped pickles (about 12 cornichons or 2 medium dill pickles)

3 tablespoons finely chopped fresh chives

2 tablespoons coarsely chopped capers

Gribiche is an old-school French sauce that I use here as inspiration for a salad component. The piquant flavors of vinegar, pickles, and capers with hard-cooked egg complement the lobster beautifully. It's ideal for a lunch with salad greens alongside, or as a starter for a dinner party. I find my box grater makes easy work of prepping the hard-cooked eggs and pickles, but you can finely chop them instead.

Remove the vein from the lobster tail meat if needed. Cut the tail across into thin slices, and cut other lobster meat into about ½-inch dice; discard any bits of shell or cartilage you come across. Put the lobster in a small bowl.

Combine the vinegar, mustard, salt, and a few grindings of black pepper in a medium bowl and blend with a fork. Blend in the oil until smooth. Spoon 2 tablespoons of the dressing over the lobster pieces and toss gently to evenly coat.

Peel the hard-cooked eggs and coarsely grate or chop them. Add the egg, pickles, chives, and capers to the remaining dressing and toss lightly with the fork to evenly blend. Taste for seasoning, adding more salt or pepper to taste. (The lobster-and-egg mixture can be prepared a couple of hours in advance, covered, and refrigerated.)

To serve, spoon the gribiche salad onto individual plates, spreading it out evenly, and arrange the lobster on top. Serve right away.

Stir-Fried Lobster with Shiitakes and Celery

MAKES 4 SERVINGS

12 to 16 ounces lobster meat, preferably raw (see page 155)

2 tablespoons mild olive oil

½ cup sliced green onion, white and green portions

2 tablespoons julienned fresh ginger (from about a 1-inch piece of ginger)

2 cloves garlic, thinly sliced

4 ounces shiitake mushrooms, stems trimmed, caps sliced (about 2 cups)

3 to 4 celery stalks, cut on bias into ½-inch pieces (about 1 cup)

¼ cup Shellfish Stock (page 183), clam juice (see page 22), or water

1 tablespoon regular or low-sodium soy sauce

Steamed rice, for serving

¼ cup coarsely chopped tender celery leaves

Raw lobster meat is best for this stir-fry to avoid overcooked, tough lobster. If you use cooked lobster meat instead (page 150), add it later in the cooking process to just heat through. For the celery stalks and leaves, those from the interior of the bunch will be more tender and milder in flavor.

Remove the vein from the lobster tail meat if needed. Cut lobster tail meat across into about ¾-inch pieces. Claw and knuckle meat can be used as is. Discard any bits of shell or cartilage you come across.

Heat a wok or large skillet over medium-high heat. Add the oil and heat for a few seconds, then add the green onion, ginger, and garlic and cook, stirring, until aromatic, 30 to 60 seconds. If using raw lobster meat, add it and cook, stirring, until the meat is mostly opaque on the surface, 1 to 2 minutes. Add the shiitakes and sliced celery stalks and cook, stirring frequently, until nearly tender, 2 to 3 minutes. Add the stock and soy sauce (and cooked lobster meat, if using) and reduce the heat to medium, stirring until the liquid reduces to a light sauce that evenly coats the lobster, 2 to 3 minutes. The lobster should be opaque through the center (for raw) or heated through (for precooked). If needed, cook another 1 to 2 minutes.

Spoon the lobster and vegetables over steamed rice, scatter with the celery leaves, and serve right away.

Removing Raw Meat from Lobster Tails

Some specialty markets may have raw lobster meat available, possibly in frozen form. Plan ahead to thaw slowly in the refrigerator if using this.

Otherwise, you can pull the meat from raw lobster tails. Use kitchen shears to cut through the membrane on the underside. Carefully bend back the sides of the tail, exposing the meat but careful to avoid the sharp points on the shell. Slide a finger between the meat and the shell to begin working the meat away down the length of the tail. After the tail meat has been removed, make a shallow slit along the top of the meat and remove the vein, which is often dark in color. Lightly rinse the meat and dry well.

Yield will vary depending on the size of tail you start with. I get about 60 percent yield of raw meat from the tails I use: about 1¼ to 1⅔ pounds of lobster tails will produce the 12 to 16 ounces meat called for here.

CRAB

My west coast roots definitely show through in this chapter. Dungeness is my hometown crab and the one I know the best of the bunch. Though I was fortunate enough to enjoy fresh-from-the-water king crab in Alaska years ago, and have had some great blue crab experiences on travels to the mid-Atlantic. One notable example was a side-by-side crab-off with freshly caught blue crab and a couple of big Dungeness crab overnighted from Seattle, which I ate with some fellow crab fans sitting steps away from a cove on Virginia's Eastern Shore. The delicious indulgence didn't dissuade me from being a Dungeness devotee. But it did exemplify that—hometown preferences aside—there is very good reason to make the most of any time a good crab opportunity knocks, whatever species it may be.

Dungeness crab reigns on the West Coast, found from Southern California to the Gulf of Alaska. The East and Gulf Coasts are home to the blue crab. Both of these crab evoke strong devotion from their biggest fans, people for whom no cookbook is needed—they know just how they like to cook and eat the beautiful crustaceans. For those not blessed to live within close proximity, we have great seafood markets and direct-order options for sourcing them in whole form, whether live or precooked.

It's fun to see the occasional whole king crab in a live tank, more often in a specialty restaurant than in a retail store. If you see them in a restaurant, consider indulging. It's a memorable experience to be served the whole king crab to share with friends; it may come in a couple of courses prepared different ways.

Prime commercial Dungeness season is winter into spring, though there are pockets of other harvest times—particularly in Alaska summer and fall—through most of the year. Blue crab harvest seasons vary with the region; generally volumes are at the highest over the summer and into fall.

A couple of other crab species you may come across include peekytoe and Jonah from the East Coast, primarily as picked meat. Blue crab are most often available in hard-shell form, but seasonally (or frozen) as soft-shell crab when their new shell is still papery and thin enough be edible. They require particular cooking techniques and are not interchangeable with other crab recipes here. Big, meaty stone crab claws from Florida are harvested mid-October to mid-May.

Because these are wild shellfish, specific seasons and harvest amounts can vary year to year due to a number of factors. Frozen product helps assure it's possible to enjoy most of these crab year-round.

SHOPPING AND STORING

Whole uncooked crab must be alive up to the time that you cook them; the livelier the better when you pick them out at the store. Live Dungeness will have a bricky-maroon color, and blue crab, a greenish-gray carapace and vivid blue coloring on the legs.

Dungeness in the shell are most often available in cooked form (evident from orange shell color), whole, or in clusters. These will often be frozen crab, though sometimes freshly cooked. With frozen crab, plan ahead to thaw it in the refrigerator overnight. Shells of cooked crab shouldn't have punctures or cracks. Blue crab can also be purchased precooked, to be reheated before serving. King and snow crab are rarely seen whole in stores, particularly live—imagine how big a pot you'd need for that! Instead, they're most often available precooked and frozen, in clusters or leg portions, and for snow crab, sometimes just its claws for an ideal snack serving.

Crabmeat already picked from the shells is a convenient option. It will be sold in bulk, by the pound, or packaged in tubs. With blue crab, the meat comes in a range of grades—such as jumbo lump, lump, and claw—good for different uses and budgets. With Dungeness, the bulk meat is usually a mix of flakier body meat and nuggets of leg meat. On occasion you may see Dungeness "fry legs" available, just the decadent whole pieces of leg meat perfect for a cocktail or salad.

CLEANING

Crab in the shell should require little cleaning before cooking, perhaps just a quick rinse under cold running water.

COOKING

Cooking crab from their whole, live form is not the most convenient option for most home cooks. For that reason, I have included just one recipe that's intended for whole Dungeness. That and other in-shell recipes also work great with precooked crab. Precooked crab just needs reheating, so those cooking times will be brief. Taking a few minutes to lightly crack the shells in advance allows extra flavor to penetrate while it cooks.

The remaining recipes call for crabmeat. In a couple of cases I suggest purchasing a specific grade if you have a choice at the store.

Portioning Cooked Crab

Preparing whole cooked Dungeness for serving is pretty easy and doesn't take long once you get the hang of it. It can be messy, though. I do the work in my sink, working inside a disposable bag to collect the discarded parts for easy disposal. Preparing hard-shell blue crab follows generally the same steps, short of the last couple of portioning steps.

1 Use your thumb to lift up the back side of the carapace (top shell) and remove it.

2 Turn the crab upside down and pull back and remove the "apron," a flap of shell lying on the abdomen.

3 Turn the crab upright again; pinch away and discard the feathery gills along either side of the body.

4 Break away and discard the mandibles, or mouth parts, that protrude a bit from the front of the shell.

5 Scoop out and discard the viscera from the body (The yellowish crab "butter" has devotees, but it's safest not to eat it.) Rinse the crab well under cold water.

6 The crab can be served as is, or halved through the center with a knife. To portion further, cut through the body meat, between the legs, with the claw and first leg in one portion and the remaining three legs in the other.

1

2

3

4

5

6

Lemongrass-Ginger Steamed Crab

MAKES 2 TO 4 SERVINGS

2 Dungeness crab (about 2 pounds each), live or precooked (see sidebar)

3-inch piece fresh ginger, peeled (about 2 ounces)

½ cup (1 stick) unsalted butter

1 tablespoon dry sake (optional)

Pinch kosher salt

2 stalks lemongrass, trimmed, cut into roughly 2-inch pieces and lightly smashed

Adding aromatics such as the lemongrass and ginger here imparts subtle flavor to crab, a quick and easy addition to the basic steaming technique. With the bonus of making your kitchen smell fabulous. For just a couple of live crab, a large pot with a steamer basket in the bottom should work fine, but check before getting to the point of cooking in case it's not big enough and you might need to cook them one at a time. Portioned cooked crab shouldn't be a space issue. Consider serving with steamed or fried rice with sautéed broccoli to round out this meal.

If using live Dungeness crab, you can lay them on a tray and put them in the freezer for 15 to 20 minutes (not longer) to sedate them. (This can make handling the crab a bit easier but if you don't have freezer space for it, you can omit this step.)

Finely grate enough of the ginger, preferably on a Microplane, to measure ½ teaspoon and cut the remaining ginger into thin slices. Melt the butter in a small saucepan over medium heat. Take the pan from the heat and stir in the grated ginger, sake, and salt.

Put the lemongrass and ginger slices in the bottom of a large pot and add about 2 inches of water. Add a collapsible steamer rack, cover the pot, and bring the liquid to a boil over high heat. Use tongs to carefully add the crab,

CONTINUED

cover, and reduce the heat to medium-high. Steam the live Dungeness for 18 minutes, a couple of minutes more or less based on the weight of your crab. If using precooked crab, steam for about 8 minutes to heat through.

Use tongs to transfer the steamed whole crab to a rimmed tray and let sit until cool enough to handle, then portion the crab (see page 160). If you steamed crab portions, they can be served directly.

Arrange the crab on a platter or individual plates. Rewarm the melted butter, stir, and pour it into individual dishes for serving alongside. Have a bowl available for discarded shells.

Cooked Dungeness in the Shell

If using Dungeness in the shell that are already cooked—which you may find whole or in clusters, possibly frozen—you're just reheating and infusing a dose of flavor while doing so. If the cooked crab is whole, I recommend portioning first (see page 160), which makes it easier to fit into the pot and exposes more of the crab to the aromatic steam. Taking a few minutes to lightly crack the leg and claw shells allows even more flavor to penetrate the meat but avoid cracking so much as to break apart into pieces. You can also use king or snow legs (about 2½ pounds or so), cutting them into smaller pieces as needed to fit into the pot.

Crab and Leek Cakes with Spiced Yogurt

MAKES 3 TO 6 SERVINGS

For the spiced yogurt

1 cup Greek yogurt or strained plain yogurt (see note)

¼ cup chopped fresh cilantro

½ teaspoon ground coriander

¼ teaspoon kosher salt

⅛ teaspoon Aleppo pepper or red pepper flakes

12 ounces crabmeat

4 tablespoons mild olive oil, divided, plus more if needed

2 pounds leeks, trimmed and cleaned, white and light-green portions thinly sliced (about 4 cups)

1½ teaspoons ground coriander

¾ teaspoon kosher salt

Coriander seed is one of my favorite spices; its slight citrusy character goes well with so many foods. Cilantro is the fresh herbal version of coriander seed, an ideal pairing in the yogurt topping. This is a good use for flake or body meat, but any larger lump meat in the mix makes the cakes even more exquisite. Serve as an appetizer or as a main course with lentils and/or roasted vegetables alongside.

To make the spiced yogurt, combine the yogurt, cilantro, coriander, salt, and pepper in a small bowl. Stir well to mix. Taste the yogurt for seasoning and add a bit more salt or pepper to taste, keeping in mind the flavor will develop a bit as it sits. Cover and refrigerate until needed. (The spiced yogurt can be made a day ahead.)

Pick over the crabmeat to remove any bits of shell or cartilage and squeeze the meat gently to remove excess liquid.

Heat 2 tablespoons of the oil in a large skillet over medium heat. Add the leeks and cook until very tender, about 15 minutes, stirring frequently. The leeks should not brown; reduce the heat to medium-low if needed. If the skillet becomes dry before the leeks are tender, you can add 1 to 2 tablespoons water, but there should be no residual moisture in the skillet when finished. Stir in the coriander and salt with a few grindings of black pepper.

CONTINUED

Freshly ground black pepper

1 large egg, lightly beaten

⅓ cup plus ½ cup plain dried bread crumbs, divided, plus more if needed

Transfer the leeks to a large bowl and let cool, stirring occasionally to help them cool more quickly. Clean out the skillet for cooking the cakes.

Add the crabmeat, egg, and ⅓ cup of the bread crumbs to the cooled leeks and stir gently but thoroughly to evenly blend. The mixture should hold its shape when formed into a cake; if necessary, add more bread crumbs, a tablespoon or so at a time. Form the leek and crab mixture into 6 cakes about 3½ inches in size. Put the remaining ½ cup bread crumbs on a small plate and press both sides of each cake into the crumbs, patting to remove excess. (The cakes can be made up to 2 hours ahead, covered, and refrigerated.)

Heat the remaining 2 tablespoons oil in the large skillet over medium heat. (If the skillet isn't large enough to cook the cakes all at once without crowding, cook them in 2 batches, adding more oil to the skillet as needed.) Cook the cakes until nicely browned on one side, 3 to 4 minutes. If the cakes are browning too quickly, reduce the heat a bit. Turn the cakes and continue cooking until no longer eggy at the center and nicely browned, about 3 to 4 minutes longer.

Arrange the cakes on individual plates, spoon some of the spiced yogurt alongside, and serve right away, passing extra yogurt separately.

NOTE: If you have regular plain yogurt on hand, you can strain it to use here. It may not be as thick as Greek yogurt but works well for this use. Plan on starting with about 1⅓ cups of whole or low-fat yogurt to get the 1 cup strained. Put it in a fine-mesh sieve, set it over a bowl, and refrigerate for 2 to 3 hours.

2017
Marsannay
DOMAINE JOSEPH ROTY

Soy-Garlic Grilled Crab

MAKES 2 TO 4 SERVINGS

2 Dungeness crab (about 2 pounds each), precooked and portioned (see page 160)

2 tablespoons regular or low-sodium soy sauce

2 tablespoons mild olive oil

2 tablespoons rice vinegar

2 cloves garlic, pressed or grated

Just a few pantry ingredients create a delicious coating for crab before it hits the grill, making for some delicious finger-licking while you eat too. You can roast the crab instead, in a large oblong baking dish at 475 degrees F until aromatic and heated through, 7 to 10 minutes. Serve with sautéed mushrooms and green beans to make this a meal.

Lightly crack the leg portions of the crab to allow some of the seasonings to work in, but avoid cracking so much as to break apart into pieces. Put the crab in a large bowl or other large container (you need enough room to toss the crab with seasonings).

Stir together the soy sauce, oil, vinegar, and garlic in a small bowl. Pour this over the crab pieces and toss to coat as evenly as you're able. Refrigerate while the grill heats.

Preheat an outdoor grill for direct medium-high heat.

Toss the crab in the soy mixture one last time, then arrange the crab on the grill and cook, turning every couple of minutes, until lightly browned and aromatic, about 6 to 8 minutes. By this time, the crab should be fully warmed, but larger pieces may need a few extra minutes.

Arrange the grilled crab on a platter and serve right away.

Crab and Grapefruit Salad with Crisp Shallots

MAKES 4 TO 6 SERVINGS

1 medium shallot, cut into ⅛-inch slices

¼ cup plus ½ teaspoon extra-virgin olive oil, divided

2 teaspoons all-purpose flour

1 large grapefruit (about 12 ounces)

1 teaspoon minced fresh mint

¼ teaspoon kosher salt

Freshly ground black pepper

8 ounces crabmeat

4 cups thinly sliced romaine lettuce (about ½ head, or 4 ounces)

2 cups watercress leaves (about 2 ounces)

1 cup thinly sliced radicchio (about ¼ small head)

One medium to large grapefruit should be enough for this salad, but if the grapefruit you find are on the small side, you can use two. If there's not enough grapefruit juice to use in the dressing, just add red or white wine vinegar to make up the difference. You can use other salad greens, or just romaine, in place of this particular combination if you'd like. Feel free to splurge with more crab too. This salad is perfect as a light lunch or first course.

Preheat the oven to 350 degrees F. Line a rimmed baking sheet with parchment paper or a silicone baking mat.

Separate the shallot slices into rings and put them in a medium bowl. Drizzle ½ teaspoon of the oil over and toss well to evenly and very lightly coat the shallot. Sprinkle in the flour and toss well to lightly coat the rings. Scatter the shallot rings evenly on the baking sheet, preferably not touching, and bake until lightly browned and aromatic, 15 to 20 minutes. It's likely that some of the rings will be brown before others; remove them along the way and continue baking the rest. Set the baking sheet on a wire rack to cool, adding back any rings removed earlier.

Cut the sections from the grapefruit (see page 80), work ing over a medium bowl. Use a fork to lift the grapefruit sections from the bowl and set them aside on a plate. Cut or break each section into 2 or 3 pieces. Add any accumulated juice from the plate to the juice in the bowl and measure it; you'll want 3 tablespoons for the dressing. Return that juice to the bowl, add the remaining oil, mint, and salt with a couple of grindings of black pepper. Stir well with the fork to blend.

Pick over the crabmeat to remove any bits of shell or cartilage. Squeeze the meat gently to remove excess liquid. Set aside about half of the crab—larger pieces, if there are some—for topping the salad. The rest will be tossed with the greens.

Combine the romaine, watercress, and radicchio in a large bowl and use tongs to mix. Add the grapefruit sections, crisped shallots, and half of the crab. Restir the dressing to mix, and drizzle it over the salad, tossing well to evenly mix.

Arrange the salad on individual plates, top with the reserved crab, and serve right away.

Fettuccine with Crab and Blistered Cherry Tomatoes

MAKES 4 SERVINGS

For the parsley pesto

1 clove garlic

2 cups moderately packed fresh flat-leaf parsley leaves

¼ cup finely grated Parmesan cheese

½ cup mild olive oil, plus more if needed

••••

8 to 12 ounces crabmeat

12 ounces dry fettuccine

12 ounces cherry or grape tomatoes, halved if large

Kosher salt and freshly ground black pepper

2 tablespoons mild olive oil

There's no sauce for this pasta, exactly; instead the fettuccine is tossed with cherry tomatoes that have been sautéed until they burst, adding their flavorful juices to the skillet. With crabmeat added and parsley pesto drizzled on top, this is a quick dinner to get on the table for any weeknight—just add a green salad and maybe some garlic bread (see page 132). You can use a classic basil pesto instead of this parsley version if you like, whether homemade or purchased; a half cup will be plenty. Extra pesto can be used in other pasta dishes, added to tuna salad, added to vinaigrette dressing—there are so many uses.

To make the pesto, pulse the garlic clove in a food processor (a mini processor is ideal) to finely chop, scraping down the sides once or twice. Add the parsley and Parmesan and process until the leaves are more or less evenly chopped. Add the oil about one-third at a time, blending well after each addition, then continue blending until smooth. Transfer the pesto to a small bowl and taste for seasoning, adding a bit of salt if needed (the Parmesan may be salty enough).

Pick over the crabmeat to remove any bits of shell or cartilage. Dry the tomatoes if needed, to limit spattering when cooked.

CONTINUED

FETTUCCINE WITH CRAB AND BLISTERD CHERRY TOMATOES, CONTINUED

Bring a large pot of generously salted water to a boil. Add the fettuccine and cook until just tender, still with a bit of a bite at the center, 10 to 12 minutes. Carefully scoop out about ½ cup of the water and set aside, then drain the pasta well.

Heat the oil in a large skillet over medium-high heat. Carefully add the cherry tomatoes and cook, stirring occasionally, until most of the tomatoes have burst and some skins are lightly browned, 2 to 3 minutes (note that they'll spatter as they cook and the skins burst). Reduce the heat to medium, add the pasta and crab, tossing with tongs to combine, then drizzle in about half of the reserved pasta water to moisten. Cook just until heated through, 1 to 2 minutes. The tomatoes should give off enough liquid to create a light sauce of sorts; add a bit more of the pasta water if needed.

Arrange the pasta, crab, and tomatoes on individual plates, drizzle each with a couple of tablespoons of the pesto, and serve right away.

Chilled Crab and Asparagus with Green Onion Aioli

MAKES 4 TO 6 SERVINGS

For the green onion aioli

1 egg yolk

2 teaspoons freshly squeezed lemon juice

1 teaspoon Dijon mustard

¾ cup mild olive oil

¼ cup finely chopped green onion, white and light-green portions (reserve the dark-green tops for serving)

1½ teaspoons minced or pressed garlic

½ teaspoon kosher salt

••••

24 asparagus spears, tough ends trimmed

12 ounces crabmeat

For such a simple presentation as this, with a couple of star ingredients, it's an ideal time to splurge on lump crabmeat if that's an option. The aioli flavor will be more developed if made an hour or two before serving but is at its best served the same day it's made; see the note for a short-cut alternative to homemade. This makes a wonderful first course or a light supper with a simple fresh pasta dish or grain salad alongside. Note that all parts of the green onions are used, the white and light-green parts in the aioli, the green tops for garnish.

For the aioli, whisk together the egg yolk, lemon juice, and mustard in a medium bowl. Begin adding the oil a few drops at a time, whisking constantly until the yolk begins to turn pale and thicken slightly, showing that an emulsion has begun to form. Continue adding the rest of the oil in a thin, steady stream, whisking constantly. Whisk in the green onion, garlic, and salt. Refrigerate the aioli, covered, until ready to serve.

Half-fill a sauté pan or large deep skillet with generously salted water and bring the water to a boil over high heat. While the water is heating, prepare a large bowl of ice water. Add the asparagus to the boiling water, reduce the heat to medium, and simmer until evenly bright green and the tip of a paring knife meets little resistance through the end of one of the larger spears, 2 to 3 minutes.

CONTINUED

CHILLED CRAB AND ASPARAGUS WITH GREEN ONION AIOLI, CONTINUED

NOTE: To make a quick aioli, stir the green onion, garlic, and salt into ½ cup prepared mayonnaise. The flavor will be best if made a few hours ahead, covered, and refrigerated. It won't be quite as richly flavored as home-made, but a decent alternative.

Use tongs to transfer the asparagus to the ice water and let sit until fully chilled. Transfer the chilled asparagus to a clean kitchen towel to drain.

Trim each asparagus spear to a length of 5 to 6 inches, saving the bottom trim. Return the spears to the kitchen towel, roll them up in the towel, and refrigerate until ready to serve. Thinly slice the trimmed ends and put them in a medium bowl. Thinly slice the reserved dark-green onion tops and set aside to use for garnish.

Pick over the crabmeat to remove any bits of shell or cartilage and squeeze the meat gently to remove excess liquid. Add the crab to the bowl with the sliced asparagus and add ¼ cup of the aioli. Toss to evenly mix, without breaking up the crab pieces too much. There should be just enough aioli to hold the crab and asparagus together; add a bit more if needed. Taste for seasoning, adding more salt if needed. Cover the bowl and refrigerate for about 30 minutes to chill and allow flavors to meld.

To serve, arrange the chilled asparagus spears alongside each other on individual plates. Spoon a mound of the crab mixture into the center of each raft of asparagus, scattering some of the green onion tops over all. Serve right away, passing extra aioli separately.

Crab and Endive Gratin

MAKES 2 MAIN COURSE SERVINGS
or 6 appetizer servings

8 to 12 ounces crabmeat

1 pound Belgian endive (about 4 to 6)

¾ teaspoon kosher salt, divided

Freshly ground black pepper

2 tablespoons unsalted butter, plus more for the dish

2 tablespoons all-purpose flour

1 cup Shellfish Stock (page 183) or whole milk, warmed

½ cup grated Gruyère cheese (about 2 ounces)

One of my favorite preparations for Belgian endive is the indulgent French classic that wraps it in ham to bake as a gratin with creamy sauce and cheese on top: pure comfort. I find the delicate flavor of crab works well with the endive too. The simple white sauce is typically made with milk. But if you have some shellfish stock on hand, using that here instead of milk adds an extra dose of fabulous shellfish flavor. The gratin can be served in smaller portions as a first course, or as a main course with a spinach salad and sliced baguette alongside.

Preheat the oven to 425 degrees F. Butter a 12-inch oval gratin dish or similar shallow baking dish.

Pick over the crabmeat to remove any bits of shell or cartilage. Squeeze the meat gently to remove excess liquid.

Discard any bruised or damaged outer leaves from the endive and trim the base. Cut each in half lengthwise, through the core. Arrange the endive cut side up in the gratin dish in as even a layer as you can manage; it's okay if they're snug because they'll shrink as they cook. Sprinkle with ½ teaspoon of the salt and a couple of grindings of black pepper. Cover the dish with aluminum foil and bake until the endive is partly tender (the leaves will have darkened in color, the cores still a bit firm), 12 to 15 minutes.

While the endive is baking, melt the butter in a small saucepan over medium heat. When melted, add the flour and whisk to evenly blend with the butter. Cook until the mixture bubbles up and has the slightest nutty aroma, about 3 minutes, whisking constantly; the flour shouldn't brown, reduce the heat if needed. Add the warm stock and cook, whisking often, until thickened, about 3 minutes; take care to whisk into the edges of the pan to avoid scorching. Take the pan from the heat and whisk in the remaining ¼ teaspoon salt and a couple grindings of black pepper.

When the endive is ready, take the dish from the oven and carefully remove the foil so the steam escapes away from you. Rearrange the endive if needed so it is evenly distributed. Scatter the crab over the endive, then pour the sauce over in a relatively even layer, spreading it out a bit if needed. Sprinkle with the cheese and return the dish, uncovered, to the oven. Bake until the top is lightly browned and the sauce bubbling around the edges, about 15 minutes; you can turn on the broiler for the last couple of minutes to prompt more browning if you like. Let sit for a few minutes before serving.

Use a spatula to transfer the endive and crab to individual plates and serve right away.

Deviled Eggs with Crab and Wasabi

Universally loved deviled eggs take on extra allure with crab added and some peppery zing from wasabi. I prefer the powdered form of wasabi, which stores well in the pantry for making paste as needed for a particular recipe. If you're already a fan of wasabi's peppery punch, start with 2 teaspoons, otherwise use 1½ teaspoons and work up.

MAKES 4 TO 6 SERVINGS

4 ounces crabmeat

6 large eggs, hard-cooked and cooled (see note)

⅓ cup mayonnaise, plus more if needed

1½ to 2 teaspoons wasabi paste, plus more if needed

¼ teaspoon kosher salt

NOTE: Put the eggs in a medium saucepan and add enough cold water to cover them by about 1 inch. Set the pan on medium-high heat and bring the water just to a boil. Take the pan from the heat, cover, and set aside for 15 minutes. While the eggs sit, prepare a medium bowl of ice bath. Use a slotted spoon to transfer the eggs to the ice bath and let cool completely, 15 to 20 minutes.

Pick over the crabmeat to remove any bits of shell or cartilage, and squeeze the meat gently to remove excess liquid. Break up large pieces to make stuffing the eggs easier. Reserve a couple of tablespoons of crab for garnish.

Peel the cooled eggs and cut each in half lengthwise. Scoop the yolks into a medium bowl and arrange the whites on a serving plate or platter. Mash the yolks with a fork, then add the mayonnaise, wasabi, and salt and continue mashing until smooth. Add all but the reserved crabmeat and stir to incorporate with the yolk, keeping the texture of the crab intact for the most part. Taste for seasoning, adding more wasabi or salt if needed. If the filling is stiff, you can add more mayonnaise as well. If not serving right away, store the filling and egg whites in the refrigerator separately, both covered, for up to 8 hours.

Use 2 small spoons to fill the cavity of each egg white with the crab filling, mounding it moderately. Top the eggs with the remaining crabmeat and serve.

Shellfish Stock

MAKES ABOUT 2½ QUARTS

About 1½ pounds crab, lobster and/or shrimp shells (not including carapaces), rinsed

1 medium yellow onion, coarsely chopped

2 large or 3 medium stalks celery, sliced

8 to 12 fresh parsley stems (optional)

2 or 3 sprigs fresh thyme

1 bay leaf, preferably fresh

8 to 10 whole black peppercorns

About 3 quarts cold water

NOTE: Salt is omitted here so you have control over seasoning whatever dish the stock will be used in. This is particularly important if the stock will be reduced, which would amplify its saltiness if salt is used.

One benefit of the effort you put into picking crab, lobster, and shrimp from the shell is not only the luscious sweet meat, but the leftover shells that harbor wonderful flavor. For an extra dose of flavor, there's the option of roasting the shells before simmering, which brings out a richer, slightly nutty/toasty character. Use only shells that have been cooked very simply, without added seasonings. The carapace, or large top shell, from the crab or lobster should be discarded, using shells just from legs and body for the stock. Be sure viscera are removed from the bodies and that the shells are well rinsed. If you only have shrimp shells, you may want to make the simpler shrimp stock instead (see page 184).

You can collect shells from a few different occasions, tucking them into an airtight container in the freezer until you have enough. If you have other vegetable trimmings, such as the tough stalks from a fennel bulb or the dark-green tops from a leek, feel free to add them here.

You can freeze the stock in portions so you can thaw just what's needed for later use; I usually freeze in quarts. This stock would also be fabulous in seafood-oriented risottos, stews, soups, and sauces.

As an optional first step, roast the shells. Preheat the oven to 400 degrees F. Scatter the shells in a large baking dish and roast until they are aromatic and lightly browned, 20 to 25 minutes, gently stirring once or twice for even roasting. Transfer the shells to a stockpot. If any juices are baked

CONTINUED

onto the baking dish, add a cup of warm water and stir to dissolve them, adding the liquid to the pot.

If not roasting the shells, put them directly in the stockpot. Add the onion, celery, parsley stems, thyme, bay leaf, and peppercorns to the shells with enough cold water to mostly cover the ingredients, and bring just to a boil over medium-high heat. Reduce the heat to medium and simmer until aromatic, about 1 hour. The water should just bubble lightly rather than roil; reduce the heat if needed. After the simmer, take the pot from the heat and let cool until almost room temperature, which allows more time for the flavors to be drawn from the ingredients.

Line a fine-mesh sieve with a thin clean kitchen towel or a double layer of cheesecloth (in a pinch, use a dampened paper towel). Set the sieve over a large bowl and slowly pour the stock through it. Discard the shells and vegetables and set the stock aside to cool. Store the stock in airtight containers for a few days in the refrigerator or up to 6 months in the freezer.

Shrimp Stock

As far as stocks go, making a batch of shrimp stock is about as easy as it gets. The thin shells give off their flavor quickly, worth simmering even with just a few handfuls of shells. You can follow the general idea of the shellfish stock recipe, scaling back the proportions (maybe ½ cup each onion and celery, a thyme sprig, a bay leaf, a few peppercorns). Or just simmer the shells in water alone to draw out good shrimp essence worth preserving. Simmer time can be cut to 20 to 30 minutes.

ACKNOWLEDGMENTS

MANY THANKS TO Susan Roxborough, executive editor at Sasquatch Books, for suggesting this project to me. And my great appreciation to the rest of the Sasquatch team who shepherded this book so expertly: Jill Saginario, Tony Ong, and Erin Cusick.

Many people working in the industry helped me suss out shellfish details shared here. Lyf Gildersleeve from Flying Fish Company in Portland, Oregon; Lissa James Monberg from Hama Hama Oyster Company; Bill Taylor from Taylor Shellfish Farms; and Margaret Pilaro from the Pacific Coast Shellfish Growers Association were particularly generous. My sincere thanks also to Jim and Mona Stone from Alaska Weathervane Seafoods, Heather Lusk from H. M. Terry Company, Bob Rheault from the East Coast Shellfish Growers Association, Marianne LaCroix from the Maine Lobster Marketing Collaborative, and Laura Diederick from NOAA Fisheries.

To have Jim Henkens's gorgeous images accompanying the book's content is such a joy. Thank you, Jim, for bringing out the best in these shellfish.

Cheers to my recipe testers: Cathy Silvey, Dick Wood, Michael Amend, Joanne Koonce-Hamar, and John Starbard. With extra thanks to Susan Volland, who helped with testing and was a great sounding-board through the process. Many other friends piped in with shellfish stories and input.

And while I regularly thank my husband, Bob, for his support, my appreciation in this case is doubled. A couple of months before this book was due, he helped with final recipe testing while I recovered from a broken leg, me coaching from a nearby stool. I'm incredibly grateful for that extra boost of support this time around.

INDEX

Note: Page numbers in *italic* refer to photographs.

A

B

C

D

E

F

M

O

P

Q

R

ABOUT THE AUTHOR

CYNTHIA NIMS is a lifelong Northwesterner who reveled in growing up surrounded by great food—both in her mother's kitchen and exploring the region with her family, whether eating grilled oysters on a San Juan Island beach or huckleberry pancakes while backpacking in the Olympic Mountains. After graduating from the University of Puget Sound, having majored in mathematics and French literature, Cynthia followed her dreams and went to France to study cooking at La Varenne Ecole de Cuisine. There, she received the Grand Diplôme d'Etudes Culinaires and worked on numerous cookbooks with the school's president, Anne Willan, including *Great Cooks and Their Recipes, Château Cuisine,* and ten in the *Look & Cook* series.

The author of over a dozen cookbooks, Cynthia's most recent is *Shellfish*, with *Salty Snacks* and *Gourmet Game Night* among other books she has written. In her magazine work, Cynthia has served as editor of *Simply Seafood* and food editor of *Seattle Magazine*, in addition to contributing to *Cooking Light, Coastal Living, Alaska Airlines* magazine, and other publications. She is an active member of the International Association of Culinary Professionals (for which she served as president of the board) and Les Dames d'Escoffier. Her website is MonAppetit.com and her newsletters, *Seafood Savvy* and *Long Live the Recipe Box*, are available on Substack. Cynthia and her husband live in Seattle.

Printed in China

SASQUATCH BOOKS with colophon is a registered trademark of Blue Star Press, LLC

Part of *Essential Shellfish Collection*, published 2025.
ISBN: 978-1-63217-635-6
Not for Individual Sale

29 28 27 26 25 9 8 7 6 5 4 3 2 1

The authorized representative in the EU for product safety and compliance is Authorised Rep Compliance Ltd., Ground Floor, 71 Lower Baggot Street, Dublin D02 P593, Ireland. www.arccompliance.com

Editor: Susan Roxborough
Production editor: Jill Saginario
Photographs: Jim Henkens
Design: Anna Goldstein
Cover art: Molly Reeder
Copyeditor: Michelle Hope Anderson

The recipes contained in this book have been created for the ingredients and techniques indicated. Neither publisher nor author is responsible for your specific health or allergy needs that may require supervision. Nor are publisher and author responsible for any adverse reactions you may have to the recipes contained in the book, whether you follow them as written or modify them to suit your personal dietary needs or tastes.

Sasquatch Books
1325 Fourth Avenue, Suite 1025
Seattle, WA 98101

SasquatchBooks.com

MIX
Paper | Supporting responsible forestry
FSC www.fsc.org FSC® C188448

CRAB

CRAB

Recipes with the Fresh Taste of the Sea

CYNTHIA NIMS

Photography by Jim Henkens

SASQUATCH BOOKS | SEATTLE

To Bob, who means the world to me

CONTENTS

BASICS

ICONIC CRAB

When captain george vancouver explored the Strait of Juan de Fuca at the north edge of Washington State's Olympic Peninsula in the late eighteenth century, he happened upon a stretch of land that reminded him of a point on the English Channel called Dungeness. When he gave this Washington spit the same name, Vancouver inadvertently established the namesake for what would become one of the Northwest's most iconic foods. The beautiful Dungeness crab was at first known simply as "edible crab" or just "crab." But as the fishery for this delectable, sweet crab became more significant in the early twentieth century, it took on the name "Dungeness." Today the Dungeness crab is one of the foods mostly closely identified with the Pacific Coast.

This is just one of many crab that grace dinner tables and backyard summertime spreads around the country, though. Of them, I know Dungeness best and will, without apology, call it my favorite. But devotion to other crab species runs just as strong elsewhere. In this book I take my love of Dungeness as a starting point and branch out to contemplate a number of crab that contribute to some of the most delicious eating experiences available. Blue crab from the Atlantic and Gulf coasts, stone crab from Florida, and king and snow crab from Alaska: they're all iconic in their own ways.

When it comes to enjoying crab, simple is best for most seafood fanatics: freshly cooked, with melted butter and/or lemon wedges, plenty of napkins, and a crisp, cold beverage. It's hard to imagine ever tiring of that brand of delicious. From this minimalist starting point (see Northwest Crab Boil, page 146), crab proves to be surprisingly versatile in the kitchen. In the shell crab can be boiled, steamed, stewed, roasted, and grilled. The rich, sweet-briny meat adds panache to recipes from breakfast, through lunch (in soups, salads, and sandwiches), into cocktail hour, and finally on the dinner table. I stop just short of making crab ice cream, but trust me, it's out there.

A BRIEF HISTORY

Of the dozens of crab species found in the waters of the Pacific Coast, three contribute most to the commercial and culinary character of the region: Dungeness, king, and snow crab. The latter two are fished primarily in the deep, frigid waters of Alaska, while Dungeness are found from Alaska to California.

The San Francisco Bay area reported some of the earliest commercial activity with Dungeness crab along the Pacific Coast. Early fishing records date back as far as 1848, when Italian settlers to the region began harvesting and selling local fish. This dawning industry grew quickly as the California Gold Rush gained steam, bringing new customers to the region as well as disillusioned prospectors who turned their attention from hopes of gold to heaps of seafood. It is believed that crab were initially an incidental catch—fishermen intending to catch anchovies, sole, or sardines would sometimes find crab trapped in their nets.

By the early 1860s crab were being marketed along the San Francisco waterfront and crabbing had become a more targeted fishery. Early crabbing records farther north on the Pacific Coast don't appear until near the end of the 1800s. Those early commercially harvested crab didn't make it far from the dock where they were landed, though, since there weren't yet systems in place to reliably distribute the perishable shellfish.

It wasn't until the 1920s and 1930s that a more significant crab fishery developed up and down the West Coast, in tandem with advances in refrigeration and processing techniques as well as development of transportation networks. It was about this time too that the name "Dungeness" became attached to the distinctive reddish-purple crab so abundant here. Today the Washington coastal town of Sequim, which grew out of an early settlement on the Strait of Juan de Fuca, embraces the crustaceous critter that shares its name with the nearby Dungeness Spit, the historic New Dungeness Lighthouse, and the Dungeness River that spills out into Dungeness Bay. The Cedars at Dungeness golf course in Sequim even boasts a crab-shaped sand trap they call "Old Crabby" on hole number three.

Substantial domestic commercial harvest of king crab in Alaska wasn't really rolling until the 1940s, though Japanese and Russian fishermen had been catching the crab in good volumes from the north Atlantic the decade prior. By the 1960s American harvest of king crab was dominating, with important operations out of the Bering Sea and around Kodiak Island. This is about the time that commercial harvest of snow crab was just beginning.

Commercial harvest of blue crab goes back well over a century on both the Atlantic coast and in the Gulf of Mexico.

Though just as for Dungeness, the crab didn't make it very far from where they were harvested until advances in refrigerated transportation took shape. By the early 1900s that began to change, and the industry became well developed—particularly in the Chesapeake Bay area—in the first half of the century. In more recent decades the commercial harvest has extended down the coast and around into the Gulf of Mexico. Today the top states harvesting blue crab are Maryland, Virginia, North Carolina, and Louisiana.

By contrast to these long-exploited crab, the stone crab industry is a more recent development. Though the crab themselves had been prolific, and caught for subsistence and personal use, for countless generations, early forays into commercial harvest had limited distribution and not great consumer demand. It was later into the 1960s when the fishery and burgeoning market for the claws (beyond what could be consumed at the original stone crab–claw mecca of Joe's Stone Crab in Miami) began to boom.

WEST COAST CRAB

While editor of *Simply Seafood* magazine, I had the rare treat of spending a week on Alaska's Kodiak Island, traditional home to not only the great Kodiak brown bear (of which I got a disarmingly up-close, though safe, view) but also to king crab. A most unforgettable feast during my visit was prepared by my hosts—seasonal salmon fishing families from the Lower 48 as well as locals from the village of Akhiok at the southern end of the island. The centerpiece in the midst of the salmon pirog (a pastry-topped savory pie), salmon quiche, and salmon pasta salads was a huge bowl of king crab legs, which only hours earlier were still scurrying along

the ocean floor. I'd been out in the skiff when the pots were brought up and was absolutely flabbergasted at the sight of those creatures, so big (they can attain up to five feet or more from the tip of one leg to the other) and intimidating with their thorned shells.

Back on shore, a huge pot of seawater was brought to a boil over a propane burner while the crab were cleaned. In no time we were all gorging ourselves on the incredible briny-sweet-rich meat. It was enough to have me swearing off king crab prepared any other way (experiences like that are once in a lifetime, and rightfully so). That was until a more recent development that saw more king crab being transferred live to markets and restaurants in larger cities. Crab are rather sturdy creatures and can survive a day or more out of water in the proper conditions. The king crab are put in large boxes and well chilled, which in addition to preserving the quality of the meat, dulls their senses to keep them docile in transit. Upon arrival at their destination, generally less than twenty-four hours later, the crab go into saltwater tanks and are fully revived. Now it can be possible to enjoy freshly cooked king crab without making that trek to Alaska.

These deep-sea creatures thrive in the frigid waters of the North Pacific, and treacherous ocean conditions there have helped make king crab fishing among the most dangerous professions in the world. Back in the mid-1960s, Kodiak Island was Alaska's largest producer of king crab, landing nearly ninety-one million pounds in 1966. But stocks in those waters declined significantly in the couple decades since peak harvests of Alaska king crab were recorded in the 1980s. Today there is no commercial king crabbing on Kodiak (it's primarily out in the Bering Sea now), but limited subsistence crabbing allowed on the island maintains the tradition.

Red king crab (*Paralithodes camtschatica*) is the most broadly distributed of the major king species, a huge crab that's maroon red when alive, turning bright orange red when cooked. Alaska harvest is from waters that span the Bering Sea, Aleutian Islands, and Gulf of Alaska. The size of red king crab generally ranges from four pounds to ten pounds but can weigh as much as twenty-four pounds. Similar in size is the blue king crab (*Paralithodes platypus*), so named because of the slight bluish hue on the shells in its live state. When cooked, these blue kings turn a similar fiery color as red king crab. A slightly smaller king is the golden (or brown) king crab (*Lithodes aequispinus*), which is fished in deeper waters of the North Pacific. King crab can live long lives, up to thirty years.

What's in a Name

I had always loved how Cancer magister rolls off the tongue, and the regal nature of Dungeness that the name calls to mind. That, and it was among few scientific species names that I knew without hesitation, should I find myself on Jeopardy! someday answering a five-hundred-dollar question in the crustacean category. But as I was reviewing notes about Dungeness crab for this book, I was surprised to find many resources that label it Metacarcinus magister instead. Despite the fact that the taxonomic change means nothing relative to the cooking and eating experience, I was intrigued. Apparently recent research has determined that what had been a subgenus, Metacarcinus, in fact fulfills all the characteristics of a full genus, and therefore scientists elevated it to such status, displacing its longtime Cancer genus. Though not all scientists agree—so some, whether out of habit or scientific difference of opinion, continue using Cancer magister. You know I'm a fan.

Snow crab is the common name that can be attached to two closely related species of crab: *Chionoecetes opilio* and *C. bairdi*. Bairdi, which also sometimes goes by the name tanner crab, are harvested only in Alaskan waters, while the opilio crab are fished also around Newfoundland and Labrador in the North Atlantic. Their common genus, *Chionoecetes*, translates to "snow inhabitant," reflecting their home in those frigid northern waters. Most consumers will just see "snow crab" available, with no distinction made between the species, but that may be changing as the market for the two species evolves. The opilio crab tends to be smaller (about two pounds), bairdi a bit larger (up to five pounds), though they're generally indistinguishable to the untrained eye. Snow crab is often associated with all-you-can-eat buffets or high-volume restaurants, which might make you a little skeptical. When well handled, the meat has a bright, sweet flavor that's quite wonderful.

It's pretty easy to tell the difference between snow and king legs: king crab legs are rounder with sharp, thorny bumps (be careful!), and snow crab legs, aside from being smaller, are flatter with rough but far less spiky shells.

There's little doubt that the premier Pacific Coast crab is the Dungeness. Its Latin name, *Cancer magister*, is a clue to the cultural status this creature holds. The fishery for Dungeness reaches from the Gulf of Alaska down to Southern California. Limited amounts of Dungeness are caught as far south as Santa Barbara, though the bulk of the fishery is from Morro Bay northward. To emphasize how prized this crab is, the Oregon state legislature in 2009 passed a bill naming Dungeness crab the official state crustacean.

BLUE CRAB
DUNGENESS CRAB
KING CRAB
STONE CRAB CLAWS
SNOW CRAB

EAST COAST CRAB

Two prime crab species that are in commercial production along Eastern Seaboard and Gulf of Mexico waterways are blue crab and stone crab. There is some commercial harvest of peekytoe crab and Jonah crab, though in much smaller volumes and very limited availability relative to the blue or stone.

Blue crab are nearly a religion unto themselves, particularly around the Chesapeake Bay and along Gulf Coast spots where the crab are abundant. Their Latin name, *Callinectes sapidus*, means “beautiful savory swimmer,” perfectly reflecting both the look and the deliciousness of the crab. The back two legs of these crab are flat, more like paddles than legs, called swimmerets. They do indeed permit the crab to swim around should they wish, while other crab must content themselves with simply walking along the sea floor. They’re most always enjoyed quite simply: steamed or boiled whole with seasonings of choice (a choice about which, also, passions can run deep) and piled on a paper-covered table outside for contented cracking and slurping with lots of friends. After all they sell these crab by the bushel, about forty pounds or so, maybe six to eight dozen depending on their size. (See page 148 for more on crab feeds.)

These are smaller crab than most others, which affords them a unique trait that other crab don’t have: that of being delectable (some would say outrageously so) in their soft-shell form. All crab have hard exoskeletons, so the only way for them to increase in size as they mature is to slip out of their shell and produce a new shell one size larger into which they’ll grow over the subsequent weeks. When captured at just the right moment—within a window of as little as an hour or two—the thin, nearly translucent shell of a blue crab is fine enough that the crab, once cleaned, can be eaten whole, shell and all. The only caveat is choosing a cooking method that fully crisps that soft shell to make it palatable (it'd be quite tough otherwise), which means either pan-frying or deep-frying. Darn, right?! Check out my recipe for the delicacy on page 95.

The other dominant crab of the eastern United States is stone crab (*Menippe mercenaria* and *Menippe adina*, very closely related and treated as one species by the industry). It, too, has a rather unique characteristic in that only its claws are harvested. And its claws are surely the envy of all other crab in the sea: they can grow inordinately large calling to mind Popeye's disproportionately large arms. The crab can regenerate a lost claw within twelve to eighteen months. Once the claw is removed from the crab, the meat holds up much better in cooked form than raw, so the industry standard is to cook the claws immediately, whether onboard the vessel or right after docking. Stone claws are, therefore, always ready-to-eat and the majority of them are enjoyed chilled, right out of the shell. The classic accompaniment is mustard sauce (of which I have a variation on page 79), though lemon butter, cocktail sauces, and other seafood-friendly dips are good choices too. Though the meat is not often picked from the shells to use in recipes, it certainly makes for a luxurious option in the simplest of recipes in which the crabmeat will stand out.

SEASONAL CRAB HARVEST

The commercial season for Dungeness crab is a long one, extending nearly year-round in various openings up and down the Pacific Coast. December is when one big push hits, with the opening of the ocean fishery in many areas (typically on December 1, mid-November in some areas). The bulk of the year's catch will come in the first month or two—and higher

supply tends to mean lower prices, making it traditionally a good time to splurge on a big crab feed for family and friends. Alaska's Dungeness season, primarily from off Kodiak Island and in Southeast Alaska, begins in the spring and peaks during the summer. These fisheries, coupled with inland commercial harvest from areas such as Washington's Puget Sound, cover quite a lot of the calendar with retail crab supplies, though the volume available (and relative price point) varies through the year. All commercial crab operations taper with molting season, when crab are biologically sensitive and when their shells are less filled with meat, making them less desirable as well. Late fall commercial openings are generally contingent on confirmation by fishery agents that the bulk of crab in a particular district have fully hardened shells.

In addition to the annual fluctuation of supply and prices, there are also longer cycles that see Dungeness crab supplies rise and fall over an average of seven to ten years, though the pattern is anything but consistent. It's true all along the Pacific Coast, where harvests in recent decades might drop by 30 percent from one year to the next, but rebound by even more in another year or two. There seems to be no single reason for this fluctuation, but influences can include climate, predators, and general oceanic conditions. Such is the nature of wild seafood. Given our modern food chain that's been well tailored to fit our love of consistent availability and prices, it can be frustrating to deal with the vagaries of nature for the supply of our favorite delicacies. But the best things in life—like crab at a price that has you calling friends over for a bountiful crab feed—are always worth waiting for.

Up in Alaska, the prized red king crab is fished commercially for just a couple of months in the fall, while other types such as blue and golden may be harvested from winter into spring. Likewise, snow crab species are generally harvested in Alaska from October through winter and spring, while just the opilio crab are also a significant fishery in waters off eastern Canada, where it is fished in the spring and summer.

Blue crab are harvested quite broadly, found in United States waters from Texas, around Florida, and up the Atlantic coast as far as Maine, though prime fishing grounds don't extend much north of Chesapeake Bay. The seasons vary with the harvest area, sometimes dependent on the weather, but generally volumes are highest in the summer months and into early fall. Gulf states such as Louisiana and Florida harvest the crab year-round and help meet demand for the delicious crustacean when seasons slow down to the north.

Stone crab are harvested, almost exclusively in Florida, with a consistent season that runs October 15 to May 15 of each year.

SPORT CRABBING

True crab lovers shrug at whatever the price of crab may be or uncertainty about which store will have the best product. Instead they jump in the car and head to their favorite crabbing spot to harvest some themselves. In fact, it may be that recreational crabbing is on the rise *because* of higher crab prices in the markets. That, and catching your own crab is right up there with hunting for mushrooms and picking berries on a vacant lot, bringing out the hunter-gatherer instincts in us while we collect exquisite food to enjoy.

Recreational crab fishing seasons for the different varieties of crab vary throughout the country and often licenses are required—check with the Department of Fish and Wildlife, or its equivalent, in your area to find out about regulations before you head out.

One friend says that all he needs to stay stocked in Dungeness is "$1.79 worth of turkey meat for bait and an extended lunch break," with his car or kayak pointed in the general direction of Westport, Washington, or to any nearby Puget Sound pier. Others head to their Whidbey Island cabin, another to a family home on Hood Canal. They get all the crab they can eat, and sometimes more, which is why I find myself occasionally rendezvousing in a Seattle parking lot to take some extra crab off their hands. Why yes, we are spoiled.

While technically recreational harvest is allowed on many parts of the Pacific Coast, ocean conditions can be uninviting, with some estuaries and other protected spots more conducive to crabbing for fun. The inland waters of greater Puget Sound (including Hood Canal and other offshoots) in Washington State are a plentiful crab habitat that keeps countless sport crabbers happy through the summer months, with priceless beachside crab feeds ensuing. During summer, many commercial fishers have their eyes on salmon up in Alaska and other prize harvest elsewhere. When the casual crowd is ready to pull their boats in for the season, the commercial folks are back and ready to drop their pots.

East and Gulf coasters have a pretty profound devotion to crabbing for blues as well, no doubt about it. My blue-crab correspondent from Delaware said that most people in that area have been doing it all their lives, and that nothing says "summer" in blue-crab country like those signs seen in coastal areas touting "hot fat crab and cold beer." The blue crab is caught in various types of traps or on trot lines onto which bait is attached. The lines are let out, you sit and have a cold one, then you slowly pull up that line. If a crab's attached to the bait that he's determined to eat, he'll hold on tight as long as the line's drawn in slowly enough. With a net ready to nab the crab as soon as it's visible, the crabber is one count closer to dinner.

ESTABLISHED
1971

Whatever crab they're catching, sport fishers are decidedly enthusiastic about their fishing spot, their bait and gear, and whatever particular rituals and habits they have about the craft of crabbing. And it's an infectious enthusiasm. Some days I wonder if there are enough turkey and chicken necks available for all that go into crab pots and on trot lines to lure in those luscious crab. While, sure, crab are known to be scavengers that will eat pretty much any dead thing they come across on the sea floor—my intel on bait choices found crabbers preferring to lure with fresh meat (chicken or turkey legs or necks) and occasionally seafood, such as salmon or tuna heads and salmon bones. More than one crabber pointed out that they'd rather eat a crab whose last meal was something fresh.

SUSTAINABILITY

Crab is a seafood that you can indulge in with a clear conscience regarding its sustainability, which is to say the health of its populations, environmental impact of its fishery, and how well its harvest is managed. All the domestic harvest of the species featured in this book generally rank well, if not very well, with sustainability watchdogs.

The Dungeness crab, for one, is nearly a poster child for sustainability. The fishery has had a management strategy known as "3-S" in place for decades. This references sex (only males can be harvested), size (a minimum carapace width ensures all males harvested have had at least one season to mate), and seasonality (varies regionally but avoids disturbing crab postmolt when shells are soft and they are biologically vulnerable). In recent years there has been concern about some instances of humpback whales being entangled in pot lines. Though this is generally considered to be a rarity, given the whale's endangered status, it is nonetheless a call to action for the industry to take measures to reduce likelihood of entanglements.

King crab have had some challenges over the years. It was a prolific and very profitable fishery for decades, until a distinct crash in the 1980s that put the brakes on much of the harvest. There had been a kind of Wild West race-for-the-crab derby approach before: the season opened and it was each boat for itself to get as much crab as it could until the season closed. For a long time that worked, until suddenly it didn't. A number of possible factors have been cited for this crash, including limited recruitment (survival of crab larvae) and changes in climate and ocean conditions, though overfishing is also a likely culprit. Tough but crucial limits on harvest and changes in industry practices, such as annually determined quotas limiting how many crab can be caught based on surveys of that year's population, seem to have paid off. In recent years the populations of king crab in Alaska have clearly rebounded. Reports indicate that populations in the Bering Sea are back to levels two to three times what they were in 1985, though rebound in other Alaska waters has been slower to materialize.

Snow crab are deemed to have healthy stocks, risk little harm to the environment or other sea creatures, and are fished under solid management practices. Like for king crab, if authorities have data suggesting lower abundance of snow crab in a given year, they'll reduce the quota sizes to assure enough mature crab remain to support solid populations in the future. Given the inherent cyclical nature of crab abundance, there's sure to be a boom year not long after one that's slim.

Domestic blue crab too are pretty consistently given the green (or at least yellow) light from sustainability monitors. Biologically, the species has a short but fecund life, which contributes a sizeable cohort of juveniles each year though their survival is contingent on everything from weather to predation. Effective management of stocks and other oversight has helped stabilize the fishery that had—particularly in the Chesapeake Bay—some challenging years not long ago. (Blue swimmer crab from Asia, a different species, can show up in US markets. Concerns about less stringent oversight

Science Says

So, we know that crab is a gastronomic delicacy on our dinner plates. But what is crab's status in the biologist's lab? First, crab are part of a large group of creatures called arthropods—invertebrates with segmented bodies and jointed legs—which includes insects, spiders, and centipedes. Of those subsets, crab are—along with shrimp, lobsters, and crayfish among others—crustaceans. Within that class, crab are designated as decapods, because they have ten legs.

From this point the crab population falls into one of two groups: brachyurans and anomurans. The former are considered to be the "true" crab because, true to decapods, they sport ten visible appendages: four pairs of legs and one pair of claws. Brachyurans include Dungeness, snow, blue, and stone crab. The anomura crab are also technically decapods, though only the claws and three pairs of legs are visible, the fourth set dwarfed and tucked under the back shell edge. Anomuran crab include the glorious king crab, as well as an array of hermit crab, box crab, and the wild-looking heart crab.

of fishery practices means consumers are generally recommended to check the provenance of the blue crab they're purchasing to ensure it is from a well-managed source.)

Stone crab get high marks for sustainability as well. The fishery is closed five months of the year during prime spawning season, minimum claw size (at least two and three-quarters inches from tip of the immobile half of the claw to the first leg joint) assures harvest from only mature crab, egg-bearing females must be returned to the water with both claws still intact, and it's illegal to harvest whole crab.

The Monterey Bay Aquarium's Seafood Watch program is a particularly good resource to help consumers make informed choices about the seafood they purchase. It's available online, as a great mobile app, and in pocket-size paper guides. Established through the Vancouver Aquarium in British Columbia is Ocean Wise, which evaluates seafood species from around the globe as well. And the Marine Stewardship Council (MSC) supports an elaborate program that certifies sustainable fisheries. But bear in mind that this is an "opt-in" program. This means a particular fishery organization that hopes to be certified must initiate the process, not to mention budget a good deal of time and money for the review process that's required. Not seeing your favorite seafood on the MSC list does not mean that the fishery is unsustainable.

It pays to do some research about your favorite seafoods, learn more about the regions where they're harvested, the fishing methods used, and what, if any, environmental impact the fishery has in order to make a decision about what you're comfortable eating. It is rarely as easy as a blanket "good" or "bad" about any single seafood species. So many variables come into play, including when, how, and where the seafood is caught. Informing yourself and asking questions of restaurant staff and retail vendors will go far to help you consume seafood with a clear conscience.

WHAT TO DRINK WITH CRAB

Looking for ideas about what to sip alongside your delectable crab? The short answer is crisp white wine, great sparkling wine, or a nice cold beer. Countless aficionados don't stray far from those options, often having long ago picked favorite selections that are near and dear to their crab-loving hearts. There are a number of options within those three categories, where variations abound.

Let's start with wine. I'll draw a pretty sweeping, though perhaps not all that bold, generalization that West Coasters are more in the wine-with-crab camp while in the East they're more likely to be drinking beer. Not because, necessarily, wine is better suited to Dungeness and beer to blues. It has a lot to do with the native wine culture, with Washington, Oregon, and California all producing a slew of crab-friendly options within a short drive of those crab grounds. Wine is a big part of the culinary landscape. Un- (or only moderately) oaked chardonnay, pinot gris, dry riesling, and dry gewürztraminer can be solid contenders for crab.

Chardonnay is grown around the world and produced in myriad styles. For the simplest of crab preparations with few other flavors and ingredients in the mix, lighter chardonnay with a minimum of oak is ideal. But as the dishes become richer, perhaps in fritters or served with a buttery sauce, the more buttery, lush styles of chardonnay that may have more pronounced oak do quite well. Among my (and many others') favorite chardonnays are those made in Burgundy, where the grape takes on a particular elegance and the wines have a rounded, moderate lushness that makes them wonderful alongside crab.

Generally, wines with some body, not too steely-dry and austere, do best with crab. With oysters I want supercrisp, a good dose of acidity, and striking minerality. With crab it goes more toward lush and rounded with lighter acidity and a bit more fruit character to complement the sweeter, richer-tasting (though technically very lean) meat. Albariño, not-too-fruity viognier, and grüner veltliner are among other solid options.

Ahhhhh, Champagne! Not only is it elegant, delicious, and inherently festive, it is also one of the most broadly food-friendly beverages available. And when it comes to crab, the partnership is particularly brilliant. Speaking now of true Champagne from the namesake region of France, winemaking requirements and the natural environment assure wines that have a bright acidity to counterpoint the rich sweetness of crab, along with complexity from the aging process that elevates the flavor of the crab. Vintage Champagne, in particular, has even more character with its minimum of three years' aging, which shifts flavors from the fruit-forward more toward the savory and earthy.

If you think that rosé Champagne is suited only for "ladies who lunch" occasions, think again. The pink color does not reflect girly sweetness, but instead reflects some red wine influence that gives the Champagne more structure and further boosts its food friendliness. In particular, it remains a strong partner for bolder flavors, elevating and complementing spice where other wines may be overpowered by them.

Sparkling wines are made around the world, though in that broader context the variations in style and flavor are just too vast to generalize for crab pairing. I would recommend focusing on those that have bright flavor, moderate acidity, and minimal sweetness. There are worse tasks than sipping a few different sparkling wines with crab to figure out which one you like best.

And beer? No, I wasn't going to forget beer. In fact, philosophically, one might argue that it is an exemplary crab partner given how well beer echoes the casualness of outdoor summer crab feasts. Given the relatively delicate, slightly sweet flavor of most crab, go for a lighter style of beer such as lager, pilsner, or wheat beer (which sometimes goes by hefeweisen). They tend to be low on the hoppy-bitterness scale and have a cheery brightness that complements crab well.

All this being said, beverage pairing is very much to each his or her own. Our palates are incredibly personal; if breaking any pairing "rule" produces a flavor combination that knocks your socks off—all the more power to that partnership.

Diverse Tastes

To make all these pairing considerations more interesting, remember that not all crab taste exactly the same, which becomes clearer when you get a chance to taste different varieties side by side. Dungeness is sweet, lightly salty, with a touch of richness; blue is more sea-breeze, delicate, less salty; king is very rich and the briniest of them all; snow can be even more sweet-salty than Dungeness; and stone is quite sweet, with minimal saltiness, and almost meaty. So while there certainly are beverages that pair well with all five, even those slight variations might lead you toward some species-specific preferences as you explore options.

PACKING
TO TRAVEL
24 HOUR
PACK-$5.00
48 HOUR
PACK $10.00

IN THE KITCHEN

BUYING & STORING CRAB

When buying live crab, choose ones that are visibly active. Let the professionals drop their arms into those live tanks, but you get to accept or reject their choices. An added confirmation of quality (in the case of Dungeness) would be a pinch of one of the back legs to be sure it's fully hard. If it gives rather than feeling solid, the crab may still be filling out after its last molt and not in prime form (there will be less meat and it can be on the soft side).

Keep the crab cool in transit, asking for a bag of crushed ice at the seafood counter if it's warm out or if you won't be home right away, and refrigerate the crab as soon as you get home. Live crab need air, so open up the packaging. I like to clear out a vegetable bin for storing crab, to help contain any water draining. Live crab will be somewhat dulled by the chill of the refrigerator, so don't expect them to rummage around much in there. Don't be tempted to keep them in water (even salted) or on ice, which will do more harm than keeping them in open air. It's best to plan cooking live crab the day you purchase them.

For cooked, whole crab, look for those without punctures or other breaks in the shell. The crab should feel heavy in your hand, indicating that it is full of meat. Check that all its legs, especially the claws, are intact. Blue crab are blue and grayish green when alive, Dungeness a purplish-brown color, both turning a vivid orange red when cooked. The orange-red color is a clue for cooked crab that are ready to eat. Though cleaning Dungeness crab is easy, it can get a little messy, so consider asking the fishmonger to clean the cooked crab for you. In some regions cooked Dungeness is available frozen, either whole or in cleaned sections. See below for info on frozen king and snow crab related to choosing and thawing.

Bulk crabmeat should smell sweet and slightly briny. Avoid any crabmeat that looks dried out or has a heavy "fishy" aroma. Cooked crab, whether in the shell or not, will keep for a few days if well chilled, but it will be at its best for flavor and moistness if used within a day or two of buying it. (If buying packaged crabmeat, refer to the label for storage guidelines.) You should never catch a whiff of ammonia smell with crab, either in the shell or picked meat. That's a clear indicator of a product past its prime.

King and snow crab are commonly sold frozen in sections. Carefully check any exposed flesh that's visible: it should be white and not look dried out, which indicates freezer burn or other poor handling. Often the leg portions will be covered in a thin glaze of ice, which is a good thing. These crab are cooked shortly after hitting the docks, then quickly frozen to preserve the quality of the meat (and help assure the meat doesn't cling to the shells), then glazed with ice to protect them, especially from contact with air. Thaw the crab legs in the refrigerator overnight, in a deep pan (such as an oblong baking dish) to catch the water melt.

Blue crab, both hard-shell and soft-shell, are available—depending on the season—in both fresh and frozen form. Selecting and storing hard-shell blue crab require similar criteria to Dungeness. Soft-shell crab are clearly distinct, though a fresh, clean aroma if fresh and lack of blemishes in either state are key factors to look for.

Stone crab claws are available fresh in season and frozen through much of the year. The shells may have been scored by the processor to make cracking easier; otherwise the shells should appear unbroken. They should have a sweet, briny aroma, if any aroma at all. Plan ahead to allow frozen claws time to thaw slowly in the refrigerator, as noted for king and snow.

In a Can

Not all crabmeat is created equal. In fresh form crabmeat may be sold in plastic tubs or bulk at a seafood counter to purchase by the pound. You may also see crab in a can at the seafood counter, which is pasteurized to protect the contents and extends shelf life a bit, but it has no other ingredients added and must be refrigerated.

The shelf-stable canned crab you'll find alongside canned tuna and anchovies in your grocery store is different: it's generally packaged with additives and preservatives. And these products typically rely on crab harvested in Asia, which is often not the most sustainable option. While crabmeat from bulk trays, plastic tubs, and pasteurized in cans with nothing added are all great products to use in these recipes, I am not a fan of using shelf-stable canned crab in its place.

I generally never recommend that we home cooks freeze seafood in our home freezers. Seafood that's frozen commercially is done so at temperatures far lower than our freezers can attain, and those extra-low temperatures mean quick freezing and formation of very, very small ice crystals. When we put a piece of fish in our home freezer, it takes longer to freeze, the ice crystals that form are larger, and they become like little knives puncturing cell walls of the meat, altering the texture and reducing the flavor quality the crab will have once thawed.

That being said, if you ever find yourself with more delicate, fresh, sweet crabmeat than you can use (which might sound unlikely, but it can happen) the last thing you want to do is throw it away. One friend tipped me off to the freezing-in-milk option, apparently an old fisherman's trick. After picking meat from the shells and removing any shell bits and cartilage, put the meat (I package it in recipe-friendly eight-ounce portions) in a heavy-duty ziplock bag and add just enough milk to cover. Draw out as much excess air from the bag as you can, seal well, and freeze. When ready to use, thaw overnight in the refrigerator, then drain off the milk and squeeze the excess liquid from the crabmeat before using. The quality holds up quite well. You wouldn't want to use this on a crab Louis salad or for crab cocktail, but it's a great option for soup, risotto, quiche, and many other cooked recipes.

LIVE CLEANING

This is an option for cleaning blue and Dungeness crab that is practiced by some crabbers and the most ardent of crab cooking fanatics. It involves cleaning the crab from its live state, rather than after it has been cooked. There are a few benefits, which include being able to fill a pot with more cleaned, portioned crab than you can whole crab, for more efficiency when cooking lots of crab. It also leaves the meat more pure white and slightly milder in flavor, since the yellowish viscera is not in contact with the body meat unlike when crab are cooked whole. Lastly, whatever seasoning you may be adding to the cooking process will have better access to the exposed meat, and the crabmeat will better absorb those other flavors.

Cleaning crab live is a bit less daunting a task with smaller blue crab, as they're simply easier to manage. To mellow both the crab and the cook before starting, many put the crab in a big bowl of ice water for five minutes or so to dull it a bit and reduce its activity.

I've cleaned live Dungeness at home and it's doable, but messier than cleaning cooked crab and a little unnerving.

Ultimately this cleaning process is the same as the process for cleaning cooked crab: remove the carapace (top shell), remove the apron, pinch away the gills, and clean out the guts. One slight variation some employ is to cut the crab in half from the abdomen side with a large, sharp cleaver while the carapace is intact (definitely not recommended with a chef's knife or a hesitant cook), which immediately kills and halves the crab in one gesture.

For me, live cleaning is a technique best suited to beach cleaning, where aficionados go through the motions in a matter of moments, first removing the carapace, carefully grabbing the claws and legs together in each hand and breaking the crab in half, shaking out the viscera and quickly swishing the halves in seawater to rinse. Much easier to do so outdoors than in our home kitchens.

Top-quality seafood markets with crab in live tanks should be happy to clean the crab for you. Be sure to keep live-cleaned crab cold in transit and cook them within a few hours.

BOILING & STEAMING CRAB

These are the two most basic ways to cook crab. Boiling is often the first step for just-harvested crab, both for commercial processors and for recreational crabbers. Cooking crab just out of the water captures them at peak freshness and makes transporting and storing easier than for live crab. And for purists, that's all the work needed before taking the crab to the table for a feast. Steaming, too, can perform this task for just-caught crab, whether to be eaten right away or stored for two or three days in the refrigerator before using. But steaming can also double as a means to reheat precooked crab for serving warm. Boiling is not recommended for this; some of the crab's delicate flavor would be lost into the hot water while steaming does a better job of preserving it.

You need a big pot to cook whole crab at home, particularly if you're feeding a crowd. When a crab feed is on the menu, consider using a pot as big as twelve to sixteen quarts to get through the volume of crab to keep everyone happy, or have a couple of smaller pots boiling away at the same time. Even for just one or two Dungeness crab or a dozen blue crab, eight quarts in volume will be best. If cooking lots of crab might become a regular habit, consider larger two-piece pots made with just this in mind, either with a large basket that fits snugly inside the pot for easy adding and removing of the crab, or with a shallower lower portion to hold the liquid and seasonings and a larger pot that sits atop it with the crab perched over for steaming.

TO BOIL CRAB: Fill a large pot with water up to a few inches below the top. Add plenty of salt, about one-half cup per gallon of water. Cover the pot and bring the water to a boil over high heat. If boiling a whole live crab, put it in the freezer to chill and make it docile while the water is heating. (The crab shouldn't freeze, so don't leave it in the freezer for more than fifteen or twenty minutes.) When the water's at a full rolling boil, grab the crab securely at the back of the carapace and carefully but quickly slip the crab into the water head-first. Reduce the heat to medium high so the water's actively gurgling but not boiling over. Cook the crab for eighteen minutes for a two-pound whole crab (a few or less based on other sizes); cook for about ten minutes if using cleaned crab portions or blue crab.

TO STEAM CRAB: Put about three to four inches of water in a large pot and add a collapsible steamer basket to the bottom of the pot. (If you don't have a steamer basket, you could use a few tuna cans with both top and bottom removed.) Cover the pot and bring the water to a boil over high heat. Sedate the crab in the freezer as noted above. When the water's at a full rolling boil, add the crab to the steamer basket, cover, and steam for about twenty-two minutes for whole Dungeness crab, or about fifteen minutes for crab portions or blue crab. Keep an eye on the water level during cooking to be certain that the pot doesn't boil dry; if necessary, add another cup or two of very hot (preferably boiling) water.

Drain the cooked crab in the sink. If serving the crab chilled, put them in a sink full of ice water to cool quickly, then drain well, clean them if not already cleaned, and refrigerate until ready to serve. If serving the crab hot, give them a quick rinse under warm water, clean them, and you're ready to go.

CLEANING & PORTIONING CRAB

Dungeness & Hard-Shell Blue Crab

To clean a cooked crab (see pages 36 to 37 for photos), begin by removing the carapace by inserting your thumb under the edge of the carapace at the back edge and lifting it up and away from the body. If you're a fan of crab butter (see page 39), spoon out the soft, yellowish material and set aside in a small dish. Otherwise, discard it with the remaining innards that are tucked in the body cavity. Turn the crab over, then lift up and remove the small flap of shell known as the apron. (This apron being narrow and fingerlike, by the way, identifies the crab as a male, as it must be for legal Dungeness; on a female crab the apron is more broad and dome-like, which you may see on blue crab.)

Pinch off the feathery gills that are on either side of the body cavity. Break away the mandibles, or mouth parts, that protrude a bit from the front of the shell. Rinse the crab well under cold water. Use a large, heavy knife to cut the body in half where it narrows at the center. If you have a crab cleaned for you at the market, this is what you'll be taking home. And for blue crab this is generally the last step before cooking or serving.

There are two ways to proceed for portioning Dungeness crab, though for a crab feed, you can leave them in these larger portions. One option is to pull the legs away from the body, then cut each body half into two or three pieces. I prefer a different method that leaves some body meat attached to each leg portion. Set the half crab upright on the chopping board with the legs up and the body portion flat on the surface. Using a cleaver or other large sharp, heavy knife, make a swift downward chop between each of the legs (though I'll keep the last two smaller legs together), through the soft shell of the body. Use whichever method appeals to you.

For precooked crab that is to be used in a recipe, lightly crack the shells of the legs so that flavorings from the other ingredients will more easily penetrate the meat. This is also a jump-start for your guests, making it easier for them to get at the meat. Use crab crackers or a wooden mallet and try to avoid crushing the shell into the meat. Ideally, the legs will remain intact.

If you're serving the crab as is, it's ready for the table. Be sure to provide your guests with crab crackers and small seafood forks for removing the meat from the shells. When you get to the big luscious claws, the meat will come out more easily if you first remove the loose claw joint: grab the pincer and bend it backward, pulling it away from the claw. It should come away with a thin membrane that runs down the center of the claw meat. When serving the crab, have a bowl or two on the table for guests to discard shells as they go.

Other Crab

It's pretty rare to come across a king or snow crab live in retail stores—and if you did, think about how big a pot you'd need to cook it once home! King and snow crab are most always precooked, available as individual leg portions or clusters with a few legs together. And they'll likely be frozen as well, so you'll have to thaw the crab overnight in the refrigerator before using (see page 29). From this point there's not much you need to do to clean or portion these crab. Though some legs, particularly king, can be quite long and unwieldy for cooking and serving, so you may wish to cut them in half or thirds before using. If a joint is conveniently located for this, simply bend one side backward to separate

How to Clean a Crab

1. Lift up and remove the carapace. **2.** If you're a fan of crab butter, spoon it out and set it aside. **3.** Turn the crab over and remove the apron. **4.** Pinch off the feathery gills.

5. Break away the mandibles. 6. Rinse the crab well under cold water. 7. Use a large, heavy knife to cut the body in half. 8. Set the half crab upright on the chopping board with the body portion flat on the surface. Make a swift downward chop between each of the legs.

it from the other portion at the joint. If not, use a cleaver or a heavy chef's knife to cut through the shell in desired portions.

Note that king and snow crab shells aren't quite as hard as those of Dungeness crab, so crab crackers are less effective to get at the meat. Instead use a pair of slender-bladed kitchen shears to cut down the length of the leg portions and pry apart the shell to expose the meat. Larger poultry-type shears will mangle the meat as they pass down the length of the shells. If you don't have a slender-bladed option, use a heavy, sharp knife to halve the legs lengthwise.

Don't underestimate those spiny protrusions that are particularly pronounced on king crab; they can puncture your skin if you're not careful. You may wish to hold the legs with a kitchen towel or hot pad to grip them securely while you're cutting the shells to avoid hurting yourself.

Soft-shell blue crab are quite distinct from their hard-shell versions, particularly since the shell remains intact through the cooking and eating. But it is important the crab be cleaned before cooking. Some vendors may sell them precleaned, which is a bonus. Lift up one side of the top shell and see if the feathery gills are still intact, which indicates they haven't been cleaned. In this case use your fingers to pinch away the gills from both sides. Then use a pair of kitchen shears to cut away the front portion of the crab body, just about one-half inch behind the eyes and mouth. Flip the crab over and pull up and pinch off the apron flap. Rinse the crab well.

When it comes to stone crab, since only the claws are harvested and they're precooked, you won't need to do much in the way of preparation of this particular crab, aside from a quick rinse under cold water. Since these are some of the hardest crab shells you'll encounter, you're more likely to need a mallet than traditional crab crackers to break through. A small wooden mallet is ideal, but avoid pounding too hard and imbedding broken shell into the meat. Each "claw" is really a three-sectioned leg, with two knuckles that have lovely nuggets of meat inside, and the oversized main claw portion. This claw, as for other crab, has a flat piece of membrane that runs down the center of the meat; take care to avoid that when eating.

Crab Butter

Crab "butter" is one of those wonderful culinary euphemisms, like sea urchin "roe" (gonads) and "sweetbreads" (thymus gland . . . but oh so delicious!). Also known as tomalley or mustard, this yellow-amber soft material (it's more grayish green when raw) is found clinging to the underside of the carapace and in the body cavity of the crab. It is mostly hepatopancreas, an organ that serves a number of purposes for the crab, which includes acting something like our liver.

Devotees of crab butter swear by stirring it into sauces to serve with crab or simply eating it as is. And they like the flavor that it imparts to the adjacent body meat. But others find the flavor too strong, and some agencies don't recommend people consume the crab butter as it's where any toxins harbored in the crab will be concentrated. In fact, some go so far as to recommend that you clean the crab live (see page 30) to remove the viscera before cooking to avoid any potential exposure to toxins or other contaminants.

ABOUT THE RECIPES

Many of the recipes in this book were made with Dungeness crab in mind, simply because it's the prime crab in the Northwest where I've been doing my cooking for a few-plus decades. But as they say, variety is the spice of life, so there's plenty to love about exploring other types of crab. All five types of crab featured in the book are unique characters in terms of size, shape, and flavor. Taken as a whole, these crab offer a broad range of options in the kitchen and many opportunities for some delicious considerations.

A handful of the recipes rely on in-shell crab, in which case the form (claws, legs, a mix) and the size (from small blue crab to huge king crab) have a big impact on how well a particular crab will work in a specific recipe. You'll find that I clarify in the recipes the best options—or possible variations to suit different species—to help steer you in the right direction. When using precooked crab in a recipe the goal is to just heat them through and give them enough time to mingle flavors with other ingredients—too much extra cooking and they'll start to lose their sweet character.

Most of the recipes rely on bulk crabmeat. It's easily the most versatile form for cooking: it's more broadly available than whole crab and allows for more flexibility between the different species. When buying Dungeness meat, you rarely get a choice of meat type; it will generally be a mix of both the flakier body meat and larger pieces of leg meat. Though on rare occasion you may see "fry legs," just the lovely whole nuggets of meat from the larger legs, sold. Blue crab, however, is sold by meat type: jumbo lump (the largest of unbroken pieces from the body), lump (unbroken pieces from the body), backfin or special (remaining body meat, broken lumps and/

or flaked meat), and claw meat (smaller pieces tinged reddish brown from the claws).

There are recipes where lump meat is ideal or at least a luxurious option to showcase the premium meat, and I note this in recipes where it's appropriate. Other times its specialness would be lost in a recipe that blends the crab into a batter or stirs it into a soup. In fact in those recipes flake can be ideal because it more readily distributes and blends with the other ingredients. Throughout the recipes I offer notes about what meat type to consider using, though to simplify across species I reference just flake or lump, with the understanding Dungeness customers often don't have a choice. The information will help you lean one way or the other when you do.

Note that some recipes are more crab-forward than others. For instance the Firecracker Crab Cocktail (page 75) is all about the crab with an embellishment of homemade cocktail sauce, while for the Choux Puffs with Curried Crab (page 81), the meat is blended with seasonings and other ingredients for a filling that's not boldly crab-heavy in flavor. In this way I try to offer a range of crabness to suite different tastes and crowds where perhaps not everyone is a crab fiend. Some recipes offer a range in the amount of crab you could use, so you can embellish that Crab Louis (page 120) more or less luxuriously according to your whim and budget.

In crabmeat recipes I redundantly remind you to pick through the meat to remove shell and cartilage before using it. Small bits of shell tend to stand out visually simply because of their color, but the thin material that surrounds sections of body meat and the strips of cartilage that run down some leg portions are pure white and often hard to see against the white crabmeat. It pays to take an extra few moments to run your fingers through the crab to double check if any hard bits are lingering.

Crabmeat can harbor a lot of liquid, which is a hindrance in some recipes where the added moisture would alter the recipe's results. In those cases I suggest you squeeze the crab gently to remove some of that excess liquid before using it. Just grab a handful and squeeze gently over the sink. In other recipes that liquid is not an issue and in fact melds well with other ingredients.

It's tempting to believe that when you're using a recipe that calls for crabmeat, you'd save money picking the meat yourself from a whole Dungeness crab. But crab economics don't always work out that way. In a rough average I have found that the yield of meat from a whole cooked crab will be about 25 percent of the original weight, though it varies with the thoroughness of picking and with the crab itself—a larger crab will generally have a better meat-to-shell ratio than a smaller one. If your two-pound crab costs eight dollars per pound, that's sixteen dollars. Since you'll get about one-half pound of meat from that crab, you're paying roughly thirty-two dollars per pound for the meat itself. If the price for the bulk meat is in that range, you'll save yourself plenty of time at little or no extra cost buying prepicked meat. Though, on the down side, you won't have crab shells with which to make Crab Stock (page 111). Blue crab have a much lower yield and the crab are so much smaller, I think it's never a debate about buying blue crabmeat versus picking it yourself.

RECIPES

BREAKFAST & BRUNCH

Fines Herbes Omelet with Crab

MAKES 1 SERVING

Crab: any cooked crabmeat, mix of flake and lump ideal

2 large eggs

1 tablespoon water

2 ounces crabmeat

1 tablespoon unsalted butter

½ teaspoon minced fresh chives, plus more for serving

½ teaspoon minced fresh chervil, plus more for serving

¼ teaspoon minced fresh flat-leaf (Italian) parsley, plus more for serving

¼ teaspoon minced fresh tarragon, plus more for serving

Kosher salt and freshly ground white or black pepper

Coarsely chopped fresh herbs, for garnish (optional)

Eggs and fresh herbs are, to me, a magical combination of ingredients that play beautifully off each other. Crab is perfectly at home in the mix. This single-serving omelet makes a lovely presentation and is quick enough to make that you'll have two on the breakfast table in no time flat: the perfect tête-à-tête Sunday brunch. The trick to an ideal fluffy omelet is to cook the eggs slowly over moderate heat, so they remain tender and moist. Overheating quickly turns eggs dry and flavorless.

Crack the eggs into a medium bowl and beat them with a fork until partially blended. Add the water and continue beating until the eggs are evenly blended and a little frothy. Pick over the crabmeat to remove any bits of shell or cartilage. If using king or snow crab leg meat, cut it into small dice. Squeeze the crab gently to remove excess liquid.

Melt the butter in a small skillet, preferably nonstick, over medium heat. Add the minced chives, chervil, parsley, and tarragon to the eggs, along with a pinch each of salt and pepper, and stir just to mix. Slowly pour the eggs into the skillet and cook until they are nearly set, 2 to 3 minutes.

During this time, slowly draw a wooden spoon across the bottom of the pan in a spiral, starting at the outer edge and working your way to the center, then back out. Keeping the eggs in motion helps them cook evenly. When there is almost no liquid egg left, stop stirring, scatter the crabmeat evenly over, and cook until the omelet is set, 1 to 2 minutes more.

Take the skillet from the heat. Using a heatproof spatula, fold one third of the omelet toward the center, then fold that center portion again toward the opposite edge of the skillet. Carefully roll the omelet from the skillet onto a warmed serving plate. (Ideally, the "seam" will be on the bottom, though it doesn't really matter.) Serve right away, with a sprinkle of chopped herbs across the top if you like.

Fine Indeed

Fines herbes is a French term for the combination of chervil, chives, parsley, and tarragon. Although the blend is commonly available in dried form, for this dish I'd recommend that you use only fresh. Chervil is a delicate herb with lacy, parsley-like leaves and a flavor reminiscent of anise. The herb can be hard to find fresh in markets but is easy to grow, so consider adding it to your kitchen garden or window box. You could use extra chives or parsley to replace the chervil if you are unable to find it. If you happen to have any chives blossoming in your garden, pluck the little purple blossoms and scatter some over the omelet for a striking garnish.

Breakfast Bruschetta with Crab & Goat Cheese

MAKES 4 SERVINGS

Crab: any cooked crabmeat, lump is luxurious

4 slices country-style bread, about ¾ inch thick

8 ounces fresh goat cheese

1 tablespoon minced fresh dill or other tender herb, plus more for garnish

Kosher salt and freshly ground black pepper

4 to 6 ounces crabmeat

1 large vine-ripe tomato, cored and cut into 8 thin slices

Slices of toasted rustic bread serve as an open-faced foundation on which goat cheese, crabmeat, and vine-ripe tomatoes are layered—a wonderful waker-upper. Mix and match other ingredients to suit your taste and the best of what's available at the market. Add other minced fresh herbs to the goat cheese. When summer's tomatoes are no longer available, you could top the sandwiches with oven-roasted or sun-dried tomatoes, fresh leaves of baby spinach, or a few sprigs of parsley to add a bright finish.

Preheat the broiler. Toast one side of the bread slices about 4 inches from the broiler element until lightly browned, 1 to 2 minutes, then turn and lightly toast the other side, 1 to 2 minutes more. Set aside on a wire rack to cool.

Crumble the goat cheese into a small bowl and mash it with a fork to soften the cheese slightly. Add the dill with a pinch each of salt and pepper and stir to mix well. Spread the goat cheese mixture over the bread slices.

Pick over the crabmeat to remove any bits of shell or cartilage. If using king or snow crab leg meat, cut it into medium dice. Squeeze the crab gently to remove excess liquid. Arrange the crab over the goat cheese. Lay the tomato slices over the crab, garnish with the dill, and serve.

Crab & Leek Quiche

MAKES 8 SERVINGS

For the pastry dough

1½ cups all-purpose flour

½ teaspoon kosher salt

½ cup unsalted butter, cut into ¾-inch pieces and chilled

About 5 tablespoons ice water, plus more if needed

....

2 tablespoons unsalted butter

2 large leeks, white and pale-green parts only, split, cleaned, and thinly sliced

Kosher salt and freshly ground black pepper

8 ounces crabmeat (any cooked crabmeat)

1½ cups grated Gruyère cheese (about 6 ounces)

3 large eggs

1½ cups half-and-half

The simple glory of quiche: when eggs, cream, and cheese combine to cradle ingredients in a flaky crust. Gruyère is the cheese of choice (though Swiss can be used). It's an ideal option for breakfast, brunch, or lunch, or even as an appetizer.

To make the pastry dough, in a food processor, combine the flour and salt and pulse once to mix. Add the butter pieces and pulse to finely chop the butter and create a mixture with a coarse, sandy texture. Transfer the mixture to a medium bowl, drizzle with 3 tablespoons of the water over and stir with a fork to quickly blend. Repeat with the remaining 2 tablespoons of water, stirring well. The dough has the proper amount of liquid if it feels neither dusty-dry nor sticky when you squeeze some between your fingers; stir in a bit more water if needed.

Turn the dough out onto a work surface, form it into a disc, and wrap it in plastic. Refrigerate the dough for at least 30 minutes before rolling it out.

Melt the butter in a small saucepan over medium heat. Add the leeks and cook, stirring occasionally, until just tender, about 5 minutes. The leeks shouldn't brown; reduce the heat if needed. Season lightly with salt and pepper and set aside to cool.

Preheat the oven to 400 degrees F.

Roll out the chilled dough on a lightly floured surface to a roughly 12-inch circle, and use it to line a 9- to 10-inch quiche or pie pan. Press the dough gently down the sides of the pan to be sure it is evenly covering the bottom. Using kitchen shears or a small knife, trim the outer edge of the dough to a ½-inch overhang, then fold that edge under and use your fingers to flute the pastry edge.

Prick the bottom of the shell with the tines of a fork, line the pastry shell with a piece of foil or parchment paper, and add pie weights or dry beans to cover the bottom. Bake the pastry shell until the edges are set, about 10 minutes. Take the pan from the oven, remove the foil and weights, and continue baking the crust until it is lightly browned and the bottom no longer looks raw, 3 to 5 minutes more. (If the bottom of the shell starts to puff up, prick the dough again.) Take the crust from the oven and let cool for about 15 minutes; reduce the oven temperature to 375 degrees F.

Scatter the sautéed leeks over the bottom of the pastry shell. Pick over the crabmeat to remove any bits of shell or cartilage. If using king or snow crab leg meat, cut it into medium dice. Squeeze the crab gently to remove excess liquid. Arrange the crab evenly over the leeks and sprinkle the Gruyère over the crab.

In a medium bowl, whisk together the eggs to blend, then whisk in the half-and-half with a good pinch each of salt and pepper. Pour the custard over the filling. Bake the quiche until the top is lightly browned and a knife inserted in the center comes out clean, 30 to 40 minutes. Let it sit for about 5 minutes before cutting it into wedges to serve. The quiche can also be served at room temperature, though it needs to be refrigerated if you won't be eating it right away.

Hash Brown Cakes with Crab

MAKES 6 SERVINGS

6 to 8 ounces crabmeat (any cooked crabmeat, mix of flake and lump ideal)

½ cup finely chopped onion

¼ cup finely chopped fresh flat-leaf (Italian) parsley

Kosher salt and freshly ground black pepper

2 medium russet potatoes (about 1½ pounds)

1 large egg, beaten

Mild olive oil, for cooking

When everyday hash browns won't do, there is nothing like a dose of gorgeous crabmeat to rise to the occasion. These aren't quite diner-style hash browns, and not trying to be latkes. Somewhere in between, you'll get the crisp crunch of fried potato on the surface, and a tender inside with the pockets of sweet crabmeat throughout. Serve them alongside your favorite egg dish for breakfast or brunch.

Pick over the crabmeat to remove any bits of shell or cartilage. If using king or snow crab leg meat, cut it into medium dice. If any of the other meat pieces are quite large, break them into a few smaller pieces. Squeeze the crab gently to remove excess liquid.

In a large bowl, combine the crabmeat, onion, parsley, and a good pinch each of salt and pepper. Stir to mix.

Heat a large, heavy skillet over medium heat. Preheat the oven to 200 degrees F.

While the skillet is heating, peel the potatoes and coarsely grate them on the large holes of a grater. Grab a good handful of the grated potato and squeeze it well over the sink to draw off excess liquid, then add the potato to the bowl with the crab. Continue squeezing the remaining potato in the same way. When all the potato has been added, add the egg and toss the ingredients well to thoroughly blend.

Add about ⅛ inch of oil to the heated skillet. Scoop up about ¼ cup of the potato mixture and carefully add it to the skillet, using a spatula to help form a tidy mound if some of it goes astray. Repeat with more portions of the potato mixture, allowing about 1 inch between the cakes so they're not crowding the pan. Cook the cakes undisturbed until nicely browned on the bottom, 4 to 5 minutes. About halfway through that time, use the flat side of the spatula to press down evenly on each cake to compress it a bit.

Turn the cakes over and continue cooking until nicely browned on the other side, 4 to 5 minutes more. Transfer the cakes to a wire rack set on a baking sheet and keep warm in the oven while cooking the remaining potato mixture in the same way. You will likely need to add more oil to the skillet for each batch; they won't brown and crisp well without it. You should get about 12 cakes total.

Crab Benedict

MAKES 4 SERVINGS

Crab: any cooked crabmeat, lump is luxurious

For the hollandaise sauce

½ cup unsalted butter

2 tablespoons water

2 large egg yolks

1 tablespoon freshly squeezed lemon juice

½ teaspoon finely grated orange zest

¼ teaspoon finely grated lemon zest

Kosher salt and freshly ground white pepper

••••

2 plain English muffins

4 ounces crabmeat

2 tablespoons distilled white vinegar

4 large eggs

1 teaspoon minced fresh chervil or chives

Already an indulgence, with its combination of freshly poached eggs and rich hollandaise sauce, this breakfast classic is made even more special when plump crab replaces the traditional ham as a bed for the eggs. Because the crab-egg-hollandaise combination is so rich, I suggest just one muffin half per serving, but for heartier appetites you could serve two. For an extradecadent brunch, you could skip the muffins and crabmeat and use one of the West Coast Crab Cakes (page 141) or East Coast Crab Cakes (page 144) instead as a base for the poached egg and sauce.

Here the hollandaise sauce, traditionally flavored only with lemon juice, gets added flavor from a touch of lemon and orange zest, making the sauce a bit brighter in flavor. It's important to cook the hollandaise sauce over low heat so the egg yolks cook gently and thicken smoothly without becoming grainy. If your burner won't maintain low heat, cook the sauce in a double boiler or in a bowl set over, but not touching, a pan of simmering water.

Preheat the oven to 200 degrees F.

To make the hollandaise sauce, melt the butter in a small saucepan over medium-low heat. Once fully melted, use a small spoon to skim off and discard the milk solids that collect on the surface of the melted butter; set aside.

In another small saucepan, whisk together the water and egg yolks until blended. Set the saucepan over low heat and cook, whisking constantly, until the mixture has about doubled in volume and is frothy and thick, 5 to 7 minutes.

Take the pan from the heat and whisk in the melted butter in a thin, steady stream, leaving behind the milky sediment in the bottom of the pan. Whisk the lemon juice and zests into the sauce, along with salt and pepper to taste. Keep the sauce warm over very low heat or over a pan of hot water.

Split and toast the English muffins and set them on a baking sheet. Pick over the crabmeat to remove any bits of shell or cartilage. If using king or snow crab leg meat, cut it into medium dice. Squeeze the crab gently to remove excess liquid. Divide the crabmeat evenly over the muffins and keep them warm in the oven while poaching the eggs.

Fill a large skillet halfway with water and add the vinegar. Bring the water to a gentle boil over medium-high heat, then carefully crack the eggs into the water. (To avoid scalding your knuckles, you could first crack each egg into a small bowl, then gently tip the egg from the bowl into the water.) Reduce the heat to medium and simmer gently until the egg whites are set but the yolks are still soft, about 3 minutes. Gently slosh some of the water over the top of the eggs a few times during cooking to help set the surface of the yolks.

Scoop out the eggs with a slotted spoon, drain gently on paper towels, and set the eggs on the crab-topped muffins. Set each muffin on a warmed plate, spoon the hollandaise sauce over, and sprinkle with the chervil. Serve right away.

Crab & Mushroom Dutch Baby

MAKES 6 TO 8 SERVINGS

Crab: any cooked crabmeat, lump is luxurious

6 ounces crabmeat

7 tablespoons unsalted butter, divided

4 large mushrooms (about 6 ounces), wiped clean, trimmed, and diced

¼ cup finely chopped green onion

½ cup moderately packed slivered fresh spinach leaves (see note, page 60)

½ teaspoon kosher salt, plus more for seasoning

Freshly ground black pepper

4 large eggs

1 cup whole milk

1 cup all-purpose flour

½ teaspoon kosher salt

→

This is inspired by revisiting the beloved brunch treat, the dutch baby (or German pancake, by which name you may know it). So often served sweetly with powdered sugar and lemon or a fruit topping, this dish can also be savory. It makes quite a glorious presentation with the batter puffed up high and browned around the edges; it's a dish to consider serving from the center of the table, cutting into it only after the initial oohs and aahs have died down. Beyond brunch, this could be cut into smaller pieces and served as an appetizer as well.

There is something magic about the cast iron pan in this recipe. Its dense, heavy construction holds heat with determination and creates a very striking and brown puffy edge for this dish. I've tried it in a less substantial, everyday stainless steel skillet and while the results are delicious and worthy, they're not as dramatic and puffed-crisp around the edges as you'll get from the cast iron pan.

Preheat the oven to 425 degrees F.

Pick over the crabmeat to remove any bits of shell or cartilage. If using king or snow crab leg meat, cut it into medium dice. If any of the other meat pieces are quite large, break them into a few smaller pieces. Squeeze the crab gently to remove excess liquid.

CONTINUED

....

2 tablespoons freshly grated Parmesan cheese

NOTE: To sliver greens such as the spinach here, stack 5 to 6 leaves and roll them up lengthwise in a moderately snug cylinder. Cut across the cylinder to form thin strips, which might range from very thin (known as *chiffonade* among chefs) to broader strips of an inch thick or more, depending on the use.

Melt 1 tablespoon of the butter in a medium skillet over medium heat. Add the mushrooms and green onion and cook, stirring occasionally, until tender and any liquid given off by the mushrooms has evaporated, 3 to 4 minutes. Transfer the vegetables to a medium bowl and stir in the crab, then stir in the spinach with a good pinch each of salt and pepper (the spinach will wilt slightly, which is the plan).

Put the remaining 6 tablespoons of butter (in one single piece, not cut up) in a 10- to 11-inch cast iron skillet and put the skillet in the oven to preheat while making the batter.

Blend the eggs in a blender on high speed for 30 seconds. Add the milk, flour, and salt, then blend for 30 to 60 seconds longer until very smooth and evenly blended.

When the butter is fully melted, take the skillet from the oven and gently pour the batter into the center. Scatter the crab mixture over most of the center, leaving the outer 1-inch perimeter of the batter free of crab. Sprinkle the Parmesan over the crab, then return the skillet to the oven and bake until well puffed and nicely browned, 20 to 25 minutes.

Set the skillet on a trivet in the center of the table and cut into wedges to serve. Or, simply cut it in the kitchen and serve.

Savory Crab Blintzes with Dill

MAKES 4 TO 8 SERVINGS

Crab: any cooked crabmeat

For the crepes

1 cup all-purpose flour

½ teaspoon kosher salt

3 large eggs

1¼ cups whole milk

2 tablespoons unsalted butter, melted and cooled, plus more for cooking the crepes and for baking dish

2 teaspoons minced fresh dill

....

8 ounces crabmeat

1 (15-ounce) container part-skim ricotta cheese

½ cup small-curd cottage cheese

→

In this savory twist on blintzes, the crepe batter contains fresh dill, adding flavor, aroma, and flecks of vibrant green to enclose the rich filling of ricotta with delicate crab. Add some scrambled eggs and fresh fruit, and your day's off to a great start. Two blintzes per person is a substantial brunch main course; if you have a number of other things on the menu, you may prefer to serve one per person. And they'll be delicious as an appetizer course as well. Any extra crepes can be frozen for later use, wrapped well in plastic wrap.

To make the crepes, in a medium bowl, combine the flour and salt and stir with a fork to mix, then make a well in the center. Break the eggs into a small bowl and beat with the fork just to mix. Add the milk to the eggs and stir to blend. Pour the milk mixture into the well in the flour and begin incorporating the flour just until mixed. Avoid overmixing; the batter may have some tiny lumps, which is fine. Add the melted butter and dill and stir just to incorporate. Cover and refrigerate for 1 to 2 hours before cooking the crepes.

Lightly coat an 8-inch crepe pan or medium nonstick skillet with melted butter and heat it over medium heat (I like to use paper towel dipped in melted butter to quickly spread an even coating of the butter). Stir the batter once again

CONTINUED

2 tablespoons freshly squeezed lemon juice

2 tablespoons minced fresh flat-leaf (Italian) parsley

1 teaspoon minced fresh dill

½ teaspoon finely grated lemon zest

Kosher salt and freshly ground black pepper

to remix it. Add a scant ¼ cup of the batter to the pan and quickly but gently swirl the pan so the batter evenly coats the base. Cook the crepe until the surface turns from shiny to dull and the edges are just beginning to curl, about 1 minute. Using a small spatula, carefully flip the crepe and cook on the second side until lightly browned on the bottom, 30 to 60 seconds longer.

Transfer the crepe to a plate and continue with the remaining batter, stacking the cooked crepes one on top of the other. It's very common for the first (and sometimes second) crepe to be a total failure, so don't think twice about tossing out early crepes that don't work. You need 8 crepes for this recipe and will have batter enough to make extra (they freeze well, securely wrapped in a couple layers of plastic wrap).

Preheat the oven to 350 degrees F. Lightly butter a 9-by-13-inch baking dish.

To make the filling, pick over the crabmeat to remove any bits of shell or cartilage. If using king or snow crab leg meat, cut it into small dice. If any of the other meat pieces are quite large, break them into a few smaller pieces. Squeeze the crab gently to remove excess liquid.

In a medium bowl, combine the ricotta and cottage cheeses and stir to blend. Stir in the crab, then add the lemon juice, parsley, dill, and lemon zest and stir to blend. Season with a pinch each of salt and pepper.

Lay one crepe on the work surface with the more attractive side down. Spoon about ⅓ cup of the blintz filling into the center of the crepe and spread it out a bit to form a rectangle. Fold in the sides of the crepe over the filling, then fold down the top edge, and finally fold the bottom edge up, making a tidy rectangular package.

Set the blintz, folded side down, in the baking dish, and repeat with the remaining crepes and filling. Lightly brush the tops of the blintzes with more melted butter and bake until they are heated through, about 20 minutes.

Transfer the blintzes to individual plates, serving 1 or 2 per person.

Crab & Artichoke Frittata

MAKES 6 TO 8 SERVINGS

Crab: any cooked crabmeat

1 lemon, halved (if using fresh artichokes)

2 large whole artichokes, or 4 canned artichoke bottoms

2 tablespoons unsalted butter

½ cup thinly sliced red onion

6 to 8 ounces crabmeat

8 large eggs

Kosher salt and freshly ground black pepper

I'm an artichoke purist, I guess, finding that prepared artichokes—whether canned bottoms or bottled hearts—are always disappointing compared to their fresh counterparts. For that reason, this recipe starts with a couple of whole artichokes to be trimmed down to the bottoms and simmered. For a shortcut, you can definitely use canned artichoke bottoms; they tend to be smaller than what you'd get from a typical whole fresh artichoke, so use twice as many. You can also use blanched asparagus in place of the artichokes.

Fill a medium bowl with cold water and squeeze the juice from one lemon half into it, dropping the lemon half into the water as well. (If using canned artichoke bottoms, skip to preheating the oven.)

Using a small, sharp knife, cut the stem from one artichoke where it meets the base. With your fingers, pick off a few rows of the tough outer leaves (being careful to avoid any thorny tips) until you begin to see the bulbous outline of the artichoke bottom and the leaf bases are more pale than dark green. Using the knife, trim away the tough green skin covering the base and sides of the artichoke bottom. Rub the cut edge of the remaining lemon half over the artichoke to help avoid discoloration. Holding the remaining cone of leaves with one hand, cut away the leaves about ¼ inch

CONTINUED

above where they meet the artichoke bottom (the fuzzy choke will be removed after the bottoms are cooked). Put the artichoke bottom in the lemon water and repeat with the second artichoke.

Bring a medium pan of salted water to a boil over high heat. While the water is heating, cut a circle of parchment or waxed paper to a size about the same diameter as the pan. Add the artichoke bottoms to the boiling water, reduce the heat to medium, and lay the paper circle on the surface of the water. The paper helps keep the artichokes protected from contact with the air. Cook the artichokes until tender when pierced with the tip of a knife, 20 to 30 minutes, depending on their size. Drain the artichokes and run cold water over them to cool quickly; when cool enough to handle, scoop out the choke with a small spoon and discard it. Set the artichoke bottoms aside.

Preheat the oven to 375 degrees F.

Melt the butter in a medium ovenproof skillet, preferably nonstick, over medium heat. Add the onion and cook, stirring, until it just begins to soften, 3 to 5 minutes. Take the skillet from the heat and spread the onion out evenly over the bottom of the skillet. Cut the artichoke bottoms into ¼-inch slices and arrange them over the onion. Pick over the crabmeat to remove any bits of shell or cartilage.

If using king or snow crab leg meat, cut it into medium dice. Squeeze the crab gently to remove excess liquid. Scatter the crab over the vegetables.

Whisk the eggs in a medium bowl until well blended, then whisk in a good pinch each of salt and pepper. Pour the eggs gently into the skillet and return it to medium heat until the bottom is set and the edges are beginning to firm up, 5 to 7 minutes. Transfer the skillet to the oven and bake just until the top is set and the eggs are cooked through (no longer jiggly in the center when the skillet is nudged), 5 to 7 minutes more. Slip the frittata onto a cutting board, cut it into wedges, and serve right away.

Sourdough Bread Pudding with Crab

MAKES 8 SERVINGS

Crab: any cooked crabmeat

Unsalted butter, for buttering

1 small loaf day-old rustic sourdough bread (about 1 pound), cut into ½-inch cubes, divided

2 cups grated sharp cheddar cheese (about 8 ounces), divided

½ cup minced onion

8 to 12 ounces crabmeat

8 large eggs

3 cups whole milk

2 tablespoons minced fresh flat-leaf (Italian) parsley

1 tablespoon minced fresh chives

Kosher salt and freshly ground black pepper

Bread pudding shows up in a lot of guises these days, making an appearance here at the breakfast table with tangy sourdough bread holding sweet crabmeat in an herby custard. Feel free to use a non-sourdough bread if you prefer.

Preheat the oven to 350 degrees F. Generously butter a 9-by-13-inch baking dish.

Scatter about half of the bread cubes evenly in the baking dish, and sprinkle 1½ cups of the cheese over the bread, followed by the onion. Pick over the crabmeat to remove any bits of shell or cartilage. If using king or snow crab leg meat, cut it into small dice. Scatter the crab over the onion, then top the crab with the remaining bread cubes.

In a medium bowl, whisk the eggs to blend, then whisk in the milk, parsley, and chives with a good pinch each of salt and pepper. Pour the egg mixture over the bread and let sit for about 10 minutes, pressing the cubes down so they evenly soak up the custard.

Sprinkle the remaining ½ cup cheese over the top and bake the bread pudding until the top is lightly browned and a knife inserted in the center of the dish comes out clean, about 45 minutes. If the top is well browned before the eggy custard is cooked, loosely cover the dish with a piece of foil. Let the bread pudding sit for a few minutes before cutting it into pieces to serve.

APPETIZERS

Fresh Spring Rolls with Crab

MAKES 4 TO 8 SERVINGS

Crab: any cooked crabmeat, lump is luxurious

For the dipping sauce

3 tablespoons unseasoned rice vinegar

3 tablespoons freshly squeezed lime juice (from 1 to 2 limes)

1 teaspoon fish sauce, plus more if needed

½ teaspoon minced or pressed garlic

½ teaspoon sugar

½ teaspoon sriracha or other hot chile sauce, plus more if needed

••••

1½ ounces dry cellophane (bean thread) noodles

8 to 12 ounces crabmeat

8 (8-inch) round rice paper wrappers

Fried spring rolls can be addicting for their crispness, but I prefer the unfried version that allows the flavors of individual ingredients to shine more boldly. Fresh herbs and plump crab—with crunch from lettuce and body from cellophane noodles—make these simple spring rolls as easy to enjoy as they are to make. Rice paper wrappers come in brittle, semitranslucent rounds that need to be dampened before using. Look for them in Asian markets or on well-stocked grocery shelves near other Asian products.

To make the dipping sauce, in a small bowl, combine the vinegar, lime juice, fish sauce, garlic, sugar, and sriracha and stir to mix. Set aside while making the spring rolls.

Put the cellophane noodles in a small heatproof bowl and pour boiling water over them to cover. Let soak until tender, about 5 minutes, then drain well and let cool. When cool, cut the noodles into sections about 3 inches long, using kitchen shears or a knife. Don't worry about the evenness of the pieces; you're just making the noodles easier to handle by portioning them a bit.

Pick over the crabmeat to remove any bits of shell or cartilage. If using king or snow crab leg meat, cut it into roughly 2-inch sections. If any pieces are quite thick, halve them lengthwise. Squeeze the crab gently to remove excess liquid.

8 small green lettuce leaves, rinsed, dried, and halved (ribs discarded)

1 cup coarsely grated carrot

½ cup loosely packed fresh mint leaves

½ cup loosely packed fresh cilantro leaves

Fill a shallow dish, such as a pie pan, with water. Dip one of the rice paper wrappers in the water until evenly moistened, 5 to 10 seconds, and lift it up to allow excess water to drip off. Lay the wrapper on the work surface (it will become fully pliable in less than a minute) and begin layering ingredients on the wrapper, first setting a piece of lettuce horizontally just below the center point. On top of the lettuce, arrange even layers of about one eighth each of the cellophane noodles, carrot, mint leaves, and cilantro leaves, then set one-eighth of the crabmeat on top. Fold the bottom of the wrapper upward over the filling, then fold in each side and roll the package away from you to fully and snugly enclose the filling in a cylinder. Repeat with the remaining wrappers and filling ingredients.

Cut each of the spring rolls in half crosswise, at a slight angle, and arrange the halves on individual plates or a platter. Stir the dipping sauce to remix and taste for seasoning, adding a bit more fish sauce and/or sriracha to taste. For individual servings, provide a small dish of dipping sauce for each diner, or leave the sauce in a single bowl if serving from a platter.

Firecracker Crab Cocktail

MAKES 6 TO 8 SERVINGS

Crab: any cooked crabmeat, lump is luxurious; good dip for stone claws

For the cocktail sauce

½ cup ketchup

¼ cup chili sauce

2 tablespoons horseradish, preferably freshly grated

2 tablespoons freshly squeezed lemon juice (from about 1 small lemon)

2 teaspoons minced green onion tops

½ teaspoon Worcestershire sauce

• • • •

Hot pepper sauce

12 to 16 ounces crabmeat

1 lemon, cut into wedges, for serving

Here's an example of "simple is best": no lettuce, no filler, no frills, just crab and good homemade cocktail sauce. You could use three-quarters cup of ketchup rather than both ketchup and chili sauce, though the latter adds more texture to the mix. To be clear, this is old-school tomato-based chili sauce in a bottle, not a hot, peppery sauce.

I like to put a bit of the cocktail sauce in the dish first so that when you get to the bottom you still have some of the zesty sauce for the last of the crab.

To make the cocktail sauce, in a small bowl, combine the ketchup, chili sauce, horseradish, lemon juice, green onion, Worcestershire, and hot pepper sauce to taste and stir to mix. Refrigerate until ready to serve. The flavor will be best if it's made at least 1 hour before serving, to allow the flavors to meld, but it can be made up to 2 days in advance.

Just before serving, spoon about 1 tablespoon of the cocktail sauce into individual small dishes. Pick over the crabmeat to remove any bits of shell or cartilage. If using king or snow crab leg meat, cut it into medium dice. Divide the crab among the dishes. Spoon the rest of the cocktail sauce over the crab, set the dishes on small plates, and place the lemon wedges on the plates.

Crab Pizza with Arugula & Fresh Mozzarella

MAKES 4 SERVINGS

Crab: any cooked crabmeat, lump is luxurious

For the pizza dough

1 cup all-purpose flour, plus more for flouring

½ teaspoon kosher salt

⅓ cup warm water (105 to 110 degrees F)

1 teaspoon active dry yeast

1 tablespoon mild olive oil, plus more for oiling

••••

6 to 8 ounces crabmeat

4 ounces fresh mozzarella, cut into ⅛-inch-thick slices

Fine cornmeal, for sprinkling

2 tablespoons extra-virgin olive oil, divided

This simple pizza recipe has no sauce to speak of, just a brush of extra-virgin olive oil over the dough before it is topped with crab and fresh mozzarella. The peppery crunch of arugula added just before serving makes a delightful finish. And I like the unexpected touch of heat from red pepper flakes too, though that's an optional element. This small, thin-crusted pizza is meant to be served in wedges as a first course or snack, but it could also be served whole as a single main course serving.

Try to find fresh mozzarella for this recipe. You can use firmer, more shreddable mozzarella, though its flavor and texture aren't as luscious as fresh.

To make the pizza dough, in a medium bowl, stir together the flour and salt, making a well in the center. Pour the warm water into the well and sprinkle the yeast over the water, stirring it into the water gently. Let sit until the yeast is frothy, about 5 minutes. Stir the dough, gently drawing in the flour from the edges and adding the mild olive oil as you go. When the dough becomes cohesive and forms a ball, transfer it to a lightly floured work surface and knead for a few minutes until it becomes smooth and satiny.

Put the dough in a lightly oiled bowl (it can be the same bowl you mixed the dough in), and turn it to evenly but lightly coat the dough with oil. Cover the bowl with a clean kitchen towel and set aside in a warm place until the dough has risen by about half, about 1 hour.

¼ teaspoon dried red pepper flakes (optional)

2 handfuls arugula, rinsed, dried, and tough stems removed (about 1 cup moderately packed)

Preheat the oven to 450 degrees F. (If using a pizza stone, follow the manufacturer's instructions, which generally include preheating the stone with the oven.)

Pick over the crabmeat to remove any bits of shell or cartilage. If using king or snow crab leg meat, cut it into medium dice. Squeeze the crab gently to remove excess liquid. Lay the mozzarella slices on a double layer of paper towel to drain. Drawing off excess moisture from the crab and cheese will help keep the pizza from getting soggy.

Turn the risen dough out onto a lightly floured work surface and knead it gently. Press the dough into a rough circle and roll it out to about 12 inches across. (If using a baking sheet rather than a pizza stone, roll the dough into a more rectangular shape that will easily fit on your baking sheet.) The dough may start springing back after a bit of rolling. When this happens, let the dough rest for a minute or two before continuing.

If using a pizza stone that is preheated in the oven, sprinkle a thin layer of cornmeal on a peel or on an upside-down baking sheet, and lay the dough on top. Otherwise, simply sprinkle the cornmeal on a heavy baking sheet and top with the dough. Brush about 1 tablespoon of the extra-virgin olive oil over the dough, leaving a 1-inch perimeter that is not oiled. Scatter the crabmeat evenly over the oiled dough and lay the cheese slices over the crab, in a random pattern. Sprinkle with the pepper flakes.

CONTINUED

For the pizza-stone bakers, slide the pizza carefully but quickly from the peel onto the preheated stone (manufacturer's instructions should have pointers on this trick). Otherwise, put the baking sheet in the oven and, either way, bake until the crust is firm and the cheese is gently melted, 12 to 16 minutes. Take the pizza from the oven and scatter the arugula leaves evenly on top. Drizzle the remaining 1 tablespoon of extra-virgin olive oil over the arugula, cut the pizza into wedges, and serve.

Stone Crab Claws with Mustard-Horseradish Sauce

MAKES 4 TO 6 SERVINGS

Crab: made with stone crab claws in mind, but can be a dip for other cooked crab

2 tablespoons yellow or brown mustard seeds (or a blend of both)

2 tablespoons water

2 tablespoons white wine vinegar

½ cup mayonnaise

¼ cup sour cream

1 teaspoon prepared horseradish

½ teaspoon Worcestershire sauce

½ teaspoon kosher salt

2 to 3 pounds cooked stone crab claws, thawed if frozen, shells partially cracked

Stone crab claws are a special treat, there's no doubt about it. To showcase the rich-tasting meat, the claws are usually served very simply, often with the longstanding traditional accompaniment of mustard sauce. Given the sweetness of the meat, I thought a subtle dose of peppery horseradish would be a welcome addition to the mustard. Stone crab claws range in size (and price per pound); any claws will work here. About half a pound per person is ideal for an appetizer portion.

For some homemade flair in the sauce I start here with whole mustard seeds, which need to soak for a couple of days before grinding into the sauce. The result is a mustard with a deeper, more peppery mustard flavor. You can certainly skip that step and simply use three tablespoons of Dijon mustard (smooth or grainy) and omit the mustard seeds, water, and vinegar. If using the seeds, finishing the sauce at least a few hours before you plan to serve it will be a good idea, to allow the flavors to meld.

In a small bowl, combine the mustard seeds, water, and vinegar and stir to mix. Loosely cover the bowl and let it sit at room temperature until the seeds are plumped and more tender, about 2 days, stirring a few times each day.

CONTINUED

STONE CRAB CLAWS WITH MUSTARD-HORSERADISH SAUCE, CONTINUED

Drain the seeds from the liquid, reserving both. In a food processor, put the seeds and 2 tablespoons of the liquid (the rest can be discarded) and pulse 10 or 12 times to break up some of the mustard seeds, scraping down the sides of the bowl 2 or 3 times. Add the mayonnaise, sour cream, horseradish, Worcestershire sauce, and salt. Pulse a few quick times to blend, then process for 30 seconds until well blended, scraping down the sides once or twice. (Refrigerate the sauce if not serving right away.)

Transfer the mustard sauce to individual dishes. Arrange the crab claws on plates, with the sauce alongside for dipping.

Choux Puffs with Curried Crab

MAKES 4 TO 6 SERVINGS

Crab: any cooked crabmeat, flake ideal

1 cup water

½ cup unsalted butter, cut into 1-inch pieces

1 teaspoon kosher salt

1 cup all-purpose flour

4 large eggs

For the filling:

1 tablespoon unsalted butter

⅓ cup finely chopped green onion

1 teaspoon curry powder

6 ounces crabmeat

1 tablespoon dry sherry

Kosher salt and freshly ground black pepper

→

This recipe comes with a wink and a nod to Trader Vic's restaurants, founded by Victor Bergeron, which helped bring the exotic flavors of the Pacific Islands to the United States during the white-bread era of the mid-twentieth century. I can still remember what an adventure it was to eat at his Seattle restaurant, long closed but once an exotic refuge in the Westin Hotel (originally the Washington Plaza Hotel) downtown.

The choux puff recipe will make about twice as many puffs as you'll need, but it's not practical to make in smaller batches. You can either double the filling recipe if you will be serving a crowd, or freeze the extra puffs: once cooled, arrange them on a baking sheet and freeze them until solid, then transfer them to an airtight container to freeze for up to one month. When you're ready to serve them, simply arrange the frozen puffs on a baking sheet and reheat at 350 degrees F before using. It's an outstanding shortcut to have on hand for future cocktail snacks!

Preheat the oven to 400 degrees F. Line 2 baking sheets with parchment paper or silicone baking mats.

To make the *choux* puffs, in a medium saucepan over medium heat, combine the water, butter, and salt and warm until the butter is fully melted. The liquid should not boil; reduce the heat if needed. Add the flour all at once and stir gently with a wooden spoon until fully incorporated.

CONTINUED

½ cup (4 ounces) cream cheese, softened at room temperature

¼ cup finely chopped water chestnuts or celery

Continue to stir the flour, a bit more vigorously now, until it forms a smooth dough that pulls away from the sides of the pan, about 1 minute longer.

Take the pan from the heat and add 1 of the eggs. (To help avoid any shell getting into the dough, you can first break the egg into a ramekin or other small dish. After removing any stray shell bits, tip the egg into the saucepan.) As soon as the egg is added, stir well to blend fully into the dough. Add the remaining eggs one at a time in the same fashion, creating a smooth and glossy dough.

Spoon the *choux* dough into a pastry bag fitted with a ¾-inch plain tip. Pipe the dough into rounds of about 1½ inch in diameter on the lined baking sheets, with 1 inch between them. (Alternatively, form the dough with two spoons—see Alternative to Piping on the facing page.) The tops of the mounds should be smooth; if there are any peaks, even them out with the back of a spoon or your finger. When one baking sheet is filled, bake until browned and well puffed, about 25 minutes. Shortly before the first tray is done baking, pipe the remaining dough onto the second baking sheet and bake as for the first. Let the *choux* puffs cool for a few minutes on the baking sheets, then transfer them to a wire rack to cool completely.

To make the filling, melt the butter in a medium skillet over medium heat. Add the green onion and cook, stirring, until softened and aromatic but not browned, 1 to 2 minutes. Add the curry powder and stir to mix, cooking for about 1 minute longer. Set the skillet aside to cool.

Pick over the crabmeat to remove any bits of shell or cartilage. If using king or snow crab leg meat, cut it into small dice. If any of the other meat pieces are quite large, break them into a few smaller pieces. Squeeze the crab gently to remove excess liquid. Add the crabmeat and sherry with a good pinch each of salt and pepper to the curry mixture and stir to mix, then stir in the softened cream cheese and water chestnuts until evenly blended. You can make the filling up to 4 hours ahead and refrigerate; let it come to room temperature before serving.

Preheat the oven to 450 degrees F.

Use a small serrated knife to halve 16 *choux* puffs and spoon a generous tablespoon of the crab filling into each, topping with its lid. Arrange the puffs on a baking sheet and warm in the oven for 3 to 5 minutes. The filling won't be heated through, just lightly warmed, and the tops of the *choux* will crisp up a bit. Transfer the puffs to a platter and serve.

Alternative to Piping

It's traditional to use a pastry bag to pipe choux dough onto baking sheets, forming tidy little mounds. But if you don't have a pastry bag, don't fret. Use a couple regular spoons, scooping up about a generous tablespoon of the dough in one, and using the other to tidily scrape it onto the baking sheet. Do your best to form neat shapes, though they'll self-correct a bit in the oven.

Chirashi Sushi with Crab

As much as I like sushi, it's not something for which I get a hankering to make at home. Sushi chefs are well-armed with the skills, tools, and wide array of top-quality ingredients at hand that make ordering, rather than making, sushi so fully enjoyable. *Chirashi* means "scattered"—this home-style sushi is not wrapped in nori but instead served in a bowl with selected toppings. A particular delight is how much room there is for variations, using different toppings and seasonings to suit your taste.

MAKES 4 TO 6 SERVINGS

Crab: any cooked crabmeat, lump ideal

1 cup short- or medium-grain rice

2 cups plus 2 teaspoons cold water, divided

Kosher salt

1 to 2 teaspoons wasabi powder

⅓ cup unseasoned rice vinegar

2 teaspoons soy sauce

1 teaspoon sugar

8 ounces crabmeat

2 large eggs

1 tablespoon mild olive or vegetable oil

¼ cup slivered fresh shiso leaves (optional)

2 tablespoons minced peeled ginger

2 ounces daikon radish sprouts, or ¼ cup coarsely grated red radish

→

In a medium saucepan, combine the rice, 2 cups of the water, and a good pinch of salt. Bring the water to a boil over medium-high heat, then cover the pan, reduce the heat to low, and cook until the rice is tender and the water fully absorbed, about 20 minutes. Fluff the rice gently with a fork, then cover with the lid to keep warm.

Put the wasabi powder in a small bowl, add the remaining 2 teaspoons water, and stir to make a smooth paste. Stir in the vinegar, soy sauce, and sugar until well blended.

Pick over the crabmeat to remove any bits of shell or cartilage. If using king or snow crab leg meat, cut it across into pieces about 2 inches long; if any of those pieces are quite thick, halve them lengthwise. Put the crab in a medium bowl. Drizzle about 2 tablespoons of the vinegar mixture over and toss to mix; set aside.

CONTINUED

¼ cup slivered nori (see note below)

1 tablespoon toasted sesame seeds

4 to 6 thin lemon slices, for serving

Transfer the warm rice to a medium bowl and pour the remaining vinegar mixture over, stirring well with the fork to evenly coat the rice. Set aside to cool.

In a small bowl, beat the eggs with a pinch of salt. Heat half of the oil in a medium skillet, preferably nonstick, over medium heat. Add half of the egg mixture and swirl the pan so it evenly coats the base. Cook until set, about 1 minute, then flip the egg over to cook for about 30 seconds on the other side. Transfer the egg to a cutting board and repeat with the remaining egg, setting the second cooked round on top of the first. Let cool, then roll the egg into a loose cylinder and cut across into roughly ¼-inch slices, separating the slices with your fingers.

Stir the shiso and ginger into the cooled rice and arrange it in an even layer in the bottom of individual bowls. Scatter the slivers of egg over the rice, followed by the daikon sprouts. Arrange the crab evenly over the sprouts, then form a small mound of the nori slivers in the center. Scatter the sesame seeds over all, add a lemon slice to the side in each bowl, and serve.

NOTE: Nori—thin sheets of dried seaweed—comes in rather large packets that may be quite a lot more than you'd likely get through in other recipes. Thankfully, small toasted (and often seasoned) sheets of nori have become a popular snack item. You may find the snack-size packets of nori that can be used for the slivered nori that is among the rice toppings. I'd opt for the plain type rather than seasoned, though a little sesame flavor would be nice. Kitchen shears will be the easiest way to sliver the sheets, whichever type you use.

Crab Cornmeal Fritters with Lime Aioli

MAKES 4 TO 6 SERVINGS

Crab: any cooked crabmeat, flake ideal

For the lime aioli

1 large egg yolk

1 tablespoon freshly squeezed lime juice

2 cloves garlic, finely chopped

¾ cup mild olive oil

½ teaspoon finely grated lime zest

Kosher salt and freshly ground white pepper

••••

6 ounces crabmeat

Vegetable oil, for frying

½ cup cornmeal

¼ cup all-purpose flour, plus more if needed

1½ teaspoons baking powder

→

These fritters hint at hush puppies; the nuttiness of cornmeal is a tasty complement to the sweet crabmeat. This is ideal for flakier meat that will blend well into the cornmeal batter, though a few larger pieces of meat here and there provide decadent nuggets to bite into. For notes on a manual version of making the aioli, see Making Mayo on page 153.

Temperature control when deep-frying is important, not only for your safety but to assure that the fritters will be cooked through, not still gooey, when the outside is nicely browned. It's best to use a cooking thermometer to keep tabs on the heat level while you're frying. The fritters will be at their best if served right away.

To make the lime aioli, in a food processor, combine the egg yolk, lime juice, and garlic and pulse to blend. With the motor running, begin adding the oil, a few drops at a time, until the mixture starts to thicken, showing that an emulsion is beginning to form. Continue adding the oil in a thin, steady stream. When all the oil has been added, add the lime zest, with a good pinch each of salt and pepper, and pulse a few more times to mix evenly. Transfer the aioli to a bowl, cover with plastic wrap, and refrigerate until ready to serve. The aioli will have a more pronounced flavor if made a couple of hours before serving, but let it sit at room temperature for at least 10 to 15 minutes before serving. (Makes 1 scant cup.)

CONTINUED

1 teaspoon finely grated lime zest

½ teaspoon kosher salt

⅛ teaspoon freshly ground black pepper

¼ cup whole milk, plus more if needed

1 large egg, lightly beaten

Lime wedges, for serving

Pick over the crabmeat to remove any bits of shell or cartilage. If using king or snow crab leg meat, cut it into small dice. If any of the other meat pieces are quite large, break them into a few smaller pieces. Squeeze the crab gently to remove excess liquid.

Preheat the oven to 200 degrees F.

In a large, heavy saucepan heat about 2 inches of oil (the oil should not come more than halfway up the sides of the pan) over medium heat to about 350 degrees F (use a deep-fry thermometer to check the temperature). While the oil is heating, in a medium bowl, combine the cornmeal, flour, baking powder, lime zest, salt, and pepper and stir to mix. Add the milk and egg and stir to make a smooth batter. Add the crab to the batter and stir to blend evenly. The batter should be moist and firm enough to hold its shape when lifted in a spoon, but not stiff. If on the stiff side, stir in a bit more milk. If too soft, stir in a bit more flour.

When the oil is hot enough, scoop up a generous tablespoonful of the fritter batter and use another spoon to transfer it gently into the hot oil. Cook 4 or 5 fritters at a time until they are nicely browned and cooked through, about 3 minutes, carefully turning them once or twice so they cook evenly. Scoop out the fritters with a slotted spoon and drain on a wire rack set on a baking sheet and keep them warm in the oven while cooking the rest of the batter. Allow the oil to reheat as necessary between batches.

Arrange the warm fritters on individual plates, spoon some of the lime aioli alongside, and add a lime wedge to each plate. You can also serve the fritters on a platter, with the aioli in a bowl at the center and lime wedges scattered around. Serve right away.

Keeping Warm & Crisp

For so long I would drain just-fried foods such as these fritters on a double layer of paper towels or maybe brown paper on occasion. But depending on how moist the food is that's been fried and how long it will be held, the portion touching the paper can get a little humid and lose some of its crisp character, not to mention sit in the draining oil. I'm now more likely to set these just-fried foods on a wire rack instead, which helps preserve the crispness. I have one such rack that fits perfectly within my favorite rimmed baking sheets. This is particularly handy for items to be kept warm in a low (about 200 degrees F or so) oven—one easy unit to handle. To catch oil drips, you can lay some paper towels or brown paper beneath the rack if you like.

Crab & Corn Soufflé

MAKES 4 TO 6 SERVINGS

Crab: any cooked crabmeat, flake ideal

3 tablespoons unsalted butter, plus more for buttering

Dry bread crumbs, for coating

6 ounces crabmeat

1 ear tender sweet corn (white or yellow), husks and silk removed

¼ cup all-purpose flour

1 cup half-and-half

1½ teaspoons Dijon mustard

½ teaspoon kosher salt

⅛ teaspoon freshly ground white or black pepper

¼ cup finely chopped green onion

2 large egg yolks

4 large egg whites

It's much easier to make a soufflé than you may think, and there's nothing quite so impressive when it comes fresh from the oven, all puffed and richly browned. The simple combination of flavors from the corn and crab is quite wonderful, but if you'd like to add herbs, feel free. I'd suggest a couple tablespoons of minced fresh chives, chervil, or parsley. This soufflé could also be served as a light main course.

Preheat the oven to 375 degrees F. Generously butter a 1½-quart soufflé dish and coat it with dry bread crumbs, tapping the dish gently while it's upside-down to remove the excess. Pick over the crabmeat to remove any bits of shell or cartilage. If using king or snow crab leg meat, cut it into small dice. If any of the other meat pieces are quite large, break them into a few smaller pieces. Squeeze the crab gently to remove excess liquid.

Trim the stem end of the ear of corn and set it upright on a cutting board. Use a sharp knife to cut downward to remove a few rows of the kernels at a time, turning the ear and repeating until you have cut away all of the kernels. Try to avoid cutting too deeply, so you get mostly tender kernels and not the tougher core. Using the back of the knife, repeat the same motion around the ear again, this time scraping away any of the tender corn still clinging to the core. You should have about 1 generous cup of corn.

Melt the butter in a medium saucepan over medium heat. Add the flour and cook until it foams up and smells slightly nutty, stirring often with a whisk, 2 to 3 minutes. Add the half-and-half and whisk to mix well. Continue cooking, whisking often, until well thickened, 2 to 3 minutes more. Whisk in the mustard, salt, and pepper. Transfer the soufflé base to a large bowl and stir in the crabmeat, corn, green onion, and egg yolks. Set aside. (The base can be made a few hours in advance and refrigerated, but let it sit at room temperature for a bit to take the chill off before continuing.)

In a medium bowl, using a hand mixer or large whisk, beat the egg whites until moderately stiff peaks form; do not overbeat or they will become grainy. Add one-quarter of the egg whites to the crab mixture and stir to lighten the soufflé base. Gently fold in about half of the remaining egg whites, then fold in the last of the egg whites until thoroughly combined.

Pour the soufflé mixture into the prepared dish, smoothing the top a bit. Bake until it is puffed up and nicely browned on top, 35 to 40 minutes. Serve immediately, using two large spoons to scoop out the soufflé onto individual plates.

Crab & Avocado Tostadas

MAKES 6 TO 8 SERVINGS

Crab: any cooked crabmeat

6 ounces crabmeat

1 ripe but firm avocado

3 tablespoons freshly squeezed lime juice (from 1 to 2 limes)

1 tablespoon minced fresh cilantro

½ teaspoon minced jalapeño

Pinch ground cumin

Kosher salt

6 corn tortillas

2 to 3 tablespoons vegetable oil

2 to 3 tablespoons sour cream (optional)

About ¼ cup loosely packed fresh cilantro leaves

This variation on the tostada makes great cocktail party fare. The tortilla pieces can be cut and toasted in the morning and then stored in an airtight container after they are fully cooled. Or, for a major shortcut, use good store-bought corn chips in place of the home-toasted tortillas, though the long, slender triangles used here make for a more elegant presentation and are sturdier than many commercial chips. The topping is best made not more than an hour before serving.

Pick over the crabmeat to remove any bits of shell or cartilage. If using king or snow crab leg meat, cut it into small dice. Squeeze the crab gently to remove excess liquid. Put the crab in a medium bowl.

Peel and pit the avocado, cut it into small dice, and add it to the bowl with the crab. Drizzle the lime juice over the mixture, and use a fork to lightly mash the avocado while gently blending it with the crab. Add the minced cilantro, jalapeño, and cumin, with a pinch of salt. Stir gently to mix and refrigerate until ready to serve. The crab/avocado mixture should be a bit chunky rather than smooth.

Preheat the oven to 350 degrees F.

Lightly brush both sides of each tortilla with some of the oil. Cut each tortilla in half, then cut about ½ inch from the rounded edge opposite the diameter cut, to square off each half a bit. (These trimmings can be discarded or toasted with the rest of the tortillas as a snack for the cook.) Halve the tortilla pieces diagonally to make two long, slender triangles, and lay the pieces on two baking sheets.

Toast the tortilla pieces in the oven until crisp and lightly browned, about 10 minutes, switching the baking sheets halfway through. Alternatively, you could toast the triangles on one sheet, half at a time. Let the tortilla pieces cool on a wire rack.

Just before serving, scoop a spoonful of the crab/avocado mixture onto the broader end of each tortilla chip. Add a tiny dollop of sour cream, and top with a cilantro leaf. Arrange the tostadas on a platter and serve.

Pan-fried Soft-Shell Crab with Salsa Verde

MAKES 4 TO 6 SERVINGS

Crab: soft-shell blue crab

For the salsa verde:

⅓ cup chopped fresh flat-leaf (Italian) parsley

¼ cup chopped green onion

2 tablespoons drained capers

1 teaspoon chopped fresh thyme

1 teaspoon chopped fresh oregano

1 teaspoon chopped garlic

¼ cup red wine vinegar

3 tablespoons mild olive oil

Kosher salt and freshly ground black pepper

....

1 large egg

2 tablespoons water

→

An abundance of fresh herbs create a strong—and very green—foundation of flavor for this sauce, reflecting the *verde* in its name. You can use other tender herbs that you may have on hand, such as lovage, chervil, or tarragon (though a little tarragon goes a long way so I wouldn't recommend using much of it). The sauce will be most flavorful if it's made at least one hour in advance. This recipe can double as a main course as well, serving two crab per person.

Since soft-shell season is limited to generally the summer months, and the delicate creatures don't travel particularly well in fresh form, many of us will be using frozen, which hold up quite well. Thaw them slowly in the refrigerator overnight, and dry them well before cooking. These will be best fried just before serving to assure the crispest results.

To make the salsa verde, pile together the parsley, green onion, capers, thyme, oregano, and garlic on the chopping board and chop across the pile—back and forth for a minute or so—to more finely chop them and to jump-start melding their flavors together. Transfer the herb mixture to a medium bowl and stir in the vinegar and oil. Season with a good pinch each of salt and pepper and set aside at room temperature, stirring now and then. The salsa will be most flavorful if it's made at least an hour before serving, but it can be made up to 4 hours in advance.

CONTINUED

Kosher salt and freshly ground black pepper

¾ cup all-purpose flour, plus more for sprinkling

4 to 6 soft-shell crab (2½ to 3 ounces each), cleaned and trimmed (see page 38)

½ cup mild olive oil, plus more if needed

Beat the egg well with a fork in a shallow bowl. Add the water and a good pinch each of salt and pepper and beat until well blended. Spread the flour out on a plate. Sprinkle more flour onto a tray large enough to hold the crab. Dip 1 of the crab in the egg, lifting it above the bowl for a few seconds to allow excess to drip off. Lay the crab in the flour on the plate and use your dry hand to coat it well in the flour, patting to remove excess. Transfer the crab to the tray and repeat with the remaining crab, reserving extra flour.

Preheat a large, heavy skillet, preferably cast iron, over medium heat. While the pan is heating, coat the crab once more in flour, patting to remove excess.

When the skillet is hot, add the oil and allow it to heat for a few moments. Place the crab (don't crowd the pan; cook in 2 batches if needed) top-side down and cook until nicely browned, 3 to 4 minutes. Turn the crab over and continue cooking until well browned and crisp, 3 to 4 minutes more. Transfer the crab to a wire rack or paper towels to drain.

Arrange the hot crab on individual plates, spoon the salsa verde over it, and serve.

Sherried Crab & Mushrooms on Toast

MAKES 6 SERVINGS

Crab: any cooked crabmeat, mix of flake and lump ideal

2 tablespoons unsalted butter, divided

1 cup thinly sliced mushrooms

½ cup finely chopped onion

2 tablespoons all-purpose flour

1½ cups half-and-half

8 ounces crabmeat

3 tablespoons dry sherry

Kosher salt and freshly ground black pepper

6 slices white bread, crusts trimmed

2 tablespoons minced fresh flat-leaf (Italian) parsley

This is simple comfort food at its best, a recipe that can be dressed up for a fancy dinner party (serve with a small mesclun salad, tossed with a sherry vinaigrette) or dressed down for a quick midnight snack (forget trimming the bread, just serve the creamy crab mixture on a piece of toast fresh from the toaster). To garnish it in midcentury style, you could scatter some chopped hard-cooked egg on top just before serving.

Melt 1 tablespoon of the butter in a medium skillet over medium heat. Add the mushrooms and onion and sauté until tender, about 5 minutes. Sprinkle the flour over the vegetables and stir for a minute or two to evenly coat them. Add the half-and-half and cook, stirring often, until the sauce is thickened and well blended, 5 to 7 minutes.

Pick over the crabmeat to remove any bits of shell or cartilage. If using king or snow crab leg meat, cut it into medium dice. Add the crab and sherry to the sauce, reduce the heat to medium low, and cook just until the crab is heated through, 2 to 3 minutes. Season the sauce to taste with salt and pepper.

Toast the bread and cut each piece in half diagonally, forming 2 triangles. Butter the toast lightly with the remaining 1 tablespoon butter, and lay 2 triangles, slightly overlapping, in the center of each of 6 warmed small plates. Spoon the crab and sauce over the toast, sprinkle the parsley over, and serve right away.

SOUPS & SANDWICHES

Chilled Tomato Soup with Crab

A handful of sweet crabmeat is an ideal constrast for the zesty, fresh flavors of the vegetables in this gazpacho-like soup. There's no replacement for the flavor and texture of summer's fresh tomatoes—though really good, ripe hothouse tomatoes are the next best thing. Likewise, fresh corn that's tender and sweet, not starchy, is the best choice. This is the essence of summer in a bowl.

MAKES 6 SERVINGS

Crab: any cooked crabmeat, lump is luxurious

1 ear tender sweet corn (white or yellow), husks and silk removed

2 pounds vine-ripe tomatoes, cored, seeded, and coarsely chopped

1 large cucumber, peeled, seeded, and coarsely chopped

1 large red bell pepper, cored, seeded, and coarsely chopped

1 cup chopped red onion

½ cup loosely packed fresh flat-leaf (Italian) parsley leaves

¼ cup loosely packed fresh cilantro leaves

3 tablespoons mild olive oil

Trim the stem end of the ear of corn and set it upright on a cutting board. Use a sharp knife to cut downward to remove a few rows of the kernels at a time, turning the ear and repeating until you have cut away all of the kernels. Try to avoid cutting too deeply so you get mostly tender kernels and not the tougher core. Bring a small saucepan of salted water to a boil over high heat, add the corn kernels, and cook for 1 minute. Drain the corn, run cold water over it to cool, and drain well; refrigerate until ready to serve.

In a food processor, put half each of the tomatoes, cucumber, bell pepper, and onion and pulse until quite finely chopped. Do not thoroughly puree them; you want to keep some texture and crunch. Transfer the mixture to a large bowl and repeat with the remaining vegetables, adding the parsley, cilantro, oil, and garlic to this batch. Stir this mixture into the bowl along with the tomato juice.

2 cloves garlic, finely chopped

3 cups tomato juice, regular or spicy

Hot pepper sauce (optional)

Kosher salt and freshly ground black pepper

8 to 12 ounces crabmeat

(Alternatively, you can prepare the soup in a blender, chopping the vegetables in 4 or 5 batches, though the texture will likely be finer.) Season the soup to taste with hot pepper sauce, salt, and pepper, and refrigerate until ready to serve, at least 1 hour.

To serve, taste the soup for seasoning, adding more salt, pepper, or hot sauce to taste. Ladle the soup into chilled soup bowls and sprinkle with the corn kernels. Pick over the crabmeat to remove any bits of shell or cartilage. If using king or snow crab leg meat, cut it into medium dice. Arrange the crab in a small pile in the center of each bowl. Serve right away.

Lemongrass Broth with Crab Wontons

MAKES 4 SERVINGS

Crab: any cooked crabmeat, flake ideal

Cleaned shells from 2 whole cooked Dungeness crab (not including the carapace)

2 carrots, sliced

2 stalks celery, sliced

2 shallots, sliced

10 slices peeled ginger

4 stalks lemongrass, trimmed and sliced

6 makrut lime leaves, cut into slivers

8 to 10 whole black peppercorns

4 cups fish stock or chicken broth

Soy sauce

¼ cup thinly sliced green onion tops

There's no aroma quite like the herbal-citrus combination that makrut lime leaves and lemongrass add to this soup. The shells left after a crab feast also infuse the broth with a rich flavor. You can rinse and save the shells and freeze them for up to a month. Or, start with whole cooked crab, using its picked meat for the wonton filling (add any extra to the broth before serving) and the shells for the broth. If you have Crab Stock (page 111) on hand, skip the shells and use it in place of the fish stock and some or all of the water.

Preheat the oven to 400 degrees F. Scatter the crab shells in a baking dish and roast until they are aromatic and lightly browned, 20 to 25 minutes, gently stirring once or twice for even roasting.

Transfer the shells to a small stockpot and add the carrot, celery, shallots, ginger, lemongrass, lime leaves, and peppercorns. If any crab juices are baked onto the baking dish, add a cup of warm water and stir to dissolve them, adding the liquid to the pot. Add the fish stock with enough cold water to cover the ingredients by an inch or so (about 2 quarts), and bring just to a boil over medium-high heat. Reduce the heat to medium and simmer until aromatic and some of the color of the roasted shells has been imparted to the stock, about 1 hour.

For the crab wontons

4 ounces crabmeat

3 tablespoons minced green onion

1 tablespoon minced carrot

1 tablespoon minced celery

1 teaspoon freshly squeezed lemon juice

1 teaspoon soy sauce

16 thin square wonton wrappers

While the broth is simmering, prepare the crab wontons. Pick over the crabmeat to remove any bits of shell or cartilage. If using king or snow crab leg meat, cut it into small dice. If any of the other meat pieces are quite large, break them into a few smaller pieces. Squeeze the crab gently to remove excess liquid.

In a food processor, combine the crab with the green onion, carrot, celery, lemon juice, and soy sauce and pulse a few times to blend and finely chop the mixture, without making a paste. Transfer the filling to a small bowl. Lay the wonton wrappers out on the work surface and place a scant tablespoon of the filling in the center of each wrapper. Dip your finger in a small dish of warm water and use it to lightly dampen the edges of the wrappers. Fold each wrapper in half, corner to corner, pressing out as much air as possible and pinching the edges to seal securely. Bring a large pot of salted water to a boil over high heat.

When the broth is done simmering, line a fine-mesh sieve with dampened paper towel or a double-layer of cheesecloth and set it over a large bowl. This is extra-important given there are likely some tiny shell pieces that might pass through the sieve otherwise. Strain the broth through the sieve and discard the shells and vegetables. Rinse out the pot and return the broth to it, then season to taste with soy sauce and keep hot over medium heat.

When the salted water comes to a rolling boil, add the wontons, reduce the heat to medium, and simmer until they are just tender, 3 to 5 minutes. Drain well in a strainer and put 4 wontons in each bowl. Ladle the hot broth over the wontons, scatter with the sliced green onion, and serve right away.

Callaloo

MAKES 6 TO 8 SERVINGS

Crab: any cooked crabmeat, mix of flake and lump ideal

1 bunch (about 12 ounces) Swiss chard, trimmed and rinsed

4 slices thick-cut bacon, cut into ½-inch pieces

1 large onion, finely chopped

2 cloves garlic, finely chopped

1 to 2 serrano chiles cored, seeded, and finely chopped

1½ teaspoons chopped fresh thyme

3 cups Crab Stock (page 111), fish stock, or chicken broth

8 ounces okra, cut into 1-inch pieces (fresh or frozen)

Kosher salt and freshly ground black pepper

→

Callaloo comes in many forms throughout the Caribbean Islands. One common thread is often the green leaves of the taro plant or other similar greens, which themselves can go by the name "callaloo." Sometimes cooked quite simply as a vegetable dish, callaloo also shows up as stew or soup preparations that dot the islands.

Variations abound, often with crab but sometimes using conch or salt cod or no fish at all; other greens, such as Swiss chard or spinach, can easily replace the traditional greens. For a main course option that's more substantial, serve the callaloo over steamed rice or cooked black beans.

Cut the chard stems from the leaves and thinly slice the stems. Stack 3 or 4 chard leaves at a time, roll them up into a cylinder and cut across into roughly ½-inch strips.

Heat a large saucepan over medium heat. Add the bacon and cook, stirring, until the fat has rendered and the bacon begins to lightly brown, about 5 minutes (if there's much more than a couple tablespoons of bacon fat, scoop out the excess). Add the chard stems, onion, garlic, chile, and thyme and cook, stirring occasionally, until the onion and chard stems are tender, 8 to 10 minutes. Add the stock and bring to a boil. Add the chard leaves, a large handful at a time, stirring gently until each addition has wilted before adding the next. Stir in the okra with a good pinch each of salt and pepper. Allow the liquid to return to a boil,

CONTINUED

8 to 12 ounces crabmeat

1 (13.5-ounce) can reduced-fat coconut milk

1 lime, cut into wedges, for serving

then reduce the heat to medium low and simmer until the vegetables are tender and the soup has aromatic character, 20 to 25 minutes.

While the soup is simmering, pick over the crabmeat to remove any bits of shell or cartilage. If using king or snow crab leg meat, cut it into medium dice.

Stir the crab and coconut milk into the soup and simmer for about 5 minutes, until well heated. Taste the soup for seasoning, adding salt or pepper to taste. Ladle the soup into individual bowls and serve right away, with lime wedges on the side for squeezing into the soup.

Whiskey Crab Soup

MAKES 6 SERVINGS

Crab: any cooked crabmeat

2 tablespoons unsalted butter

1 cup finely chopped onion

3 tablespoons all-purpose flour

4 cups Crab Stock (page 111) or fish stock

8 ounces crabmeat

2 cups half-and-half

¼ cup whiskey, plus more for serving

Kosher salt and freshly ground white pepper

2 teaspoons chopped fresh chives

This rich recipe is in honor of Whiskey Flats at Dungeness Spit, the tidal flats at the Dungeness River delta below the bluffs where the town of Dungeness was first settled. The name is derived from an entrepreneurial spirit who was selling bootleg whiskey there long ago. If making crab stock for this recipe, the roasted version will be particularly delicious with its more pronounced flavor.

Melt the butter in a medium saucepan over medium heat. Add the onion and cook, stirring occasionally, until tender and aromatic, 3 to 5 minutes (the onion should soften but not brown). Sprinkle the flour over the onion and continue cooking, stirring until evenly coated, 30 to 60 seconds. Slowly pour in the crab stock and bring just to a boil, stirring often. Reduce the heat to medium low and simmer until the soup is slightly thickened, stirring occasionally, 5 to 7 minutes.

Pick over the crabmeat to remove any bits of shell or cartilage. If using king or snow crab leg meat, cut it into small dice. If any of the other meat pieces are quite large, break them into a few smaller pieces. Add the crab, half-and-half, whiskey, and a good pinch each of salt and pepper to the soup, stirring to blend. Simmer just until the soup is heated through, about 5 minutes.

Ladle the soup into individual warmed bowls, scatter the chives evenly over, and serve right away, passing a small pitcher of extra whiskey at the table, for diners to add a final splash to taste if they like.

Pea Soup with Crab Mousse

MAKES 4 SERVINGS

Crab: any cooked crabmeat, flake ideal

For the crab mousse

5 ounces crabmeat

1 large whole egg

1 large egg white

2 tablespoons heavy cream

1½ teaspoons minced fresh mint

Kosher salt and freshly ground white pepper

••••

2 tablespoons unsalted butter, plus more for buttering

1 cup finely chopped onion

4 cups freshly shelled peas or frozen petite peas

4 cups Crab Stock (page 111), fish stock, or chicken broth

½ cup half-and-half

This vibrant green pea soup is beautifully accented with a delicate crab mousse that is subtly flavored with fresh mint. If you're using shell peas, the general rule of thumb is that one pound in the pod will produce one cup shelled peas, so you'll need four pounds of in-shell peas. If using frozen peas, look for the "petite" variety, which tends to be more tender and flavorful than larger frozen peas.

Try to use white body meat to avoid creating a muddy color when the crabmeat is pureed. For a shortcut you can skip making the mousse and instead just toss the crabmeat with the minced mint and mound it in the center of the soup. And if you are using blue crab claw meat, that's recommended as well.

To make the mousse, pick over the crabmeat to remove any bits of shell or cartilage. If using king or snow crab leg meat, cut it into medium dice. If any of the other meat pieces are quite large, break them into a few smaller pieces. Squeeze the crab gently to remove excess water.

In a food processor, pulse the crab a few times to chop it up a bit, and then add the whole egg and egg white and pulse to form a smooth puree, scraping down the sides a few times to ensure that the ingredients are well mixed. Add the cream and pulse to mix. Transfer the puree to a small bowl and stir in the minced mint with a pinch each of salt and pepper. Refrigerate the mixture for about 1 hour.

2 teaspoons minced fresh mint

1 teaspoon slivered fresh mint

Preheat the oven to 350 degrees F. Lightly butter 4 (¼-cup) ramekins or other small ovenproof dishes (you can use larger ramekins, though the mousse will be shallower and will need a bit less cooking time).

Spoon the crab mousse mixture into the ramekins and set them in a baking dish. Add boiling water to the baking dish to come about halfway up the sides of the ramekins. Bake the mousse until it pulls away from the sides of the ramekins and is firm to touch, 20 to 25 minutes.

While the mousse is baking, prepare the soup. Melt the butter in a medium saucepan over medium heat. Add the onion and cook, stirring, until tender and aromatic, 3 to 5 minutes. Stir in the peas, and then add the stock. Bring the liquid just to a boil, reduce the heat to medium low, and simmer for 10 minutes.

Using an immersion blender or in batches in a food processor or blender, puree the soup until smooth. Return the soup to the saucepan, stir in the half-and-half and minced mint, and season to taste with salt and pepper. Gently reheat the soup over medium heat.

When the mousse is cooked through, carefully lift the ramekins from the baking dish and unmold the mousses upside down onto a plate. Ladle the soup into 4 warmed shallow soup bowls, set a mousse in the center of each bowl, and garnish the mousse with the slivered mint.

Crab Stock

MAKES ABOUT 8 CUPS

Crab: cooked crab shells (not including carapace) from Dungeness, king, snow, or blue crab

1½ to 2½ pounds crab shells, rinsed

1 cup coarsely chopped onion

2 stalks celery, preferably with leaves, sliced

2 or 3 sprigs fresh thyme

1 bay leaf, preferably fresh

8 to 10 whole black peppercorns

One benefit of that effort you put into picking crabmeat from the shell is not only the luscious, sweet meat, but the leftover shells that harbor wonderful flavor. They're used in Lemongrass Broth with Crab Wontons (page 102) to boost the flavor of fish stock for an Asian-inspired soup. The shells can be used to make a basic stock as well, simmered in water with aromatic vegetables, creating flavorful liquid that's ideal for seafood-based soups and stews. Use only crab shells that have been cooked very simply, without added seasonings. The carapace, or large top shell, should be discarded; use only shells from legs and body for the stock. For an extra dose of flavor, the shells are roasted before simmering, which brings out a richer, slightly nutty/toasty character that subtly enhances the flavor of the resulting stock, although you can skip this step.

Preheat the oven to 400 degrees F. Scatter the crab shells in a baking dish and roast until they are aromatic and lightly browned, 20 to 25 minutes, gently stirring once or twice for even roasting. Transfer the shells to a stockpot. If any crab juices are baked onto the baking dish, add a cup of warm water and stir to dissolve them, adding the liquid to the pot. (Alternatively, if not roasting the crab shells, put them directly into the stockpot.)

CONTINUED

CRAB STOCK, CONTINUED

Add the onion, celery, thyme, bay leaf, and peppercorns to the crab shells with enough cold water to cover the ingredients by an inch or so (about 3 quarts), and bring just to a boil over medium-high heat. Reduce the heat to medium and simmer until aromatic, about 1 hour. The water should just bubble lightly rather than roil; reduce the heat if needed. After it's done simmering, take the pot from the heat and let cool to room temperature, which allows more time for the flavors to be drawn from the ingredients.

Line a fine-mesh sieve with dampened paper towel or a double layer of cheesecloth. This is extra-important given there are likely some tiny shell pieces that might pass through the sieve otherwise. Set the sieve over a large bowl, slowly pour the stock through it, and let drain. Discard the shells and vegetables and set the stock aside to cool. Any extra stock can be frozen for 2 or 3 months.

Crab Club Sandwich

MAKES 2 SERVINGS

Crab: any cooked crabmeat, mix of flake and lump ideal

4 slices sandwich bread (white, wheat, sourdough, or other favorite bread)

2 tablespoons mayonnaise

2 large or 4 small leaves green lettuce, rinsed and dried

6 to 8 ounces crabmeat

½ lemon, cut into 2 wedges

4 beefsteak tomato slices, about ⅜ inch thick

4 slices thick-cut bacon, fried crisp

½ ripe but firm avocado

Traditionally, club sandwiches have three slices of bread each, but I've modified the idea to a conventional two-slice sandwich in which crab meets up with smoky bacon, sliced tomato, crisp lettuce, and—one of my favorite sandwich embellishments—slices of rich avocado. There's nothing not to like about this sandwich. Just take care to toast the bread only lightly so it doesn't become too crunchy. Old-fashioned white bread is typical for such a sandwich, but you can use any variety you like.

Lightly toast the bread in a toaster and let it cool. Spread ½ tablespoon of the mayonnaise on one side of each bread slice. Top 2 of the pieces of bread with the lettuce leaves.

Pick over the crabmeat to remove any bits of shell or cartilage. If using king or snow crab leg meat, cut it in lengths equal to the width of the bread slices, then cut those pieces lengthwise about ⅜ inch thick. Arrange the crabmeat evenly over the lettuce leaves and squeeze the lemon wedges over the crab, being careful to remove any seeds that might fall from the lemon. Lay the tomato slices over the crab and top with the bacon. Peel, pit, and thinly slice the avocado, and lay the slices over the bacon. Top with the remaining bread (mayo side down), cut each sandwich in half diagonally, and serve right away.

Green Goddess Crab & Watercress Sandwich

MAKES 4 SERVINGS

Crab: any cooked crabmeat, flake ideal

½ cup mayonnaise

2 green onions, minced

2 anchovy fillets, finely chopped

2 tablespoons minced fresh flat-leaf (Italian) parsley

1 tablespoon minced fresh chives

1 tablespoon tarragon vinegar or white wine vinegar

1 teaspoon minced fresh tarragon

Freshly ground black pepper

8 ounces crabmeat

8 slices white bread

2 ounces watercress, rinsed, dried, and tough stems removed

As an alternative to standard sandwiches, these could be served open-faced on halved or quartered pieces of bread, each topped with a bit of watercress. Or, for more cocktail-like nibbles, you could serve the crab mixture atop toasted baguette slices or crackers. Even better, scoop a bit of the salad into the slender, delicate leaves of Belgian endive, one of the world's perfect edible containers.

In a medium bowl, combine the mayonnaise, green onion, anchovy, parsley, chives, vinegar, and tarragon with pepper to taste. Stir to evenly mix, and refrigerate for at least 1 hour to allow the flavors to blend. (The mixture can be made up to 1 day in advance.)

Pick over the crabmeat to remove any bits of shell or cartilage. If using king or snow crab leg meat, cut it into small dice. Squeeze the crab gently to remove excess liquid. Add the crab to the mayonnaise mixture, stir with a fork to mix evenly, and then spoon the crab salad in an even layer on 4 of the bread slices. Top the crab with the watercress leaves, followed by the remaining bread slices. Cut each sandwich in half diagonally and serve right away.

Crab & Cheddar Melt

MAKES 4 SERVINGS

Crab: any cooked crabmeat, mix of flake and lump ideal

4 slices sourdough bread

12 ounces crabmeat

2 cups grated sharp cheddar cheese (about 8 ounces)

¼ cup thinly sliced green onion

4 to 5 tablespoons mayonnaise

What's not to love about luscious, sweet crab all melty and warm with really good cheese? This recipe was inspired by a specialty at the Bait House Café in Seattle's Ballard neighborhood, the seafaring heart of the city. You could, in fact, buy bait at the Bait House, and, while sitting there eating your crab sandwich, look out over the mouth of the ship canal and watch boats—from pleasure craft to part of the Alaska fishing fleet—saunter by on their way to or from the Hiram M. Chittenden Locks. It was a gloriously Seattle-funky little spot, but sadly is no more.

Preheat the broiler. Toast one side of the bread slices about 4 inches from the broiler element until lightly browned. Set aside on a wire rack to cool. Keep the broiler on.

Pick over the crabmeat to remove any bits of shell or cartilage. If using king or snow crab leg meat, cut it into small dice. Squeeze the crab gently to remove excess liquid. In a medium bowl, combine the crab, cheese, and green onion. Toss to mix, and then add just enough mayonnaise to hold the crab and cheese together; if you add too much, the sandwiches will be soft and weepy. Stir the mixture very well to be sure the ingredients are well blended and cohesive.

Spread the crab mixture on the untoasted side of the bread slices and set them on a baking sheet. Broil the sandwiches until the cheese is melted and the top is bubbly, 3 to 4 minutes. Transfer the sandwiches to individual plates and serve right away.

SALADS

Crab Louis

MAKES 4 SERVINGS

Crab: any cooked crabmeat, lump ideal

For the Louis dressing

¾ cup mayonnaise, preferably homemade

⅓ cup chili sauce or ketchup

3 tablespoons finely chopped green onion

1 tablespoon minced fresh flat-leaf (Italian) parsley

Dash Worcestershire sauce

Dash hot pepper sauce

Kosher salt and freshly ground black pepper

1 head iceberg lettuce, cored, leaves separated, rinsed, and dried

8 to 12 ounces crabmeat

Just who the "Louis" is who inspired this classic no one seems to know for certain, though legend leans toward San Francisco as this salad's birthplace. The legacy lives on and this time-honored recipe needs no updating. To do so would make it not a Louis but instead just another crab salad. The lettuce must be crisp, bright iceberg, the eggs hard cooked, the tomato cut in wedges. Embellish with artichoke bottoms or blanched asparagus, if you like.

And yes, the dressing is at its best made with prepared chili sauce or ketchup, to honor the dishes retro roots. For homemade mayonnaise, you can use the Lemon Mayonnaise recipe (page 152), omitting the lemon zest and using only one teaspoon of lemon juice. Though they are non-traditional options, I'll admit that blue cheese or green goddess dressing would be delicious on this salad as well.

To make the Louis dressing, in a small bowl, combine the mayonnaise, chili sauce, green onion, parsley, Worcestershire, and hot pepper sauce and stir to mix. Season to taste with salt and pepper and refrigerate until ready to serve. The dressing will be best if made at least an hour in advance, allowing the flavors to meld.

On 4 chilled plates, arrange beds of a couple of the larger lettuce leaves. Cut the remaining lettuce into ½-inch strips and pile them evenly in the center of each plate. Pick over

4 eggs, hard-cooked, peeled, and quartered (see Hard-Cooked Eggs)

2 small tomatoes or 4 plum tomatoes, cored and quartered

the crabmeat to remove any bits of shell or cartilage. If using king or snow crab leg meat, cut it into pieces about 1 inch long. Arrange the crab over the shredded lettuce, then add the egg and tomato wedges evenly around the crab, on the lettuce base. Spoon a bit of the Louis dressing over the crab, passing the rest separately.

Hard-Cooked Eggs

Technically, eggs shouldn't be "hard-boiled," the high heat of boiling producing whites that become tough and rubbery. Just a gentle simmer is better, or even better yet is the method where you remove the eggs from the heat and let the eggs sit in the water to avoid overcooking them. This is how I prefer to hard-cook eggs: Put the eggs in a pan with enough cold water to cover them by about 1 inch. Put the pan over high heat and bring *just* to a boil. Take the pan from the heat, add the lid, and set aside for 15 minutes. Drain the eggs and chill in a bowl of ice water until cold.

Crab & Soba Noodle Salad

Soba noodles are a foundation of Japanese cuisine, their distinctly nutty flavor coming from the buckwheat flour used to make them. In this recipe the noodles soak up a flavorful dressing to serve as a base for crab and crisp vegetables. This salad makes a delicious light main course, particularly on a hot summer's day, or serve it alongside a simply grilled piece of fish—salmon would be a particularly good partner.

MAKES 4 TO 6 SERVINGS

Crab: any crabmeat, mix of flake and lump ideal

For the sesame-soy dressing

⅓ cup unseasoned rice vinegar

¼ cup freshly squeezed lemon juice (from about 1 large lemon or 2 small lemons)

2 tablespoons mild olive or vegetable oil

2 tablespoons soy sauce

2 tablespoons mirin

2 teaspoons toasted sesame oil

••••

8 ounces soba noodles

8 to 12 ounces crabmeat

Bring a large pot of generously salted water to a boil over high heat for cooking the noodles.

While the water is heating, make the dressing. In a small bowl, combine the vinegar, lemon juice, olive oil, soy sauce, mirin, and sesame oil and whisk to blend. Set aside.

When the water comes to a rolling boil, add the noodles and cook just until tender, about 5 minutes. Drain the noodles in a colander and run cold water over to cool the noodles. Drain again well and put the noodles in a large bowl. Rewhisk the dressing and drizzle about three-quarters of it over the noodles, tossing to coat them evenly. Cover the bowl and refrigerate for at least 1 hour, stirring once or twice. (The noodles will soak up the dressing as they sit.)

1 large carrot, peeled and julienned

1 medium cucumber, halved, peeled, seeded, and thinly sliced

¼ cup chopped fresh cilantro

2 tablespoons toasted sesame seeds

¼ cup thinly sliced green onion tops

Just before serving, pick over the crabmeat to remove any bits of shell or cartilage, and set aside some larger pieces, if there are any, for garnishing the salad. Add the rest of the crab to the noodles along with the carrot, cucumber, cilantro, and sesame seeds. Toss to mix evenly, and arrange the noodle salad on individual plates. Scatter the green onion over the salad, drizzle with the remaining dressing, and top with the reserved crabmeat.

Crab & Green Bean Salad with Brown Butter Dressing

MAKES 4 TO 6 SERVINGS

Crab: any cooked crabmeat, mix of flake and lump ideal

1 pound green beans, trimmed and rinsed

6 to 8 ounces crabmeat

8 ounces cherry tomatoes, halved if large

For the brown butter dressing

¼ cup unsalted butter, cut into 4 to 6 pieces

¼ cup freshly squeezed lemon juice (from about 1 large lemon or 2 small lemons) or 3 tablespoons red wine vinegar

Kosher salt and freshly ground black pepper

It's just a handful of ingredients, but this simple combination tastes quite grand. Butter in salad dressing may sound a little odd, but if you're a fan of brown butter, you'll find the surprise pretty tasty. You can certainly use olive oil in place of the butter if you prefer.

Bring a large pan of salted water to a boil over high heat. Prepare a large bowl of ice water. Add the green beans to the boiling water and cook until just barely tender and bright green, 2 to 3 minutes. Drain the beans and transfer them directly to the ice water to cool quickly and avoid overcooking. When cool, drain well and scatter on a kitchen towel to dry while preparing the rest of the salad.

Pick over the crabmeat to remove any bits of shell or cartilage. If using king or snow crab leg meat, cut it into medium dice. In a large bowl, combine the drained green beans, crab, and cherry tomatoes and let sit at room temperature while making the vinaigrette.

To make the dressing, melt the butter in a small skillet over medium heat. Once melted, continue cooking until the solids have turned a medium brown and smell nutty, 2 to 3 minutes more. Transfer the brown butter to a medium bowl, being careful to scrape out the flavorful browned bits from the bottom of the skillet. Let it cool to nearly room

2 to 3 tablespoons coarsely chopped fresh herbs (flat-leaf parsley, chives, chervil, tarragon)

temperature, then add the lemon juice with a good pinch each of salt and pepper. Blend with a small whisk or fork and taste for seasoning, adding more salt or pepper to taste.

Drizzle the dressing over the salad. (If the butter has solidified a bit before you dress the salad, set the bottom of the bowl in a pan of warm water and stir until the dressing has softened and the consistency is smooth). Toss well to mix, then arrange on individual plates. Scatter the herbs over and serve.

Shaved Fennel Salad with Crab & Blood Oranges

MAKES 2 TO 4 SERVINGS

Crab: any cooked crabmeat, mix of flake and lump ideal

2 blood oranges or navel oranges

1 large fennel bulb

4 green onions, thinly sliced

¼ cup mild olive oil

2 tablespoons red wine vinegar

Kosher salt and freshly ground black pepper

6 to 8 ounces crabmeat

The aromatic citrus flavor of oranges and subtle anisey crunch of fennel make for a great start to any meal, particularly when the briny sweetness of crab is added to the mix. In larger servings this salad makes a light lunch.

Blood oranges are, as their name suggests, a variety of sweet orange that has reddish tones in the flesh that can range from a smattering of red speckles to a solid ruby red. They are available sporadically, and not all markets carry them. Winter into early spring is generally the best season for finding them. Navel oranges, while less colorful, will provide great results as well.

Cut both ends from one of the oranges, just to the flesh. Set the orange upright on a cutting board and use the knife to cut away the peel and pith (the white part under the peel), following the curve of the fruit. Try not to cut away too much of the flesh with the peel.

Working over a medium bowl to catch the juice, hold the peeled orange in your hand and slide the knife blade down one edge of a section, cutting it from the adjacent membrane. Cut down the other side of the same section and let it fall into the bowl. (Pick out and discard any seeds as you go.) Continue for the remaining sections, turning the flaps of the membrane like the pages of a book. Squeeze the juice from the membrane core into the bowl. Repeat with the second orange.

CONTINUED

SHAVED FENNEL SALAD WITH CRAB & BLOOD ORANGES, CONTINUED

Trim the root end and stalks of the fennel bulb, reserving some of the feathery fronds. Cut the bulb in half lengthwise and cut out the tough core. Using a mandoline slicer or a large, sharp knife, cut the fennel lengthwise into very thin slices, and put them in the bowl with the orange segments. Mince enough of the fennel fronds to measure 1 tablespoon, reserving 4 of the remaining fronds for garnish, and add the minced fennel to the bowl along with the green onion. Drizzle the oil and vinegar over the mixture and season to taste with salt and pepper.

Pick over the crabmeat to remove any bits of shell or cartilage. If using king or snow crab leg meat, cut it into medium dice. Add the crab to the salad and toss gently to avoid breaking up the orange pieces. Arrange the salad on chilled plates, drizzling the juices from the bottom of the bowl evenly over the salads. Top with the reserved fennel fronds and serve.

Stone Crab & Mango Salad with Chipotle Dressing

MAKES 4 TO 6 SERVINGS

Crab: stone crab or other cooked crabmeat, lump ideal

For the chipotle dressing

3 tablespoons freshly squeezed lime juice (from 1 to 2 limes)

½ teaspoon minced chipotle en adobo or ¼ teaspoon dried chipotle powder

¼ teaspoon finely grated lime zest

Kosher salt

⅓ cup mild olive oil

••••

8 ounces stone crab claw meat

1 mango, peeled, seeded, and cut into about ¾-inch cubes

1½ cups thinly shredded radicchio

1½ cups peeled julienned jicama

It is rather luxurious to take exquisite stone crab claw meat from its shell to mix into a salad. But there are times when such a daring move has delicious results. Exotically sweet mango, crisp and juicy jicama, vibrant radicchio—they all play beautifully together as a foundation for the crab. The yield of meat from stone crab is roughly one-third, so you'll need about one and one-half pounds whole claws for the meat needed here. Smaller, and less expensive, medium- or large-size claws will be just fine.

If it is simply anathema to you that the stone crab meat be mixed into the salad, you could instead serve the claws intact as usual and serve the salad alongside as an accompaniment. Save some of the dressing to offer in a small dish for optional dipping of the claw meat.

To make the dressing, in a medium bowl, combine the lime juice, chipotle, and lime zest with a good pinch of salt and whisk to mix. Whisk in the oil to blend. Set aside.

Pick over the crabmeat to remove any bits of shell or cartilage. Break up larger pieces of claw meat (knuckle nuggets can remain whole) into 2 or 3 smaller pieces. Avoid finely shredding it; there should still be nice lump portions.

CONTINUED

In a large bowl, combine the mango, radicchio, and jicama and toss to mix. Whisk the dressing to remix and taste for seasoning, adding a bit more salt if needed. Add half of the crabmeat to the salad and drizzle the dressing over. Toss lightly to mix, then arrange the salad on individual plates. Top with the remaining crab and serve right away.

Smokey-Hot Chipotle

Chipotle chiles are jalapeños that have been dried and smoked, creating a uniquely rich flavor that's spicy balanced with earthy. They're available as whole dried chiles, in ground form, and *en adobo*, which is canned in a rich red sauce. In that latter form they're plump and ready to use. A little goes a long way, particularly in a recipe like this where its character is intentionally subtle. Even the smallest cans will have much more than needed here. But the chipotle *en adobo* will keep well (transferred to a sealed jar) in the refrigerator for a couple of weeks, or they can be frozen for a few months.

Spinach Salad with Crab Toasts & Roasted Onion Vinaigrette

MAKES 4 SERVINGS

Crab: any cooked crabmeat, flake ideal

1 cup coarsely chopped onion

4 tablespoons mild olive oil, divided

4 ounces crabmeat

6 ounces cream cheese, softened at room temperature

Kosher salt and freshly ground black pepper

12 baguette slices, about ½ inch thick

¼ cup red wine vinegar

1 large bunch spinach (about 1 pound), rinsed, dried, and tough stems removed

The sharp flavor of raw onion turns sweeter when roasted, making a wonderful base for this tangy vinaigrette dressing. The rich crab toasts finish this spinach salad with a touch of luxury. It makes a great main course for a lunch or light supper, though it could also be served in smaller portions as a starter salad.

Preheat the oven to 375 degrees F.

Put the onion in a small baking dish and drizzle 1 tablespoon of the oil over it, stirring to evenly coat. Roast the onion until tender and lightly browned, about 30 minutes, stirring once or twice to help it roast evenly.

While the onion is roasting, pick over the crabmeat to remove any bits of shell or cartilage. If using king or snow crab leg meat, finely chop it. Squeeze the crab gently to remove excess liquid. In a medium bowl, combine the crab and cream cheese. Mix with a fork until evenly blended, and then season to taste with salt and pepper.

When the onion is finished roasting, set it aside to cool. Preheat the broiler.

Arrange the baguette slices on a baking sheet and toast them about 4 inches from the broiler element until lightly browned. Take the baking sheet from the oven, turn the slices over, and top the untoasted side of each with the crab mixture, mounding it slightly in the center. Return the sheet to the oven and continue broiling until the crab mixture bubbles and is lightly browned, 2 to 3 minutes. Turn off the oven and keep the toasts warm on a lower rack in the oven.

Put the cooled onion and its roasting oil in a food processor or blender and puree until smooth. Add the vinegar with the remaining 3 tablespoons oil. Puree to blend, and then season to taste with salt and pepper.

Put the spinach leaves in a large bowl, tearing any large leaves in half or thirds. Drizzle the onion vinaigrette over and toss to evenly coat. Arrange the spinach on individual plates and top each with 3 crab toasts.

Spring Farro & Crab Salad

MAKES 4 TO 6 SERVINGS

Crab: any cooked crabmeat, mix of flake and lump ideal

3 cups water

½ teaspoon kosher salt

1 cup farro

6 ounces asparagus spears, trimmed (halved lengthwise if thick)

1 cup freshly shelled peas or frozen petite peas

6 to 8 ounces crabmeat

3 tablespoons minced fresh flat-leaf (Italian) parsley

2 tablespoons minced fresh basil

⅓ cup mild olive oil

3 tablespoons white wine vinegar, plus more to taste

Kosher salt and freshly ground black pepper

The fresh flavors of asparagus, peas, and herbs are an ideal complement in flavor and color to nutty farro and sweet crabmeat in this easy salad. The recipe is also great with other grains, such as rice or quinoa—you'll need about two and one-half cups of cooked grain. You can certainly serve this salad right away, but the flavor will be even better if it sits for an hour or two before serving.

In a small saucepan, combine the water and salt and bring to a boil over high heat. Stir in the farro, reduce the heat to medium low, and cook until the farro is tender, 25 to 30 minutes. Drain the farro well and put it in a large bowl. Set aside to cool.

Trim 2 inches of the asparagus tip from each spear, then cut the rest of the spears into 1-inch pieces.

Bring a medium saucepan of salted water to a boil over high heat and fill a medium bowl with ice water. Add the asparagus pieces to the boiling water and blanch until bright green and just barely tender, 2 to 3 minutes. Scoop out the asparagus with a slotted spoon and put it in the ice water to cool.

Return the water to a boil, add the peas, and cook for 1 to 2 minutes. Drain the peas, add them to the ice water, and let cool completely. Drain the vegetables and scatter them on a kitchen towel to dry.

Pick over the crabmeat to remove any bits of shell or cartilage. If using king or snow crab leg meat, cut it into medium dice. If any of the other meat pieces are quite large, break them into a few smaller pieces. Add the crab, asparagus, peas, parsley, and basil to the farro.

In a small bowl, combine the oil and vinegar with a good pinch each of salt and pepper. Whisk to blend, then pour the dressing over the salad, stirring gently to mix evenly. Set the salad aside for at least an hour if possible. (The salad can be made up to 4 hours in advance; refrigerate if holding for more than 1 hour. Allow it to sit at room temperature before serving.)

Taste the salad for seasoning, adding more salt, pepper, or vinegar if needed, then spoon the salad onto individual plates and serve.

Cucumber & Daikon Sunomono with Crab

MAKES 4 TO 6 SERVINGS

Crab: any cooked crabmeat, lump ideal

1 large English cucumber, halved and thinly sliced

1 small daikon radish (about 8 ounces), peeled and thinly sliced

½ small sweet onion, cut into thin julienne

¾ cup unseasoned rice vinegar

1½ teaspoons sugar

1 teaspoon kosher salt

6 to 8 ounces crabmeat

5 to 6 fresh *shiso* leaves, cut into thin julienne

The fresh crunch and flavor of cucumber and daikon radish make this an exceptionally refreshing salad, similar to the cucumber *sunomono* often served at the start of a Japanese meal. Lump crabmeat will make the most of the contrast between the sweet, meaty crab and the crisp, vinegary vegetables.

The thin skin and innocuous seeds of English cucumber make it the best choice for this recipe. If you find Japanese cucumber, that would be a natural choice as well. If using a regular cucumber, peel it and scoop out the seeds from each half before slicing.

In a large bowl, combine the cucumber, daikon, and onion, and toss to mix.

In a medium bowl, combine the vinegar, sugar, and salt. Let sit for a few minutes, then stir the dressing until the sugar and salt have dissolved. Pour the dressing over the vegetables, toss well, and set aside for 15 minutes, so they absorb some of the dressing, stirring a few times. (If the vegetables sit too long, they will lose some of their crispness; the salad is best made shortly before serving.)

Pick over the crabmeat to remove any bits of shell or cartilage. If using king or snow crab leg meat, cut it into medium dice.

Drain the dressing from the vegetables into a small dish, then add the *shiso* to the vegetables and toss to mix. Arrange the vegetables on individual chilled plates, and top with the crabmeat. Drizzle some of the reserved dressing over each salad and serve.

Shiso

Shiso, sometimes known as perilla, is an herb related to mint and basil that is commonly used in Japanese cuisine. Its vivid green leaves, with their distinctly toothed edges, are also a common garnish on plates of sushi and sashimi. (There is also a purple *shiso*; its flavor is a little milder than the green *shiso*.) The subtle anise-mint flavor adds a wonderful herbal quality to the salad, though you could use mint in its place.

MAIN COURSES

West Coast Crab Cakes with Rouille

MAKES 4 SERVINGS

Crab: made with Dungeness in mind but other cooked crabmeat can be used; king or snow should be chopped

For the rouille

1 small red bell pepper

1 slice white bread, crusts removed

½ cup whole milk

3 cloves garlic, crushed

1 large egg yolk

2 teaspoons white wine vinegar

Pinch dried red pepper flakes

Kosher salt

¾ cup mild olive oil

→

The recipe for success when it comes to crab cakes is pretty simple: it's all about the crab. Other ingredients should simply help hold the cakes together and offer the slightest hint of color or flavor contrast. These can be served as an appetizer as well, with one cake per person. For an elegant sandwich serve the cakes on a small bun slathered with the rouille, or make bite-size cakes and top with a dollop of rouille for a cocktail party treat.

Rouille (which means rust in French) is a rich sauce often served with bouillabaisse. It's quite a garlicky sauce as well; if you prefer less-bold garlic flavor, use just one or two garlic cloves.

To make the rouille, roast the red pepper over a gas flame or under the broiler until the skin blackens, turning occasionally to roast evenly, about 10 minutes total. Put the pepper in a plastic bag, seal securely, and set aside to cool. While the pepper is cooling, tear the bread into pieces, put it in a small bowl, and pour the milk over it; set aside to soak.

When the pepper is cool enough to handle, peel away and discard the skin. Remove the core and seeds, and coarsely chop the pepper. Put the pepper in a food processor with the garlic and pulse to chop finely. Squeeze the excess milk from the soaked bread and add the bread to the food

CONTINUED

1 pound Dungeness crabmeat

About 3 cups fresh bread crumbs (see Fresh Bread Crumbs), divided, plus more if needed

2 large egg whites or 1 large whole egg, beaten

¼ cup minced celery

2 green onions, minced

2 tablespoons minced fresh flat-leaf (Italian) parsley

Mild olive or vegetable oil, for frying

processor with the egg yolk, vinegar, pepper flakes, and a generous pinch of salt. Process until smooth, scraping down the sides a couple of times. With the motor running, add the oil in a slow, steady stream. Transfer the rouille to a bowl and taste for seasoning, adding more salt if necessary. Refrigerate until ready to serve; the sauce will thicken slightly when chilled. (Makes about 1½ cups.)

To make the crab cakes, pick over the crabmeat, removing any bits of shell or cartilage. Squeeze the crab gently to remove excess liquid. In a large bowl, combine the crab, 1 cup of the bread crumbs, the egg whites, celery, green onion, and parsley and stir to evenly mix. Form the mixture into 8 (3-inch) cakes, pressing the cakes firmly so that the mixture holds together. The mixture should be a bit on the loose side, to best showcase the crab. But if the cakes aren't holding together well, stir in a bit more of the bread crumbs. Lightly coat each side of the cakes with the remaining 2 cups bread crumbs and set aside on

Fresh Bread Crumbs

Dried bread crumbs are a pantry staples that can be readily at hand any time, but here I recommend using fresh bread crumbs instead. They take just a few moments to make and contribute a much lighter texture to the finished cake than dried crumbs would. You'll need about 10 to 12 slices of standard white sandwich bread for the 3 cups of crumbs needed here. Tear the bread into pieces, put them in a food processor, and pulse until it has all been transformed into fine, fluffy bread crumbs.

a tray coated in more bread crumbs. The cakes will hold together better if they sit in the refrigerator for an hour or so before cooking.

Heat about ⅛ inch of oil in a large, heavy skillet over medium heat. Fry the crab cakes (don't crowd the pan; cook in batches if needed) until nicely browned and heated through, 4 to 5 minutes on each side. Transfer the cakes to a wire rack, adding more oil to the pan if needed for another batch. Serve the crab cakes warm, with the rouille on the side.

East Coast Crab Cakes with Old Bay Tartar Sauce

MAKES 4 SERVINGS

Crab: made with lump blue crabmeat in mind but other cooked crabmeat can be used; king or snow should be chopped

For the Old Bay tartar sauce

1 cup mayonnaise, preferably homemade

¼ cup finely chopped cornichon or dill pickle

1 tablespoon white wine vinegar

1 tablespoon coarsely chopped drained capers

1 teaspoon Old Bay seasoning

••••

12 saltine crackers, coarsely crushed

1 teaspoon Old Bay seasoning

The better the crab you begin with, the better your cakes will be. The very best crab cakes that you'll taste in Baltimore or other crab-serious spots in the East will be large pieces of lump blue crabmeat held together almost mysteriously by as little as possible, the sweet meat easily giving way when prodded with your fork. It doesn't get much better than that. If you can't find all exquisite lump meat, try to find meat that at least has a nice mix of both flaked and larger meat portions. These cakes can be served as an appetizer as well, with one cake per person. For homemade mayonnaise, you can use the Lemon Mayonnaise recipe (page 152), omitting the lemon zest and using only one teaspoon of lemon juice.

To make the tartar sauce, in a small bowl, combine the mayonnaise, cornichon, vinegar, capers, and Old Bay seasoning and stir well to blend. Refrigerate until ready to serve, preferably for at least an hour to allow the flavors to blend and develop. (Makes about 1¼ cups.)

To make the crab cakes, put the crushed crackers in a food processor and pulse until finely ground. Add the Old Bay seasoning and pulse a couple times to blend. (You should have about ½ cup crumb mixture.)

Pick over the crabmeat to remove any bits of shell or cartilage. Squeeze the crab gently to remove excess liquid. Put the crabmeat in a large bowl and add the crumb mixture, egg, and Worcestershire sauce. Use your hands

1 pound blue crabmeat

1 large egg, lightly beaten

½ teaspoon Worcestershire sauce

Mild olive or vegetable oil, for frying

or a spoon to lightly but thoroughly blend the mixture. Set aside for 15 minutes, then form the mixture into 8 (2½-inch) cakes, pressing the cakes firmly so that the mixture holds together. The cakes will hold together better if they sit in the refrigerator for an hour or so before cooking.

Heat about ⅛ inch of oil in a large, heavy skillet over medium heat. Fry the crab cakes (don't crowd the pan; cook in batches if needed) until nicely browned and heated through, 4 to 5 minutes on each side. Transfer the cakes to a wire rack, adding more oil to the pan if needed for another batch. Serve the crab cakes warm, spooning a bit of the sauce alongside and serving the rest separately.

Picker or Piler?

The world of crab eaters can be split into two distinct groups: pickers and pilers. The pickers enjoy the fruits of their labor as they go, while pilers are those who get all the hard work done first and then hedonistically relish the big heap of ready-to-eat meat when the work's complete. I, for one, am a picker too eager to enjoy the luscious meat to wait. In fact most people I know are pickers. The occasional piler I share a crab feast with ends up doubling his workload to include fending off the rest of us, protecting his precious stash. Surely this picker/piler phenomenon could make an interesting thesis subject for some budding psychologist.

Northwest Crab Boil

MAKES 2 TO 4 SERVINGS

Crab: made with Dungeness in mind, but live blue crab could be used

2 uncooked Dungeness crab (about 2 pounds each), live or cleaned and portioned (see page 34)

2 large lemons, cut into wedges, for serving

½ cup unsalted butter, melted, for serving

Unlike our compatriots in the eastern regions of the country, Northwesterners typically add no spice (beyond salt) to the pot when boiling crab for a feast. Having grown up here, of course I adhere to the practice, finding the flavor of the crab itself is near perfection. Some crab lovers simply scoop up clean sea water, which is clearly quite salty, in which to cook the crab. To replicate this at home use water that's been well salted (about ½ cup salt per gallon of water).

Depending on your guests' appetites and what else you're serving for dinner, the serving size can range from a half crab to a whole crab per person. If you're increasing this recipe to serve a bigger crowd, keep in mind that you'll need a much bigger pot, or plan to cook the crab in batches. See page 148 for more on crab feeds.

Bring a large pot (at least 8 quarts) of generously salted water to a boil over high heat. While the water is heating, put the live crab, if using, into the freezer to dull their senses a bit. (The crab should be well chilled but should not freeze at all, so don't leave them in the freezer for more than 15 to 20 minutes.) When the water's at a full rolling boil, if you're using live crab, grab each of them securely at the back of the carapace, and gently but swiftly drop them headfirst into the boiling water. If you're using cleaned crab portions, simply add them to the boiling water.

When the water comes back to a boil, reduce the heat to medium high so the water's gently bubbling but not boiling over. Cook the crab for about 18 minutes for whole, about 10 minutes for cleaned portions, counting from the time that the crab were added to the pot.

Drain the crab well. If you cooked portioned crab, arrange the pieces on a large serving platter with lemon wedges around the edges. If you cooked whole crab, clean and portion them (see page 34) before serving. Pour the melted butter into individual dishes for each diner, and serve the crab while still warm.

To Feed and To Feast

On the west coast we go nuts for crab feeds, while on the East Coast it's all about crab feasts.

Bring up the topic of "pinnacle Dungeness experience" and most people on the Pacific side will tell you about crab-feed traditions with family and friends: the Thanksgiving or Christmas Eve dinner table that is always piled high with freshly steamed crab or the summer ritual of gathering at the beach house to eat your fill of just-caught Dungeness. Countless public crab feeds are held up and down the Pacific Coast each year, from community fundraisers to school reunion festivities.

By one longstanding tradition, many Dungeness crab feeds are held in the late fall/early winter when the newly opened commercial season generally means good stocks of crab and some of the lowest prices of the year. That's truest for those counting on buying, rather than catching, their crab. For the recreational crabber it's more about summer: extralong daylight, warm temperatures, kids out of school, trips to the shoreside cabin, a compulsion to be outdoors. Western crab feeds have more than one season.

Not only is crab simply a delicious thing to eat on such occasions, there's something socially engaging about dining crab-feed style. For one, all pretense of formality is left at the door. It's a roll-up-your-sleeves-and-eat-with-your-hands extravaganza that puts everyone on an even playing field. Most crab feeds dispense with tablecloths and nice napkins. Instead, hosts cover the table with newspapers (comics or crossword puzzle in view, if you like, for dinnertime entertainment) and offer plenty of paper napkins or paper towels. You're at the table for a good while, rhythmically cracking the shells, picking out the meat, and relishing each bite, with intermittent swigs of beer or wine and forkfuls of coleslaw. This is gastronomic communal interaction at its very best.

Over on the East Coast, however, similar blue crab indulgences tend to be called feasts and are almost exclusively associated with summer. One friend told me of the "hot fat crab and cold beer" signs they see along the coast that time of year where she lives in Delaware. And a Marylander I spoke to had just recently been to a big feast at which about ninety people had gone through ten bushels of blue crab. "They're events here," he told me. No doubt!

These feasts are most always held outdoors, big mounds of freshly steamed crab piled high on picnic tables, with lots of sweet corn on the cob, maybe watermelon, and other summer treats alongside. Oh, and cold beer. Lots and lots of cold beer. By one account it seems that Natty Boh (National Bohemian beer, to outsiders) is something of an unofficial blue crab beer of summer.

Some may feast while others feed, but whatever coast or tradition is behind it—indulging in your fill of outstanding crab while it's at its best is definitely the name of the game.

Rosemary Roasted Crab

MAKES 2 TO 4 SERVINGS

Crab: any in-shell crab, cleaned and portioned (blue crab simply cleaned)

2 Dungeness crab (about 2 pounds each), cleaned and portioned (see page 34), shells lightly cracked if precooked

6 to 8 long sprigs fresh rosemary

1 large lemon, thinly sliced

¼ cup mild olive oil

4 cloves garlic, chopped

¼ teaspoon dried red pepper flakes

Kosher salt and freshly ground black pepper

The rosemary, lemon, and garlic roasted with the crab here penetrate the sweet meat with delicious subtlety while filling the kitchen with their wonderful aroma. This preparation is particularly good with raw crab portions, which will absorb the flavors more than precooked crabmeat will. If using king or snow leg portions, you'll one to use one and one-half to two pounds.

Preheat the oven to 450 degrees F.

Lay the crab portions in a 9-by-13-inch baking dish and top with the rosemary sprigs and lemon slices. Add the oil, garlic, and pepper flakes, and season generously with salt and pepper. Toss with your hands to coat the crab pieces with the seasonings, then arrange them in an even layer with most of the rosemary and lemon underneath. If using raw crab, roast the crab until the flesh is just opaque through (use body portions to judge doneness; their flesh will be more visible), about 15 minutes, or roast the precooked crab until it is heated through, 7 to 10 minutes.

Transfer the crab pieces to a serving platter, surround them with the rosemary sprigs and lemon slices, and serve.

Cold Cracked Crab with Lemon Mayonnaise

MAKES 2 TO 4 SERVINGS

Crab: any in-shell cooked crabmeat

For the lemon mayonnaise

1 small lemon

1 large egg yolk

¾ cup mild olive oil

Kosher salt and freshly ground white pepper

••••

2 uncooked Dungeness crab (about 2 pounds each), live or cleaned and portioned (see page 34)

Lemon wedges, for serving

Not only do we like our freshly cooked Dungeness crab steaming hot in the West, but we also relish sitting down to chilled crab as well. This recipe presumes you'll be cooking the crab yourself, but if you buy cooked Dungeness from the market, you're 90 percent to dinner. The crab just need to be cleaned (unless you asked them to do so at the market, in which case make that 95 percent). Cut up a couple lemons, dish up some sauce, tuck a napkin under your chin, and have something crisp and cold to drink within easy reach. To upgrade that scenario, this lemon mayonnaise does the trick.

To make the lemon mayonnaise, finely grate 1/2 teaspoon of zest from the lemon and set it aside, then squeeze the juice from the lemon (you should have about 2 tablespoons).

In a medium bowl, combine 1 teaspoon of the lemon juice with the egg yolk and whisk to blend. Begin adding the oil, a couple drops at a time, whisking constantly, until the yolk begins to turn pale and thicken slightly, showing that an emulsion has begun to form. Continue adding the rest of the oil in a thin, steady stream, whisking constantly. Whisk in the remaining lemon juice with the lemon zest and salt and pepper to taste. Alternatively, combine the teaspoon of lemon juice and egg yolk in a food processor and pulse to blend. With the motor running, begin adding the oil a few drops at a time until an emulsion has begun to form, then continue adding the rest in a thin, steady stream. Add the remaining lemon juice with the lemon zest and salt and pepper to taste, and pulse to blend.

Refrigerate the mayonnaise, covered, until ready to serve; it will have a fuller, more balanced flavor if made at least an hour before serving, and it can be made a day or two in advance.

Cook the crab as noted in Northwest Crab Boil (page 146). Carefully drain the crab and cool them completely in a large bowl (or sinkful) of ice water, then pat them dry. If you cooked whole crab, clean and portion them (see page 34). If not serving right away, you can refrigerate the crab for 1 to 2 hours.

Arrange the chilled crab portions on individual plates. Spoon the lemon mayonnaise into small dishes and serve it alongside the crab with the lemon wedges.

Making Mayo

Making mayonnaise by hand, with just a bowl and a whisk, is rewarding though it does take some dexterity to hold the bowl and drizzle the oil with one hand while whisking constantly with the other. One trick involves a kitchen towel: Grab the towel by opposite corners and twist them to make a long, slender roll, then wrap the roll around the base of the mixing bowl, gently tying it to secure a nest-like loop beneath the bowl. This will help keep the bowl from bouncing around too much as you work.

I've offered a quick food processor option as well—though it's important to note that if the blades of the processor aren't making contact with the little bit of liquid in the machine at the start, it can be difficult to get that initial emulsion going. Making mayonnaise by hand may take a bit more work, but you have more control over the mechanics of the process.

All-Crab Cioppino

MAKES 4 TO 6 SERVINGS

Crab: cleaned Dungeness crab portions, snow or king crab legs

1 tablespoon mild olive oil

2 cups thinly sliced leeks, white and pale-green parts only

1 cup finely chopped onion

1 cup diced celery

2 tablespoons minced garlic

3 cups Crab Stock (page 111), fish stock, or chicken broth

1 (28-ounce) can top-quality diced tomatoes

½ cup dry red wine

¼ cup tomato paste

¼ cup freshly squeezed lemon juice (from about 1 large lemon or 2 small

The origins of this recipe are a matter of effective sustenance rather that culinary splendor. It comes from the family of "catch of the day" seafood soups and stews that developed on fishing boats or docks around the globe, the crew using staple ingredients they had on hand with the addition of some of the day's catch. Often cioppino includes a range of seafoods such as clams, mussels, cubed fish, squid, and/or shrimp. I, however, think it really shines with nothing but crab, simmered in an herb- and vegetable-rich broth. Crusty bread—or better yet, garlic bread—is de rigueur alongside this redolent stew, as are plenty of napkins. Crab bibs too, if you have them. It's messy but worth it.Makes 4 to 6 servings

Heat the oil in a large pot (about 8 quarts) over medium heat. Add the leeks, onion, celery, and garlic and cook until tender and aromatic, about 5 minutes, stirring occasionally. Add the stock, tomatoes, wine, tomato paste, lemon juice, bay leaves, basil, thyme, and pepper flakes with a good pinch each of salt and pepper. Bring just to a boil over medium-high heat, reduce the heat to low, and simmer, covered, for 15 minutes. Taste the broth for seasoning, adding more salt, pepper, or lemon juice to taste.

lemons), plus more to taste

2 bay leaves, preferably fresh

2 tablespoons finely chopped fresh basil

2 teaspoons finely chopped fresh thyme

¼ teaspoon dried red pepper flakes (optional)

Kosher salt and freshly ground black pepper

3 Dungeness crab (about 2 pounds each), cleaned and portioned (see page 34), shells lightly cracked if precooked

Handful tender celery leaves, for serving

Lemon wedges, for serving

If any of the crab portions, particularly king or snow legs, are quite long, cut or break them in half crosswise for easier handling. On some legs there may be a joint near the center point, in which case you can simply bend the joint apart to separate the portions. Add the crab pieces to the pot, nestling them down into the liquids, and simmer, uncovered, until the crab is well heated, 10 to 12 minutes.

Use tongs to transfer the crab to individual large, shallow bowls, then ladle the rest of the stew over the crab. Tear the celery leaves into pieces and scatter them in the center of each bowl. Perch a lemon wedge to the side and serve.

nks, He'll Watch at Home
Wins
narrower than
couldn't agree on
CBS. So both netwo
seconds at about $300
becoming one of the

Beer-Steamed Blue Crab with Mustard Butter

MAKES 4 SERVINGS

Crab: made with live or precooked blue crab in mind, but Dungeness crab portions or king or snow crab legs could be used

½ cup unsalted butter

1 teaspoon mustard powder

2 (12-ounce) bottles light- to medium-bodied beer

5 to 6 dried red chiles, or 1 teaspoon dried red pepper flakes

2 bay leaves, preferably fresh, torn or crushed

6 to 8 sprigs fresh flat-leaf (Italian) parsley

24 blue crab, live or precooked

You can tell I'm not a native blue-crab eater, can't you? For one thing this recipe serves just a handful of folks, not a few dozen. I'm not cooking the blues by the bushel, or employing a backyard propane burner and ginormous pot. And the seasoning is subtle. This recipe is not intended to compete with the generations-old tradition of blue-crab feasts that stir up appetites in the East. This is a chance to bring some of that character inside. Cover the dinner table with newspaper to catch the scatterings of shell bits and crab while cracking through the meal. You'll be very happy come cleanup time when you can simply roll it all up for easy removal. Add corn on the cob and some cold beer—it'll be quite the minifeast.

Live blue crab don't travel all that well, though Asian markets and specialty seafood markets around the country will have them available beyond blue-crab country on occasion. Many of us must content ourselves with the long-distance second best: precooked blue crab shipped to our doorstep.

Melt the butter in a small saucepan over medium heat. Take the pan from the heat, stir in the mustard powder, and set aside.

CONTINUED

Pour the beer into a very large pot (see A Matter of Size on the following page), add the chiles, bay leaves, and parsley sprigs, and set a steamer basket in the bottom of the pot. Cover the pot and bring the beer to a boil over high heat. Add the crab, cover, reduce the heat to medium-high, and steam until the crab are evenly bright red, 12 to 15 minutes if using live crab. (There should be plenty of liquid for this cooking time, but just to be safe check near the end and add a cup of boiling water if needed.) If using precooked crab, steam until heated through, about 5 minutes.

Use tongs to transfer the steamed crab to a large platter and set it in the center of the table. Stir the mustard butter to gently remix, then pour it into individual dishes for each guest to use. Have a bowl available for discarded shells, and provide plenty of napkins.

A Matter of Size

For this recipe, pull out the biggest pot you've got. A standard 8-quart stockpot will likely hold only about a dozen blue crab at a time, but the steaming is quick enough you can cook half at a time and serve the crab in two batches (if so, be sure there's enough liquid for the second batch; add more beer or water if needed). If you have one of those oversized seafood steamer pots that run in the 16-plus-quart range, it's a great time to use it.

Fresh Pasta with Crab & Cilantro

MAKES 2 TO 4 SERVINGS

Crab: any cooked crabmeat, mix of flake and lump ideal

1¼ cups all-purpose flour, plus more for rolling out pasta

½ teaspoon kosher salt

2 large eggs

2 tablespoons finely chopped fresh cilantro

8 ounces crabmeat

6 tablespoons salted butter, cut into 6 pieces

1 cup moderately packed fresh cilantro leaves

Kosher salt and freshly ground white pepper

¼ cup toasted pine nuts

There really is nothing better than pasta you've made yourself and cooked shortly after rolling and cutting the dough. Here the dough contains cilantro, adding a dash of color as well as a fresh herbal flavor to the noodles. Whole leaves are then tossed with the steaming noodles, crab, and lush butter for a simple but sophisticated finish. If you're a cilantrophobe, you can make this recipe with flat-leaf (Italian) parsley instead.

Since the butter here acts as a sauce of sorts, it's a rare time I'd recommend using salted butter if you have some, in which case little or no added salt may be needed when you're seasoning the finished dish. For a super shortcut or if you don't have a pasta machine, you could use top-quality dry fettuccine in place of the fresh pasta

Put the flour in a food processor with the salt and pulse once to blend. Add the eggs and pulse a few times to partially blend, then add the chopped cilantro and pulse until evenly blended. Transfer the dough to a work surface, form it into a ball, and knead it for a few minutes to create a cohesive, satiny dough, adding a bit more flour if the dough is still a little sticky. Wrap the dough in plastic and set it aside at room temperature for about 30 minutes.

CONTINUED

Cut the pasta dough in half. Flatten one half with the heel of your hand into a rough rectangle that's a few inches wide and 4 to 5 inches long. Lightly dust the dough with flour, and roll it through the widest setting of a pasta machine. Fold the ends inward so that the dough is shaped like a packet about 4 inches across, flatten a bit with your hand again and run the pasta through the rollers, with the folded edges at either side and feeding one of the open edges in first. Repeat this process 4 or 5 more times to further knead the dough and make it very smooth, dusting the dough very lightly with flour as needed. Decrease the roller width by one setting and pass the full length of the pasta sheet through the rollers. Continue rolling out the dough at thinner and thinner settings until it is about 1⁄16 inch thick.

Drape the pasta on a pasta rack or over the back of a chair that's been covered with a kitchen towel. Repeat the rolling process with the remaining dough. Let the dough sheets rest for about 30 minutes before continuing.

Scatter about ¼ cup of flour on a tray or rimmed baking sheet. Cut the first sheet of dough in half crosswise to make it easier to handle, and then pass each half through the wider fettuccine blades of the pasta cutter. Set the noodles in a nest on the floured tray, tossing gently to be sure they don't stick together. Repeat with the remaining dough.

Bring a large pot of generously salted water to a boil over high heat. While the water's heating, pick over the crabmeat to remove any bits of shell or cartilage. If using king or snow crab leg meat, cut it into medium dice.

When the water is at a full boil, add the pasta and boil just until al dente, about 1 minute. Drain the pasta well. Set the empty pot back over medium heat, and let it sit for a few moments until all the water has evaporated. Add the butter to the pot and stir until partly melted, then add the drained pasta and toss to coat it evenly with the butter. Add the cilantro leaves and crab, season with salt and pepper to taste, and toss to mix. Transfer the pasta to a large warmed bowl or individual plates, scatter the pine nuts over, and serve right away.

Stir-Fried Snap Peas with Crab & Ginger

MAKES 4 SERVINGS

Crab: any cooked crabmeat

Mild olive or vegetable oil, for frying

2 tablespoons julienned peeled ginger

½ cup Crab Stock (page 111), fish stock, or chicken broth

2 teaspoons cornstarch

8 ounces crabmeat

2 tablespoons minced peeled ginger

¾ cup sliced green onion

12 ounces snap peas

½ cup sake or dry vermouth

1 tablespoon soy sauce, plus more to taste

3 to 4 cups steamed white or brown rice

Crisp, sweet snap peas make an ideal partner for sweet, tender crab in this quick stir-fry. The vibrant flavor of fresh ginger adds zip, both in the sauce and fried for garnishing the dish.

Heat about ½ inch of oil in a small saucepan over medium-high heat. When hot (test with a piece of julienned ginger; the oil should bubble actively around it when added), add the julienned ginger and fry, stirring gently with a fork to keep the strands separated, until just lightly browned, about 1 minute. Use the fork to transfer the ginger to paper towels to drain; reserve the oil. In a small dish, combine the stock and cornstarch and stir to mix.

Pick over the crabmeat to remove any bits of shell or cartilage. If using king or snow crab leg meat, cut it into 1- to 2-inch pieces.

Scoop 2 tablespoons of the frying oil carefully from the saucepan into a wok or large, heavy skillet (discard the remaining oil or save for another use). Heat the oil over medium-high heat, then add the minced ginger and cook until aromatic, 10 to 15 seconds. Add the green onion; cook for about 1 minute longer. Add the peas and stir-fry until bright green and partly tender, about 2 minutes. Add the sake and simmer until reduced by about half, 1 to 2 minutes.

CONTINUED

Stir the stock/cornstarch mixture to remix, then add it to the pan. Reduce the heat to medium low and cook until the sauce is thickened, about 2 minutes, stirring often. Add the crab and soy sauce to the peas and toss gently to warm through, 1 to 2 minutes. Taste for seasoning, adding more soy sauce to taste. Spoon the crab and peas over the rice on a serving platter or individual plates, scatter the fried ginger on top, and serve right away.

Salt & Pepper Crab

MAKES 2 SERVINGS

Crab: any in-shell cooked crab, cleaned and portioned

For the nam pla prik

¼ cup fish sauce

¼ cup freshly squeezed lime juice (from about 2 medium limes)

4 Thai green chiles, chopped

1 clove garlic, minced

1 teaspoon kosher salt

1 teaspoon freshly ground black pepper

1 teaspoon lightly crushed Szechwan pepper

2 tablespoons vegetable oil

1 cooked Dungeness crab (about 2 pounds), cleaned and portioned (see page 34), shells lightly cracked

This is one of my all-time favorite crab dishes, inspired by a dish I loved at the original Flying Fish restaurant located in Seattle's Belltown neighborhood. It will have you delightedly slurping crabmeat from its shells and licking your fingers. If you double the recipe—whether to serve four or offer a whole crab per serving—the original amount of spices will still suffice. Echoing its Asian roots, the crab is served with *nam pla prik*, a boldly flavored dipping sauce that's very quick to make.

To make the nam pla prik, in a small bowl, combine the fish sauce, lime juice, chiles, and garlic, stir to mix, and set aside. The sauce can be made a few hours in advance and refrigerated until ready to serve. Keep in mind that the longer the sauce sits, the more heat it will take on from the chiles.

In a small dish, combine the salt, black pepper, and Szechwan pepper and stir to mix. Heat the oil in a wok or large, heavy skillet over medium-high heat until just starting to smoke. Carefully add the crab pieces and stir-fry until heated, 3 to 4 minutes. Sprinkle the spice mixture over the crab and continue stir-frying until the pieces are evenly coated in the spices and they give off a slightly toasty aroma, about 2 minutes more.

Transfer the crab to a warmed serving platter. Pour the nam pla prik into individual bowls and serve alongside for dipping.

Crab & Chanterelle Risotto

MAKES 4 SERVINGS

Crab: any cooked crabmeat, mix of flake and lump ideal

4 tablespoons unsalted butter, divided

8 ounces chanterelle mushrooms, wiped clean, trimmed, and sliced

1 cup dry white wine

3 cups Crab Stock (page 111) or chicken broth

½ cup finely chopped onion

1 cup arborio rice

8 to 12 ounces crabmeat

Kosher salt and freshly ground black pepper

2 tablespoons minced fresh flat-leaf (Italian) parsley

The sweet and tender crabmeat offers a distinct contrast to the nutty rice and earthy mushrooms in this risotto. The crop of wild chanterelles is often at its peak in the damp, mild fall and generally continues until the first frost. When chanterelles aren't available, you can use shiitake, cremini, or even everyday white button mushrooms in their place.

If using homemade crab stock, the roasted version will be particularly delicious here. And you might consider one additional step to finish this risotto with an extra dash of luxurious flavor: Put a couple cups of the crab stock in a saucepan and simmer over medium-high heat until reduced to about one-third cup. It will thicken slightly and become richer in color with concentrated flavor. Drizzle some of this over the risotto just before serving.

Melt 2 tablespoons of the butter in a medium skillet over medium-high heat. Add the mushrooms and sauté, stirring frequently, until they are tender and lightly browned, 4 to 5 minutes. Transfer the mushrooms to a bowl and set aside.

Add the wine to the skillet and bring to a boil, stirring to draw up any remaining cooking juices and flavors from the mushrooms. Pour the wine into a medium saucepan, add the crab stock, and bring just to a boil over medium-high heat. Immediately reduce the heat to low and keep warm.

Melt the remaining 2 tablespoons of the butter in a medium, heavy saucepan over medium heat. Add the onion and stir until tender and aromatic, about 3 minutes. The onion should soften but not brown. Add the rice and stir gently until it is evenly blended with the onion. Scoop about 1 cup of the warm stock into the rice and cook, stirring constantly, until the rice has absorbed most of the liquid, 3 to 5 minutes. Continue adding the stock, ½ cup at a time, stirring the rice constantly until most of the liquid is absorbed before adding the next, until the risotto is thick and creamy, and the rice is tender but not too soft—there should still be a bit of resistance at the center of each grain. You may not need every drop of the stock; total cooking time will be 30 to 40 minutes.

Pick over the crabmeat to remove any bits of shell or cartilage. If using king or snow crab leg meat, cut it into medium dice. Add the crab and mushrooms to the risotto with a good pinch of salt and a pinch of pepper (more salt will be needed if using crab stock than chicken broth). Let heat for a few minutes, stirring occasionally, until warmed through. Spoon the risotto into warmed shallow bowls and sprinkle the parsley over it.

Steamed King Crab with Garlic

MAKES 2 TO 4 SERVINGS

Crab: in-shell portions of king or snow crab

2 teaspoons mild olive oil or vegetable oil

¼ cup chopped garlic (8 to 10 cloves)

8 tablespoons thinly sliced green onion, divided

1 tablespoon toasted sesame oil

2 teaspoons Shaoxing wine (Chinese rice wine), dry sherry, or dry white wine

¼ teaspoon kosher salt

2 pounds thawed king or snow crab leg portions

This echoes half of the elaborate king crab feast that's a signature experience at Sun Sui Wah Seafood Restaurant in Vancouver, British Columbia. When available, live king crab will be lounging in the restaurant's huge tanks, plucked to order, and presented in all its thorny glory to your table before being whisked into the kitchen for cooking. The crab's generally cooked two ways: the body meat portioned and stir-fried with chile peppers and coarse salt, and the legs steamed with a garlicky topping. This is my interpretation of the latter service, just a few ingredients needed to flavor the rich crab. You'll likely find king crab portions frozen, in which case budget time for thawing (see page 28 for thawing notes).

Heat the olive oil in a small skillet over medium-low heat. Add the garlic and 4 tablespoons of the green onion and cook gently, stirring occasionally, until the garlic is tender but not browned, 3 to 5 minutes. Transfer the mixture to a small bowl and stir in the sesame oil, wine, and salt.

Use a cleaver or other large, heavy knife to cut the longer crab legs in half crosswise for easier handling. On some legs there may be a joint near the center point, in which case you can instead simply bend the joint apart to separate the portions. Then use slender-bladed kitchen shears to cut a slit ¼ to ½ inch wide the length of one side of each crab portion, exposing the meat slightly so flavors infuse into it more and making it easier to extract the meat later. To decide where on the leg to make this slit, set the crab piece on the counter and see which side sits flat most naturally; cut the shell on the top side in this position.

Put a few inches of water in a wok or large pot over which a double-layer bamboo steamer basket will fit snugly. Bring the water to a boil over high heat.

While the water is heating, set a heatproof plate inside each of the steamer baskets and lay the crab pieces on the plates. Spoon the garlic mixture over the crab pieces, aiming to land across the split opening as much as possible. Stack the baskets over the boiling water, cover, and steam until the crab is heated through, 8 to 10 minutes. Transfer the crab leg portions to a platter or individual plates, scatter the remaining 4 tablespoons green onion over, and serve right away.

Grilled Crab with Charred Orange-Rum Butter

MAKES 4 TO 6 SERVINGS

Crab: Dungeness crab sections, king or snow crab legs, cleaned whole blue crab

- 2 Dungeness crab (about 2 pounds each), cleaned and portioned (see page 34), shells lightly cracked if precooked
- 1 large navel orange
- ¼ cup mild olive oil
- Kosher salt and freshly ground black pepper
- ½ cup unsalted butter
- 3 tablespoons rum
- 3 dashes Angostura bitters (optional)

If you haven't thought about grilling crab before, you're going to be happy to add this to your repertoire. It offers the traditional benefit of outdoor character that comes into play anytime you grill, with an added dose of flavor from the toasty crab shells imparting a slightly nutty flavor. In this recipe that flavor gets embellished with orange that both coats the shells before grilling and becomes part of the buttery sauce used for dipping. And the sauce has a dash of rum as well!

If any of the crab portions, particularly king or snow legs, are quite long, cut or break them in half crosswise for easier handling. On some legs there may be a joint near the center point, in which case you can simply bend the joint apart to separate the portions. Put the crab portions in a large bowl or large roasting pan (you need enough room to be able to toss the crab with seasonings).

Grate the zest from the orange and set aside ½ teaspoon for the butter sauce. Put the remaining zest in a small bowl and stir in the oil with a good pinch each of salt and pepper. Pour this over the crab pieces and toss to coat them as evenly as you're able. Set aside.

Preheat an outdoor grill to medium-high heat.

In a small saucepan, combine the butter, rum, bitters, and reserved orange zest. Add a good pinch of salt and warm over medium-low heat until the butter is melted. Set aside.

Cut the orange into eighths. When the grill is hot, grill the orange pieces until the flesh is lightly charred, 2 to 3 minutes on each of the wedges. Set the charred orange wedges aside.

Arrange the crab pieces on the grill and cook, turning every couple of minutes, until lightly browned and aromatic, about 6 to 8 minutes total. By this time precooked crab should be fully warmed; if you started with raw crab continue cooking for 5 to 7 minutes more, until the exposed body meat is cooked through and no longer translucent.

Arrange the grilled crab on a platter with 6 of the orange wedges around the crab. Squeeze the remaining 2 orange wedges into the butter sauce and stir to blend. Pour the butter into individual small bowls and set them on plates, passing the crab for guests to serve themselves

ACKNOWLEDGMENTS

AMONG THE MANY CRAB SPECIALISTS with whom I spoke, Rich Childers and Dan Ayres from the Washington Department of Fish and Wildlife; Hugh Link, executive director of the Oregon Dungeness Crab Commission; Bill Brooks at J. M. Clayton Company in Maryland; Glenn Davis with the Maryland Department of Natural Resources; Jennifer Shriver from the Alaska Department of Fish and Game; and Dan Ellinor with Florida Fish and Wildlife Conservation Commission were all exceptionally helpful with nitty-gritty details about crab.

It was a treat to reconnect with a colleague dating back to my time at *Simply Seafood* magazine. John van Amerongen, now at Trident Seafoods, helped me cover a lot of interesting (and delicious) territory related to king and snow crab. Thanks to Harry and Kevin Yoshimura and the whole crew at Mutual Fish in Seattle. Cheers also to Karl Uri at Alaska Seafood Marketing Institute for assisting with crab corralling.

Tom and Melissa Willits from Kathi's Krabs in Florida made me a very happy cookbook author by sending some gorgeous first-of-the-season stone crab claws just in time for this book deadline!

Among those who shared with me a lot of their own passion for crab include Riki Senn (my Delaware blue-crab correspondent), and fellow Dungeness enthusiasts Stephanie and Andy Hogenson, Victoria Trimmer, and Serni Solidarios.

It was a great pleasure to work again with photographer Jim Henkens. I adore his talent for capturing the essence of his subject. And many thanks to Gary, Em, Joyce, Rebekah, and the rest of the Sasquatch team!

I was fortunate to have a few great palates helping me navigate the beverage options for crab, which include Dawn Smith, Bryan Maletis, and Jameson Fink. And I'm always so thankful to dear friends who are willing and enthusiastic recipe tasters, offering great feedback and sometimes just the perfect tweak to make the recipe even better.

INDEX

Note: Photographs are indicated by *italics*.

D

O

P

Q

R

S

T

W

CONVERSIONS

VOLUME

UNITED STATES	METRIC	IMPERIAL
¼ tsp.	1.25 mL	
½ tsp.	2.5 mL	
1 tsp.	5 mL	
½ Tbsp.	7.5 mL	
1 Tbsp.	15 mL	
⅛ c.	30 mL	1 fl. oz.
¼ c.	60 mL	2 fl. oz.
⅓ c.	80 mL	2.5 fl. oz.
½ c.	120 mL	4 fl. oz.
1 c.	230 mL	8 fl. oz.
2 c. (1 pt.)	460 mL	16 fl. oz.
1 qt.	1 L	32 fl. oz.

LENGTH

UNITED STATES	METRIC
⅛ in.	3 mm
¼ in.	6 mm
½ in.	1.25 cm
1 in.	2.5 cm
1 ft.	30 cm

WEIGHT

AVOIRDUPOIS	METRIC
¼ oz.	7 g
½ oz.	15 g
1 oz.	30 g
2 oz.	60 g
3 oz.	90 g
4 oz.	115 g
5 oz.	150 g
6 oz.	175 g
7 oz.	200 g
8 oz. (½ lb.)	225 g
9 oz.	250 g
10 oz.	300 g
11 oz.	325 g
12 oz.	350 g
13 oz.	375 g
14 oz.	400 g
15 oz.	425 g
16 oz. (1 lb.)	450 g
1½ lb.	750 g
2 lb.	900 g
2¼ lb.	1 kg
3 lb.	1.4 kg
4 lb.	1.8 kg

TEMPERATURE

OVEN MARK	FAHRENHEIT	CELSIUS	GAS
Very cool	250–275	120–135	½–1
Cool	300	150	2
Warm	325	165	3
Moderate	350	175	4
Moderately hot	375	190	5
Fairly hot	400	200	6
Hot	425	220	7
Very hot	450	230	8
Very hot	475	245	9

For ease of use, conversions have been rounded.

3 HR PARKING
DOCK ST TO COVE ST LEFT SIDE
AWARD WINNING SEAFOOD

ABOUT THE AUTHOR

CYNTHIA NIMS is a lifelong Northwesterner who reveled in growing up surrounded by great food—both in her mother's kitchen and exploring the region with her family, whether eating grilled oysters on a San Juan Island beach or huckleberry pancakes while backpacking in the Olympic Mountains.

After graduating from the University of Puget Sound, having majored in mathematics and French literature, Cynthia followed her dreams and went to France to study cooking at La Varenne Ecole de Cuisine. There, she received the Grand Diplôme d'Etudes Culinaires and worked on numerous cookbooks with the school's president, Anne Willan, including *Great Cooks and Their Recipes*, *Château Cuisine*, and ten in the Look & Cook series.

The author of over a dozen cookbooks, Cynthia's most recent is *Shellfish*, with *Salty Snacks* and *Gourmet Game Night* among other books she has written. In her magazine work, Cynthia has served as editor of *Simply Seafood* and food editor of *Seattle Magazine*, in addition to contributing to *Cooking Light*, *Coastal Living*, *Alaska Airlines Magazine*, and other publications. She is an active member of the International Association of Culinary Professionals (for which she served as president of the board) and Les Dames d'Escoffier. Her website is MonAppetit.com and her newsletters, *Seafood Savvy* and *Long Live the Recipe Box*, are available on Substack. Cynthia and her husband live in Seattle.

Printed in China

SASQUATCH BOOKS with colophon is a registered trademark of Blue Star Press, LLC

Part of *Essential Shellfish Collection*, published 2025.
ISBN: 978-1-63217-635-6
Not for Individual Sale

29 28 27 26 25 9 8 7 6 5 4 3 2 1

The authorized representative in the EU for product safety and compliance is Authorised Rep Compliance Ltd., Ground Floor, 71 Lower Baggot Street, Dublin D02 P593, Ireland. www.arccompliance.com

Editor: Gary Luke
Production editor: Em Gale
Photographs (except page 7, courtesy of the author) and food styling: Jim Henkens
Design: Anna Goldstein
Copyeditor: Michael Townley

Sasquatch Books
1325 Fourth Avenue, Suite 1025
Seattle, WA 98101

SasquatchBooks.com

FSC www.fsc.org MIX Paper | Supporting responsible forestry FSC® C188448